How to Read and Write Critically

Get the skills you need to succeed!

Student Success books are essential guides for students of all levels. From how to think critically and write great essays to planning your dream career, the Student Success series helps you study smarter and get the best from your time at university.

Test yourself with practical tasks

Diagnose your strengths and weaknesses

Dial up your skills for improved grades

Visit **sagepub.co.uk/study-skills** for free tips and resources for study success

STUDENT
SUCCESS

How to
Read and
Write Critically

Alex Baratta

SAGE

Los Angeles | London | New Delhi
Singapore | Washington DC | Melbourne

Los Angeles | London | New Delhi
Singapore | Washington DC | Melbourne

SAGE Publications Ltd
1 Oliver's Yard
55 City Road
London EC1Y 1SP

SAGE Publications Inc.
2455 Teller Road
Thousand Oaks, California 91320

SAGE Publications India Pvt Ltd
B 1/I 1 Mohan Cooperative Industrial Area
Mathura Road
New Delhi 110 044

SAGE Publications Asia-Pacific Pte Ltd
3 Church Street
#10-04 Samsung Hub
Singapore 049483

Editor: Jai Seaman
Assistant editor: Charlotte Bush
Production editor: Prachi Arora
Copyeditor: QuADS Prepress Pvt Ltd
Proofreader: Derek Markham
Marketing manager: Catherine Slinn
Cover design: Shaun Mercier
Typeset by: C&M Digitals (P) Ltd, Chennai, India
Printed in the UK

Library of Congress Control Number: 2021931394

British Library Cataloguing in Publication data

A catalogue record for this book is available from
the British Library

ISBN 978-1-5297-5800-9
ISBN 978-1-5297-5799-6 (pbk)
eISBN 978-1-5297-6889-3

At SAGE we take sustainability seriously. Most of our products are printed in the UK using responsibly sourced
papers and boards. When we print overseas we ensure sustainable papers are used as measured by the PREPS
grading system. We undertake an annual audit to monitor our sustainability.

Contents

Contents

About the Author

Alex Baratta is a linguist whose research interests are focused on language and identity, to include linguistic prejudice and linguistic rights. However, his initial teaching and research experiences were centred on academic writing and critical thinking, topics he continues to write on, having taught academic writing in South Korea, the UK and his native USA, as part of English 101. *How to Read and Write Critically* is his fifth book on the subject of academic writing/critical thinking, with other books focused on accent preference within British teaching (*Accent and Teacher Identity in Britain: Linguistic Favouritism and Imposed Identities*, 2018); World Englishes (*World Englishes in English Language Teaching*, 2019); a collection of short stories with twist endings (*Sting in the Tale*, 2019); and Korean English (*The Societal Codification of Korean English*, 2021). He has published in leading journals and has presented his research at international conferences in Australia, Singapore and South Africa.

1

What Does It Mean to Be 'Critical'?

When you get to university, you can expect to come across many terms which are used regularly as part of higher education. Many such terms are associated with your particular field of study and constitute technical language, such as *hypercorrection*, *object permanence* and *zygote*, as but three examples. Beyond this, you can expect to come across various slogans, printed on flyers promoting meal deals and on-campus clubs and even the university's own slogan used to promote itself. However, one term from which there is no escape is **critical thinking**, and all its related terms such as *criticality*, *analysis*, *application* and so on. Critical thinking is so embedded a term in higher education that you can expect to find it, hear it and see it on every university campus. It can be found on posters advertising study skills sessions focused on this skill, you will hear it mentioned by your lecturers – sometimes in class and often as part of assessment feedback – and you can definitely see it written in some form as part of the assessment criteria on which you will be judged, whether an essay, exam or oral presentation. One potential problem, however, is that while this term is so absolutely important in university assessment, rarely is it explained to students. Your assessments are expected to show evidence of being critical, but has anyone so far explained what this actually means? More to the point, do you know how to achieve criticality in your assessments – do you know it when you see it?

I don't pose these questions to suggest that your university and/or lecturers are being secretive and are expecting you to figure it out for yourself. Indeed, you can expect to find all kinds of assistance on campus in terms of study skills nowadays, which will include help with your essays and overall assessments.

Your university might also benefit from having a dedicated writing centre of some kind, given that writing centres are starting to make their presence felt more and more on UK university campuses and are already a major part of US campuses. Add to this study skills websites which will often explain the components of academic assessment and what is expected – from essays to exams – and you may indeed feel that you have the help you need when you need it. But whether you feel this way or not, there is more that can be done to address such an important skill that you will need for university – and perhaps beyond. The key is to *show* you what being critical actually means, as a way to make a rather abstract word much more concrete. This is what this book will do.

While much of the discussion will be focused on academic writing, being critical is not tied solely to essays of course. Academic writing can be subdivided into additional areas anyway, such as note-taking, journals and research proposals, and the essays you write can range in length from 2,000 words to a 12,000-word undergraduate dissertation. We must also consider the different writing conventions for various disciplines, as academic writing is not one size fits all, and there are other ways to be assessed, such as exams, oral presentations and posters. However, the glue that binds all assessments together, from a psychology essay to an assessed blog written for a human geography course, is the need to be critical. This is the most important skill in your assessment – and even as part of an informal class discussion for that matter – because it demonstrates ultimately that you're thinking for yourself and this is the main purpose for your time at university. The more you show critical thinking in your assessments, the more you will demonstrate that you have carefully considered the subject at hand, thought about it deeply and then produced some insights around it. This is the stuff of higher scores. To not demonstrate this skill, however, leads to average scores and is suggestive of assessments that simply don't go far beyond the lecture/textbook/class handout content.

The need to demonstrate evidence of being critical does not mean that other aspects of your assessment (which will be discussed in Chapter Three) are not important. Far from it. It is important to present your essay content in a coherent manner (yes, I'll define 'coherent' too), use standard English and correct formatting. But overall, most of the weight toward your assessment's final score will be carried by how well you show criticality, and not the order of your essay's topics or how well you conjugate your verbs. Therefore, it makes sense to focus on the skill of being critical primarily, as this represents a macro-level aspect of your assessments and, therefore, needs to be addressed before you worry about word choice, punctuation and whether or not to use Harvard referencing. Having introduced the importance of being critical, and before I offer a simple, but effective, formula for it, I first wish to present some examples of critical thinking in the real world. After all, you probably engage with this skill more often than you think.

Critical thinking in the real world

Let us consider the business of criticality from a non-academic perspective, as a means to help make it even more accessible. Being critical involves taking a subject of some kind (everything from government policies to pop culture) and disseminating it in our minds. The purpose is to interpret it and, from here, arrive at our personal understanding – whether an agreement, disagreement, example to provide to others, explanation and so on.

For example, consider the last time you pondered over something that was not academic related. This could be, but is *definitely* not limited to, any of the following:

- Reading a film review and then deciding if the film is worth your money or not
- Reading the ingredients on a food package to check on the overall health benefits, or lack thereof
- Reading a wine label to see if the flavours promised by the wine stand up to your own preferences

You can no doubt think of more examples, but taking each of the three examples above in turn, let's now see how critical thinking works and what it could look like. Of course, no two people will think in the same way even about the same subject (whether climate change or a film review); even the same person can approach the same subject differently at different times in his/her life. So the examples below are just that – examples – which show you the potential considerations that might be involved in the overall process of critical thinking. The thing is, because the subjects below are those we might encounter on a somewhat regular basis and they take place outside of academia, we probably don't stop to consider that critical thinking is actually playing a part. But of course it is, and yet we perhaps don't see it that way because the topics above might be more personal, 'fun' or at least tied to our day-to-day life (e.g. health concerns). But all you need to do is take these same skills from outside the classroom and bring them into the classroom because the process of being critical is exactly the same, whether evaluating a holiday brochure for Turkey or evaluating a scientific theory: ask yourself what the subject means to you:

- Reading a film review

    o Do you trust/respect the reviewer, or do you simply ignore what he/she says and go with your own complete judgement?
    o Is the film directed by someone whose work you admire or not?
    o Does the screenplay get your interest, even if the director does not?
    o Is the film perhaps relevant to you on a personal level, based on its story?

- o Does the advertising poster attract you with its use of colour, visuals and even the font style/size used for the title?
- o Do you consider the film review itself to be well-written?
- o What are your standards for a 'well-written' film review, anyway?

- Reading the ingredients on a food package

  - o Do the ingredients match up with the promise made on the label of being 'all natural'?
  - o For example, does a box of 'healthy' granola otherwise have high levels of sugar?
  - o What to you would be a 'high level' of sugar?
  - o Are there ingredients to which you are allergic?
  - o How do you perceive the product slogan, if there is one, along with the style of packaging and visual design?
  - o Does the same product appear to be any different if sold by a different brand (e.g. is Kellogg's cornflakes any different from the local supermarket's own brand)?
  - o Do you associate a higher price tag with more than just brand name?

- Reading a wine label

  - o Is the wine just for everyday consumption or is this a special occasion?
  - o If the latter, who is it for – a close friend, parent, boss?
  - o Based on the recipient of the wine, is there a maximum budget?
  - o Does this budget change based on who the wine is for, however?
  - o For example, are you hoping to impress the boss with a 'good' wine, but without being too ostentatious?
  - o Does the price seem reasonable for the brand of wine, assuming you know your wines?
  - o If you don't know your wines, then what seems to be a 'reasonable' price?
  - o Likewise, what seems to be an interesting combination of flavours (e.g. notes of blackcurrant and cherry)?
  - o Is this wine suitable for the menu at a dinner party you're attending that night?
  - o For example, if the dinner is serving meats, then is a bold red wine a more suitable choice than, say, a dry white wine?
  - o What is a 'bold' red wine anyway – what does this mean in terms of flavour?

I could go on and on and on, but I'll stop here. If you are involved in any of the three scenarios above on even a semi-regular basis, then you don't need me to tell you how to shop for wine or read a food label. And my bullet points above may, or may not, reflect your own thought processes which are involved with the three scenarios. But as I mentioned, critical thinking differs from person to person. The important thing is that you develop this skill. It's a skill you already have anyway in the real world – you just need to transfer it to your academic assessments using the same approach: ask yourself *what does this mean to me?*

A formula for being critical

Being critical can sometimes be discussed by using other terms, as mentioned, such as *analysing*, *critically analysing*, *unpacking* and *discussing*, as well as being explained in terms of considering the subject matter, holding it up to scrutiny, engaging with it, evaluating it and so on. Ultimately, however, being critical can be nicely summed up in one word: *interpretation*. Because in order to truly engage with, consider, evaluate (and so on) the subject under discussion – whether from a book, a film or an online debate with friends – you will need to provide an interpretation. Interpretation is the final destination for all your thinking, pondering and considering. Moreover, interpreting the subject allows for you to show your thoughts on the matter, and it is *your* thoughts which are crucial in assessment, as opposed to merely regurgitating class handouts and/or what the textbook/lecturer already told you. This is not enough. Instead, take class handouts, textbook information and whatever the lecturer's points are and use this as a springboard to then launch into your own ideas. This is an important point which I will return to, but let me make it clear now: if your assessment – whether an essay/written assignment, exam or oral presentation – is largely made up of references to the class handouts or whatever else you've been told by the lecturer, then there is little evidence of being critical. How can you be critical if you're merely repeating what someone else told you, but without a subsequent interpretation? All that this demonstrates, especially in an exam, is that you have a good memory. Again, this does not mean that your assessments should never reference lecture notes/class handout material. Rather, use such material to then launch into your own understanding and in this way, you will be adding something new to the conversation.

As for the promised formula, it is this: when you read the source material, ask yourself the following question: *what does this mean to me?* This question will prompt you into doing the things that are associated with criticality: evaluating, judging, speculating, thinking deeply and so on. And when your evaluations, judgements, speculations, thoughts and so on are written for all to see, then you're providing clear evidence of being critical. So in summary:

Read/consider the source/topic + ask *'what does this mean to me?'* = being critical

If this seems overly simplistic, it's not. This is because asking yourself such a broad question will in turn lead to a great deal of processing in your head, which can also involve staying with some evaluations, rejecting others and above all, explaining to yourself – and then to the marker of your assessment – why you feel the way you do. So while the question will sometimes essentially mean, 'what do I make of this proposition – agree or disagree?', being critical is not tied solely to making your own argument or supporting someone else's.

For this reason, 'what does this mean to me?' can also refer to the following, as a brief sample:

- What does the subject mean to me in terms of relevant literature? What literature/studies/authors should I be referring to in my assessments? For example, if you are given an assessment on the subject of social mobility, then who are the main authors within this area? Having said that, don't be afraid to go beyond the reading list for your course unit and instead, be willing to search for literature that the lecturer does not mention – a Google search of the topic might bring up a journal paper that has recently been published.
- Whose work you refer to can also relate to the current push for decolonising the curriculum. From an academic perspective, this movement is partly based on a need to question who the main authors are within a subject area and how their work has been privileged above others. Such privilege of course can refer to the fact that these authors have contributed substantial knowledge to the field, but it can also mean that other voices are excluded in the process, representing groups who also have something to say. For example, some might argue that it is the work of white male authors whose publications are, in the main, most highly regarded and promoted. What do you think? Clearly, there are other voices out there too which can be found and should be considered. Thus, being critical in this case means re-evaluating the canon within your field, asking who else might be included and, indeed, including their work within your assessments.
- Going even further, you can start to think about the content of what you're taught in your textbooks based on considering who is doing the writing. This is not to suggest a wholesale rejection of the main authors in your field and what they have to say – this would not suggest a critical approach at all. But it would be uncritical to not consider others, who represent researchers and authors who have differing perspectives on the subject you study. This can include a different way to conceptualise history, perhaps calling into question what you have been taught since childhood, and/or providing new information that was not taught to you before.
- What do the methods mean to me in terms of the best methods to use for my study? So, if you are researching undergraduate students' reasons for choosing their subject of study (or 'major'), then you would clearly want to talk to them to obtain their views. But how? What method(s) do you think would work best? Interview? Questionnaire? Online survey? Focus group?
- What does the subject mean to me in terms of the specific angle within my assessment that I want to approach the subject with? Imagine you are writing about gender and language – so far, so good. But what is the point you're approaching it from? The ways that society now uses gender-neutral language (e.g. actor, for male and female)? The ways in which society still uses sexist language in some ways (e.g. using the term 'girl' to refer to a woman)?

Indeed, thinking critically can be a long process, though not always. In fact, you might sometimes find inspiration coming to you when you least expect it.

Be prepared to sometimes wake up in the middle of the night with a great idea suddenly in your head, whether a unique angle with which to approach the assessment subject or merely a great title for your work. Likewise, your shower, dinner preparation or movie watching can all be interrupted by a sudden and unexpected burst of inspiration for your assessment, and all without having expended much effort. Yes, sometimes inspiration can strike at any moment.

On the other hand, be prepared for many experiences in which you might find yourself in front of a computer hoping for inspiration, or just simple motivation, to strike. Often, you'll find yourself out of luck. I know that I have spent an hour or more trying to find a specific 'angle' for my work, read Chapter One of my textbook, or just trying to find the energy to at least write an introduction para-graph for my essay. And 1 hour later, the book is still unopened and the computer screen is blank. This is how it sometimes is, and we simply have to force ourselves. Unfortunately, no book can magically give you the energy and enthusiasm you might sometimes lack for your assessments, whether this involves writing, researching, or reading. But armed with the information in this book, you will at least have the skills you need to tackle the important topic of being critical and, from here, find assessments easier (but not necessarily always fun).

Also, remember that the source from which your critical thinking develops is not always necessarily an academic textbook, or an academic journal or book chapter for that matter. The source text might be a website, a newspaper article or a TV interview. The source might be a film or an advertisement. The source might also be an existing theory in your discipline, before you've even started to read about it in a textbook. The source might be a comment that your lecturer mentions in class, which itself of course may have derived from his/her academic research or reading about the topic under discussion.

The reasons for the points mentioned thus far are as follows. First, to again remind you that the 'traditional method' of generating critical thinking, such as reading the class textbook, is not the only way. Critical thinking can come with-out warning, in the form of the aforementioned inspiration. So be aware of this, because for one assignment, the criticality may indeed be initiated in large part with textbook reading, only for the next assignment to have criticality largely derived from a study group session with your classmates. There is no one way to generate critical thinking – sometimes you have to make the effort for the most part and sometimes the critical thoughts appear to come to you automatically.

Second, and related to the first point, the inspiration so often needed as a part of the critical thinking process can come from multiple sources. And as I have already mentioned in this chapter, being critical is something we do every day and is not tied solely to academic assessment. As a further example, dissecting the deeper message and/or directing style of your favourite film with friends involves critical thinking skills, even though in this case you won't be tested on them after. So be open to critical thinking in terms of where it might derive from and how it might happen. A textbook is indeed a good starting point to generate some critical thinking, but there are many other ways which you will find throughout your time as a university student.

The next chapter will now discuss the various ways to demonstrate that you are being critical, in part by using the power of persuasion. However, this is not tied solely to making an argument but can, in fact, be seen in several different ways.

2

Different Ways to Show Your Criticality

More than just an argument

You will probably find that once you get to university, if not before, the skill of being critical is often linked to making an argument. Chapter Three will cover this in more detail, but for now, it is important to understand that while making an argument is indeed a very crucial aspect of demonstrating criticality, it is just *one* aspect. There is much more to being critical than making an argument. This is one aspect of this book that perhaps sets it apart from others on the market. This is not meant to be a selling point, but just my way of letting you know that you need to consider the formula for being critical from more than just a singular perspective connected to making an argument, important though this is. The examples which follow in this section are just to give you an idea; more detail will be provided in the chapters that follow. But for now, let us consider a few scenarios, all of which will require you to think critically, but for different purposes.

Scenario 1: Making your own argument

In this case, you read through an academic text and hone in on a specific idea/ theory/concept put forward by an author. Asking yourself what this means to you may well lead to an opinion formed on the validity, or not, of what the author says. From here, you formulate your own argument and present your points of support for it. For example, what do you think of the statement that 'it is easier to learn a foreign language in childhood than in adulthood'. Here's where the formula for being critical kicks in – *what does this statement mean to you*?

- How do we truly know that it's easier to learn a foreign language in childhood than in adulthood? What evidence do we have?
- Does the statement mean that adults can never truly master a foreign language? If so, then how do we explain those who have done so? We need to know more about their circumstances that allowed them to learn a foreign language proficiently.
- Does 'learning' a foreign language necessarily have to mean becoming proficient in it? What is the measuring stick here to determine 'learning'? Even a few sentences of a foreign language can be sufficient if used on holidays, for example.
- Perhaps adults, often burdened with work, money issues, and raising a family, have less time to devote to language learning, and thus, it can create additional stress – might infants and young children learn language easier because they often have less stress in their lives if compared with adults?
- Is there a cut-off point to determine 'children' and 'adult'? For example, by 'children', what is the age range we are referring to? Likewise, what is the age range for 'adult'? How about teenagers – how do they fare with language learning?
- Might some adults actually find learning a foreign language somewhat easier than children, in that they already understand more explicitly the building blocks of all languages, such as subjects, objects, verbs, nouns, verb tense and so on.
- Is language learning easier in childhood largely because it is more systematic, such as learning it in a classroom? Many adults may not necessarily learn a language this way. In fact, we need to truly understand more points before the claim under discussion can be stated so boldly. For example:
  - What is the age range under discussion?
  - Where and how are the learners actually learning the foreign language(s)?
  - What is the motivation for learning a second language, whether child or adult?

As you can see, the ideas above are varied and there is no doubt we could go even further. Likewise, I'm sure you have come up with additional points to consider based on the statement. If some of the points above did not come to your mind, this is fine. They don't have to. Interpretation is subjective to a large extent and the same text – whether a sentence is long or an entire book – is not going to be interpreted the same by everyone who reads it, as I had mentioned. Also, what we have above, while evidence of having read critically, are rather disorganised points at present. This is fine of course! It is entirely natural to have a bunch of otherwise disconnected ideas and thoughts as the first step of critical thinking, much like mind mapping.

The next step is to look within your thoughts and from there, organise them – or some of them – into a coherent whole. You probably couldn't focus on all of the bullet points above because when discussing a subject as part of your academic assessment, you need to maintain a unified focus (more on this in Chapter Three). This means that not only do you need to have a clear and consistent focus from start to finish, it also means that you need to support it with relevant topics. Finally, you should try not to cover too many topics in your assessment but, instead, go for more in-depth discussion of fewer topics. In other words, go for depth over width. A lot to consider, I know. But for now, let's go to the next stage and organise a specific focus, more than one in fact, based on the bullet points above.

Focus 1: A Comparison Between Children and Adult Learners

The assessment focus could be squarely on a comparison between children and adults who learn a foreign language. This would benefit from much-needed clarity to begin with, such as defining the age range of both groups. From here, the assessment could explore specific contexts in which both children and adults learn a foreign language, based on the various academic literature that the writer engages with:

- Primary school children learning a foreign language in the classroom.
- Adults learning a foreign language in a classroom.
- Reasons for study.

Here, we have at least a sense of like for like, in that learning is taking place in a classroom. This means that we can make a better comparison in that learning for both groups is taking place as part of formal learning, as opposed to self-study. Children's reason(s) for studying a foreign language in primary school are largely centred on such study being part of the curriculum, certainly for their first foreign language. For adults, however, there might be more variety in terms of why they study a foreign language – this can include personal desire, a need to study for a university entrance exam, or work-based reasons. This alone can mean that adults might have more motivation, in some cases, if they believe that proficiency in a language can lead to better career prospects.

The truth is, we could keep going and going with this. But for now, I have hopefully demonstrated the journey initiated from a single sentence – *it is easier to learn a foreign language in childhood than in adulthood* – to the resulting ideas that come from a critical reading of the sentence.

Focus 2: A Discussion of Nature Versus Nurture in Language Learning

The focus above, though not explicitly stated as one of the bullet prompts that followed critically reading the statement, ties in with a key argument within language learning – are we genetically predisposed to learn a language or do we simply learn in a more general way, by repetition and reinforcement? This focus often applies more to the acquisition of our first language, but there is no reason why it couldn't be applied to the learning of a foreign language after we've otherwise mastered our first. However, applying a specific theory or concept to an area in which it is not usually applied is a large part of critical thinking. Again, it starts with asking yourself what the source means to *you*. As an example, if you feel that Marxist theory can be legitimately applied to biology, then go for it. This is an example of application which in itself is an example of being critical – once again by first asking what the subject means to you and how it is then interpreted.

I'll stop here and suggest you think of an additional focus based on the bullets above or, better yet, based on any bullet points you came up with that I did not.

Focus 3

_____

_____

_____

_____

_____

_____

Scenario 2: Supporting someone else's argument

As I have mentioned, making your own original argument in your assessments is but one aspect of demonstrating that you are being critical. But it is by no means the only way. More to the point, if you do make an argument, you need to make sure that you take the necessary time to explain and illustrate your points in detail. Indeed, it is the time you take to explain why you feel the way you do that demonstrates criticality, and this is true whether you disagree – or agree – with a theory/author/concept and so on.

In fact, consider the following scenario. Imagine you read the ideas of a given author whose views and/or theories are considered out of date, or even largely dismissed. But what if you agree with them and from here make a detailed, logical and objective account as to why you agree. In this case, the fact you agree does not make the strength of the argument any less than if you were to disagree. Again, agree/disagree – both show evidence of being critical as long as you clearly explain *why* you agree or disagree.

However, it doesn't make your agreement any less if you find yourself agreeing with an author with whom everyone else within the discipline tends to also agree. Once again, it's how clearly, deeply and informatively you explain the reason for your agreement or disagreement that will show your reader the extent to which you are being critical.

Scenario 3: Considering why your research project is necessary

When you are involved with a research project for which you are in charge of selecting the subject under investigation – for example, a dissertation or thesis – then you should make sure that in chapter one, you include a rationale for your study. This is especially important the higher up you go, so a PhD thesis absolutely needs to have a clear sense of why the research being undertaken is valuable, but even an undergraduate dissertation will be stronger with a rationale and should include one.

The rationale is an answer to the question 'why should we care about your research?' It's a way of justifying the need for your research in objective terms. This means going beyond a personal interest in the subject and instead focusing on the bigger picture. Now, within the Humanities and Social Sciences – **though always check with your lecturer/supervisor** – declaring a personal interest in the subject under investigation need not be off limits as part of your rationale. In fact, it can enhance it. A personal interest may sometimes involve professional experience, such as having taught English overseas for several years and thus being in a good position to bring such experience to a dissertation focused on intercultural communication in the classroom. However, personal experience should be the starting point for a rationale, not the end point. Use personal experience, if deemed relevant, to then lead into a more objective reason(s) for undertaking your study. You might consider additional prompts to help you write your rationale, such as *how will my study benefit the subject area? How can it address problems in my field of study? How can it improve individuals' lives? Can my study address policy?* A rationale is important enough to have its own section in your dissertation's introduction chapter and one to two paragraphs is sufficient. Let's now have a look at two rationales – one average and one decidedly stronger:

Rationale 1

The focus on professional development amongst high school teachers within this dissertation stems from a personal interest, as well as experience having worked as a teacher for two years in a local primary school. During my time, it became clear that under the guidance of a firm, but fair, principal, teaching staff – the principal included – were encouraged to seek opportunities for professional development provided by the school, as well as suggest others. Staff learned new skills, such as the inclusion of online teaching in their work, as well as new languages via a language exchange amongst staff. There were additional aspects of this overall professional development and as a result, the school improved overall, recognised with a rating from OFSTED[1] of 'outstanding', with the previous rating having been 'requires improvement'. This demonstrated to myself, and other staff, that under firm leadership, necessary improvements can be made to a school which was indeed in need of such improvement. While leadership is an important topic of study, this dissertation will focus on professional development specifically, as this is an important focus as a means to reveal what is involved in terms of the potential obstacles and the strategies to overcome any obstacles. Further, my school also demonstrated that with collective professional development and working as a team, the school as a whole – namely the students – will benefit, and not just the staff.

Thoughts: The initial focus on the writer's personal and professional experience is wholly relevant and provides a useful backdrop to the dissertation that follows. The writer offers experience that explains why he/she wishes to look into this further, whether it involves interviewing teachers at a local primary school or some other method of collecting data. There is also a clear point made through the rationale above, namely that professional development is not just about the individual but, instead, individuals seeking professional development and working as a team to put such development to good use. In this case, it is a means to improve a school's rating. There might have been a few references to previous studies to help provide a bit more academic strength, but this is otherwise a competent and convincing rationale.

Rationale 2

The focus on professional development amongst high school teachers within this dissertation stems from a personal interest, as well as experience having worked as a teacher for two years in a local primary school. During my time, it became clear that under the guidance of a firm, but fair, principal, teaching staff – the principal included – were encouraged to seek opportunities for professional development provided by the school, as well as suggest others. Staff learned new skills, such as the inclusion of online teaching in their work, as well as new languages via a language exchange amongst staff. There were additional aspects of this overall professional development and as a result, the school improved overall, recognised with a rating from OFSTED of outstanding, with the previous rating having been 'requires improvement'. This demonstrated to myself, and other staff, that under firm leadership, necessary improvements can be made to a school which was indeed in need of such improvement. While leadership is an important topic of study, this dissertation will focus on professional development specifically, as this is an important focus as a means to reveal what is involved in terms of the potential obstacles and the strategies to overcome any obstacles. Further, my school also demonstrated that with collective professional development and working as a team, the school as a whole – namely the students – will benefit, and not just the staff.

The results of just one school cannot be generalised to others necessarily, but the importance of professional development is certainly not tied to just one school either. For schools in need of improvement, collective staff improvement is vital as a school can only address its deficits if the staff work together as a team to do so. Obvious though this might be, it is nonetheless put forward as a key factor for primary schools in order to raise standards and, indeed, to maintain them. Given the gap in educational attainment, child poverty levels and failing schools, it is argued that while no school can change societal inequalities, schools can nonetheless seek to address them in the classroom. In this dissertation, I will focus on this topic by revealing how improving standards for learning in the classroom begins by improving one's standards as a teacher and working with other teachers on this goal collectively.

Thoughts: This takes the first rationale to the next level, by adding an extra paragraph in which more objective information is provided. In this case, the information pertains to national issues with educational attainment gaps, which the writer's school seems to have addressed. Some references to previous studies would add even more weight to help back up some of the writer's key points above, such as 'Given the gap in educational attainment, child poverty levels and failing schools'; references to studies or government reports (even better perhaps) to support the fact that child poverty and failing schools are issues would have added credibility. Nonetheless, this is a strong rationale. It's not better than the first merely because it's longer. It's quality, not quantity, that counts. But if more writing is needed in order to provide more necessary detail, and here support, then so be it.

As part of a strong rationale, the starting point is to problematise the subject you want to research. This means finding/addressing an issue within the field, if not making a less obvious issue more explicit for the reader. In the second rationale above, it is clear that the writer has unpacked the subject area and, in so doing, identified a problem that is in need of investigation – child poverty – which is suggested to be a factor behind lower educational attainment. While this might not sound particularly original or surprising, this does not make it any less important to investigate. Moreover, the writer is taking these two issues and addressing them both through collective professional development at primary schools. Also, the reasons *why* the subject is in need of investigation are made clear for the reader. This is what makes the rationale convincing.

Problematising topics

Let's have a look at the way a topic can be made 'research ready' by first finding the issue within, as referenced in the section above. This is where the rationale for your dissertation/thesis is born – indeed the entire impetus for conducting research in the first place.

Topic of research: Mental health in schoolchildren

Problem: This has been exacerbated by the recent lockdown due to coronavirus, and yet, we still don't know what the long-term effects will be, even after children return to school.

And? This dissertation will investigate mental health issues in secondary school children and how they might have been exacerbated by the recent lockdown due to coronavirus.

Why should we care? Mental health is an ongoing problem for many in society, and given that this has been reported as having been affected by the lockdown – for people of all ages – it makes sense to investigate further. This will allow for more insights to be drawn and for teachers and parents alike to be able to find solutions for their children's mental health issues, certainly as part of education. Studies of this nature are perhaps in their infancy and more needs to be done to fill this gap in order to address the mental health issues that could last beyond lockdown when children are back in school.

Given that coronavirus is less than a year old as I write, then there might not necessarily be a great many studies in this area. However, finding a gap in the literature is not, in itself, a rationale for conducting a study. You need to say why the gap *needs* to be filled. The text above does this, and while it is not a finished rationale, it is on its way.

At this early stage, you can hopefully see that being critical does not always mean arguing at all. It involves interpreting a source text, interpreting an idea, or interpreting a subject area for your dissertation, as seen above. By asking what the source text/idea/subject area and so on means to you, this helps to lead into an interpretation, and from here, you then give your input. So while making an argument of some kind is a large part of academic culture, it is not the only way to demonstrate that you're being critical. On the other hand, you might feel that everything is, broadly speaking, an argument. After all, the rationale above is essentially saying 'here's why my dissertation needs to be written' – is this not an argument of sorts? And as we'll see in the next section, justifying your choice of methods, such as the decision to use interviews in a research study, is also a means to argue; in this case, you're saying 'this is why I think interviews are so important for my study'. If you want to conceptualise the skill of being critical as a skill that is tied to argumentation, whether direct or indirect, that's fine. Or by all means stick with my approach, in which I present interpretation – itself regarded on a broad level – as the key to being critical. In the end, it doesn't really matter how you regard criticality, as long as you know what to do to produce it for your academic assessments.

Scenario 4: Explaining the reasons for your methodological choices

Another common reason for using your critical thinking skills is when you explain to the reader the methods you have chosen for your dissertation/thesis – often this focus is in Chapter three of your dissertation. Again, there are two points to consider in terms of being critical. One, by interpreting the ideas you read, then the plans you make for your assessments and the words you actually type on the page show that you are being critical. It takes a good think about things to arrive at reasoned answers and solutions, and in this case, by asking 'what does this mean to me?' – with 'this' referring to a methodological choice – you can arrive at a clear and convincing understanding. Thus, by asking yourself, for example, why you have chosen to use interviews and not questionnaires, your explanation – justification, in fact – for this choice will sound convincing to the reader.

Two, you can also see how this process of consideration does not involve an overt argument per se. Yes, you are arguing why, for example, interviews work better than questionnaires for your particular research project. But this may not be how you otherwise considered 'argument' in the first place (more on this later). As I mentioned, feel free to conceptualise 'argument' in a much more inclusive sense if this helps you understand criticality, in which case, we can argue against an author/theory as much as we can argue for a methodological choice. But whether you view it this way, or indeed place interpretation as the key means to conceptualise criticality, the main thing is to demonstrate that you are being critical.

As an example, consider the following:

> As Jones (2018: 7) states, 'semi-structured interviews, and interviews in general, allow the researcher to probe participants' thoughts, feelings and beliefs, so crucial in coming to an understanding of a given topic'. This is crucial to my own research on the subject of working-class identity in UK society for the following reasons. First, it is argued that it is those who identify as working-class in the first instance who are best placed to inform others on the topic of what makes them working-class in their own minds. Second, class identity is something that needs to be informed beyond the literature per se. That is to say, we need real people to inform us as to what can otherwise be rather abstract theory on the subject of class. In this way, the approach taken is letting the group in question define itself.

As you can hopefully see, the above writing is critical without the need for an overt argument as to why semi-structured interviews are the best choice. Instead, the writer is explaining why semi-structured interviews are the best choice *for his/her research*. In doing so, the writer is justifying the choice that was made, and **justification** is a large part of being critical when explaining your methods (everything from the sample you chose to the data collection tools you used), as well as other areas – such as the theories/studies you refer to in your literature review (next section).

Scenario 5: Explaining the reasons for your choice of literature

In your dissertation or even in a more 'standard' essay of 2,500 words or so, justifying your decision to focus on a particular theory or concept and/or a specific author is also a way in which critical reflection is seen. Again, it is a case of essentially saying, 'I've given it some thought and here is why theory X and/or author Y are the most relevant choices for my essay/dissertation'. A bit of advice I often give my students is 'write for idiots'; in other words, spell out each and every decision you make for your assessment, more so dissertations which inherently involve a great deal more decision-making to begin with. This blunt advice refers to the need to tell us **what you did and why**, wherever applicable. No, your lecturers are not idiots of course, but we're not mind readers either. So unless you take the time to explain – hence, justify – the choices you made, we won't know why you did what you did. And this can lead to your reader essentially having to guess your rationale for the choices you made. But if you make it clear for us, this helps to 'sell' your choices as we can see the detail and logic involved with them. As I will return to later, it's a case of **the more you**

explain, the less they complain. In other words, take the time to talk your reader through your decision-making process – from methods used to literature referred to – and this means that even if your readers don't agree with your choices, they will agree with the rationale behind the choices you made.

So here's a brief example:

> This essay will largely rely on the socio-constructivist theory of identity, as this illustrates the fact that individuals exhibit, and own, multiple identities and with this comes implications for what is considered 'appropriate' behaviour or not. Thus, an individual might be, in the space of just one hour, a father, husband, and manager, each of which comes with its own societal norms for behaviour.

Just one sentence above nonetheless provides a logical justification for the choice to focus on a particular theory. Sometimes, all it takes in fact is one or two sentences to provide that much needed justification – hence, evidence of criticality – which subsequently provides your assessment with a bit of depth.

Scenario 6: Illustrating a broad concept

From my experience, a lack of illustration in students' assessments is one of the biggest issues and an issue that reflects a lack of criticality. Yet it's one of the easiest ways to be critical and help your reader understand your train of thought. When I refer to 'illustration', I simply mean providing the reader with examples of the topic you are referring to. I use the word 'illustration' and not exemplification, however, as I think that the very nature of this word – *illustrate* – is suggestive of being clear and vivid, and this is something you need to achieve in your assessed speech and writing. The key here is again to ask what the topic in question means to you as the starting point to then illustrating it. Beyond this, you should also be clear on what exactly needs to be illustrated. In this case, whenever you refer to a broad word/theory/concept within your discipline of study, you should provide an illustration to follow as much as possible. Because if you don't, then your writing will sound very abstract and be hard to fathom.

First, I would consider the terms used in your discipline which would indeed reflect a certain broadness – that is, they could refer to many different ideas, applications and definitions, and as such, by giving the reader a concrete illustration, it's your way of saying, 'Here's what *I* think'. Let's start by considering key terms as used in academia which reflect this broadness – add some of your own too:

Globalisation

Bilingualism

Scaffolded learning

Haploid

Psychodynamic

Ableism

A handful of words, from a handful of academic disciplines. Before we explore this further, don't forget that the same words can also be used very differently amongst disciplines. If we say that an experimental drug is 'controversial', then this means it could have life-threatening effects, or at least undesirable side effects. If we say, however, that *the belief that Korean is related to Hungarian is controversial* (as part of Linguistics), then this is very different.

Anyway, any time you refer to a broad word/concept and so on, whether a technical word or not, illustrate it. This doesn't mean giving a definition necessarily, but instead providing an example. But please make sure that the examples you provide are not merely cut and pasted from your class handouts and/or what the lecturer told you in class. Make sure the examples are your own, even if they were inspired by textbook reading in the first instance. If indeed the examples you provide are yours – from your *own* thinking – then the examples you give will have five benefits:

- They will make the content of your assessment more concrete and less abstract.
- They will help the reader (and marker) follow your train of thought.
- They will indeed act as evidence of your own critical thinking.
- They will act as support.
- They will prove you truly understand the topic under discussion.

Again, if the examples are immediately recognised by the lecturer as his/her ideas, then bullets three and five above are cancelled out automatically; how can a lecturer be sure you really understand and are being critical if you're simply telling them what they told *you*? You need to demonstrate that you are thinking for yourself!

Also, support does not simply mean referring to previous studies, or using quotes or paraphrase, though this is certainly a large part of support. Think about it – if you give the reader your own original examples of a broad concept, then this helps to provide a very visual means to then help them understand the subject better. This is also why bullets one and two are catered for by the provision of your own examples. Let's now see the differences between writing without, and then with, adequate illustration.

Example 1

Discrimination is unacceptable because it goes against the societal push for equality and diversity. We need to accept all people, especially those who might share a workplace with us. Laws are needed to create a fairer culture.

Thoughts: First, what are the broad words, whether technical or not, in the sample of writing above? That is to say, what words are used which by themselves could apply to many different things/ideas/subjects? It is precisely because of their broad nature that we need a concrete illustration with which to make the discussion easier to follow. Certainly, words such as *discrimination, societal, workplace* and *culture* mean so many different things that the reader, unless you spell it out for them, will have to fill in the blanks. Instead, this is *your* job.

Now have a look at the revised versions below.

Example 2

Discrimination is unacceptable because it goes against the societal push for equality and diversity. As but one example, prejudice based on those who are, or are perceived to be, disabled can be seen on many levels, reflective of the many ways the word 'disabled' is currently recognised in law. We need to accept all people, especially those who might share a workplace with us. Indeed, the workplace is perhaps one of the most relevant areas for addressing this prejudice, because excluding blind co-workers from group meetings or assuming someone in a wheelchair has an impaired intellect are but two examples of prejudices, even unintentional ones, that need to be addressed. For this reason, laws are in place in many countries, such as Australia, Bahrain and Finland to name but a few, which seek to protect the disabled from work-based prejudice in particular, seen with the Equality Act (2010) here in the UK.

Thoughts: Again, it's not a case of quantity – it's about *quality*. The addition of extra material directly above helps the reader have a firmer grasp of the subject under discussion precisely because we have evidence that the writer has a firm grasp – this is seen with original examples which together help to illustrate broad words such as *discrimination, workplace* and *society*.

Example 3

Discrimination is unacceptable because it goes against the societal push for equality and diversity. In terms of prejudice based on disability, this essentially places otherwise 'able-bodied' people as the norm, and in doing so, all those who fall outside this category are potentially treated less favourably. Thus, we have a societal dichotomy, of those who can walk, versus those who are in wheelchairs; those with limbs and those without; those with vision and those who are blind. Moreover, we need to understand this prejudice as applied to those who otherwise seem 'normal', but who might otherwise have learning difficulties. We need to accept all people, especially those who might share a workplace with us, as it is within the workplace where the sheer variety of people from all walks of life and backgrounds often come together, united in a common goal to get the job done.

Thoughts: The example above adds illustration by means of providing three examples of what would be considered disabilities and goes even further by suggesting a schism in society of, broadly speaking, disabled versus non-disabled. An illustration is then provided by means of conceptualising the workplace as a centre for people from many different backgrounds, which would involve diversity at other levels too (e.g. race, class, gender, etc.). A reference to a previous study or a quote would add even more depth (more on this later in the book), but for now, we have two examples which address the benefits of providing illustration for otherwise broad words.

So the next time you find yourself using a word in your assessment that has broad application/understanding within your discipline and/or society as a whole, provide an illustration. This will help you to help the reader, as well as giving the reader evidence that you understand the concept fully.

Example 4

It is common for infants to produce errors when acquiring their first language.

OK, which word do you think is broad – once again, I define 'broad' very spe-cifically in terms of words which could refer to multiple things and are therefore prone to potential confusion in the mind of the reader. Not because he/she doesn't 'get it', but precisely because the reader won't know what it means to *you* unless you tell them with the aid of your illustration.

Broad word: *Errors*

You don't need to be a linguist to know what an error is with regard to speaking a language, whether your own or someone else's. But what kind of errors are we talking about exactly? Grammatical? Phonological? Lexical? Pragmatic? You might also argue that *infants* is a broad word, but surely it's not broad/abstract to the extent that you can't pin it down to a central idea – namely, that infants are perhaps those who are aged from 1 to 4. Likewise, the words *first language* are broad in the sense that they could refer to potentially any one of the thousands of languages spoken in the world. But this is not what I mean by 'broadness'; I use the word 'broad' to refer to concepts/ideas/words which could refer to many different things, not necessarily to many different kinds of the same thing. Thus, *errors* can be applied to different categories, but *first language* can refer to just one thing – language – and this is clearly conceptualised, whether English, Russian, Korean, Tamil, Basque and so on.

The illustration that now follows the original sentence makes it clear for the reader:

It is common for infants to produce errors when acquiring their first language. This can be seen with hypercorrection, in which we find constructions for English speakers such as *I catched a cold.* Here, a grammatical rule is being over applied to irregular verbs which are, of course, the exception to the rule.

Do you see the difference? Let's compare with what could have made for a less effective transition; in this case, by moving from one broad term to another, without any intervening illustration:

It is common for infants to produce errors when acquiring their first language. This is the case across all world languages and errors are thus a predictable aspect of language acquisition across cultures. We can thus expect an infant who otherwise has no language learning difficulties, to nonetheless produce errors when using his/her first language.

In the example above, there really isn't any other broad word in need of illustrating. *Cultures*, like *first language*, is referring to a singular entity. Though this doesn't mean that you needn't provide an illustration for this word, it is more imperative to illustrate the word *errors*.

'Critical thinking' is actually a misleading term!

Critical thinking is a term often used at university, and yet, it is not entirely exact. This is because lecturers don't know what you're thinking – we can't read your thoughts. This is the reason why it is vital to illustrate broad terms and concepts that otherwise will be referred to in your assessments, as I have just stressed. Otherwise, we won't know what your understanding is of said terms/concepts/theories and so on. For this reason, you need to always tell us what is in your mind. This will allow us to see evidence of just how critical your thinking actually is, via critical writing (e.g. exams, essays, reports, PowerPoint slides, etc.) and via critical speaking (e.g. for an oral presentation). Critical thinking, then, is your business and is between you and you. You need to tell us what's in your mind as part of your assessment because it is only then that we will know the extent of the criticality that goes on as part of how you process information – whether it is derived from textbook reading or any other source. And very often, but not always, critical thinking is generated from critical reading. I had mentioned this earlier and again, it's a process which can be linear (sometimes!):

critical reading = critical thinking = critical writing

As I also mentioned, however, the process of getting from your information source (e.g. a journal article) to demonstrating your criticality is sometimes anything but linear, and instead, inspiration can strike when you're otherwise engaged in some other (non-academic) activity. Don't be surprised, then, when endless reading of academic texts on a given day results in very little, if any, critical thinking, versus times when you wake up first thing in the morning and have a great new idea for your research project or perhaps an original angle from which to discuss your essay's topic.

When you think about it, exams are one example of assessment in which you might depend on sudden inspiration. After all, you have a time limit of just 1 to 2 hours usually in which to say what you need to say and then that's it – time's up. For some, the time limit equates to pressure which can, in some cases, create inspiration and students then come up with some good insights. For others, this might not be the case, and for others still, there is no pressure as an exam is over fairly quickly, whereas an essay takes weeks to craft and perfect. Some prefer the extra time that comes with essay assessments, others would prefer not to drag things out and, instead, just get it 'over and done with' in an exam. But whichever type of assessment you prefer, chances are you will have a mixture of assessments throughout your time at university, to include some practical assessments perhaps, depending on the discipline.

But the main point is again that it is what you say, or write, as part of your assessments that proves to the marker that you really understand the material and, ideally, have something new to contribute in the process. So take those critical thoughts of yours and transfer them to the page, exam booklet, PowerPoint slides and/or your own voice – this is the ultimate dissemination of critical thoughts.

Note

1 OFSTED stands for The Office for Standards in Education, Children's Services and Skills, and works to assess the quality of schools in the UK.

Summary

This chapter has served to set the scene with regard to the skill of being critical. The main point again is that being critical can involve argumentation, but it is not tied to this skill alone. Instead, it is initiated with asking yourself what a given idea/topic/concept and so on means to you – what do you make of it/how do you interpret it? And interpretation is indeed the key word, as a means to help you begin the critical thinking process. So whether you're engaged with menu analysis to decide which of two restaurants is the better choice for dinner; whether you're deciding on an easier commute to work but with a higher price tag for a house closer to work, versus a lower price for a house farther away from work; or indeed, whether you're analysing the finer points of Marxian theory, all of these scenarios involve critical thinking. And all of these examples involve interpretation. Just as being critical is not tied to argumentation alone, neither is it a skill tied to academia alone. So harness this skill and its various parts when you're engaged with non-academic pursuits and start to apply it more and more to your assessments. Because the approach taken to real-world criticality (e.g. the pros and cons of a Samsung vs. an Apple) is the same as academic criticality (e.g. the pros and cons of wearing a school uniform, as part of a sociology assignment).

3

Understanding the Score Bands, and Developing Your Skills, Within Academic Assessments

The score you receive for your assessment is based on a variety of factors. Admittedly, this includes other aspects beyond being critical, though this is of course important. The purpose of this chapter is to discuss these additional areas on which you will be scored for your assessments in the UK. This does not suggest that in other countries the focus will be widely different in terms of how your assessments are judged and scored. You may in fact find similarities between the kinds of score terms used in the UK as in your own country, yet even within a given university in the UK, the score terms can be different. From my own experience in fact in the UK, the score terms differ from one programme to another, even within the same department, as well as differing when applied to a 2,000-word essay versus a 12,000-word dissertation. Despite this, I am not suggesting there is mass confusion, along the lines of 'what am I being judged on exactly from one programme to the next, from one university to the next, in one country to the next?'

Rest assured, the building blocks of your assessments' final score – the categories on which you will be scored – are largely the same, but with different terms sometimes given to them. So terminology aside, it is a matter of the kinds of *skills* you need to develop in your university-level assessments. So don't be surprised if the skill of 'critical thinking' is often referred to as 'analysis' as part of your assessment criteria. Likewise, 'grammar and style' might be referred to as 'presentation and language'. You might have other terms in use in your specific programme, within a specific department, within a specific university, within a specific country. But for this chapter, we will look into five score bands which represent five skills that you will be judged on for your assessments, regardless of differing terminologies.

Weightings for each score band

First, let us consider how each of these five score bands work together to arrive at your assessment's final score. Each score band is given its own weighting, referring to a percentage that contributes to the final score (see Table 3.1).

Table 3.1   Example score bands and weighting

Score Band	Weighting
Argument and structure	20%
Knowledge and understanding	20%
Use of sources	15%
Analysis	35%
Presentation and language	10%

Each assessment will have its own score band weightings, and it is very important for you to familiarise yourself with this for each assessment. Table 3.1 is thus nothing more than a guide. While it might reflect the weightings for assessments you must complete, it is not the same each time. What is important to note is the fact that analysis contributes the highest percentage to your final score. Though I can't guarantee this will always be the case, it would be very unusual for this skill not to have a high weighting. And consider this: if your analysis is sound, then it stands to reason that so is your knowledge and understanding. After all, your analysis of a given subject is unlikely to get a high score if you lack a basic, or even a moderate, understanding of the subject to begin with. With that in mind, a good score for these two score bands means that 55% of your final score might already be at the high end based on Table 3.1 (in the UK, this would be a final score ranging anywhere from 67 to 72, for example; elsewhere, something along the lines of a B+ to an A–). Of course, you might have great analytical skills but subsequent grammatical issues, to include typos, for example. However, even a low score for presentation and language, at just 10% of the final score here, might not offset the final score too much if your analysis is truly strong, coupled with good knowledge and understanding.

In the end, it is better to have strong evidence of analytical skills in your assessments, even if presentation and language are weak – this is a case of substance over style – and your assessment will be remembered more for its level of criticality than its grammatical weaknesses. But to have grammatical proficiency and an overall good style of writing but merely present a regurgitation of what you were told in class is clearly a case of style over substance, and your final score will reflect this. So get into the habit of carefully analysing the weighting of scores for all your assessments, as this will help give you some crucial information from the beginning as to how you're being judged and the ways in which this contributes to your assessment's final score.

I now continue with a detailed discussion of each of the five score bands.

Argument and structure

You may indeed come across the word 'argument' a great deal as part of your assessments, which is one reason why you may feel that making an argument is such an integral aspect of being critical, as well as a key feature of higher education in general. Sometimes your assessments will require you to make an overt argument, by arguing for or against a specific idea/theory and so on. However, the term 'argument' in academic contexts – specifically with regard to assessment criteria – does not always refer to an argument in the strict sense of actually *making* one. This is one definition, however. But the term 'argument' is also used in another, more broad sense as part of your assessments. In this case, the term refers to **the main point that underpins the entirety of your essay, response to an exam question, oral presentation** and so on. **This main point needs to be encapsulated in one sentence ideally** and for essays, placed firmly in your introduction (I will refer to this sentence as the 'argument sentence', though this is a term not generally used in universities). Likewise, within a response to an exam question or as part of an oral presentation, the argument should be presented at the start. You are then free to explore it as part of the body of your essay, exam question or slides. But how do we construct a 'main point'? Below is an illustration which addresses this question, followed by a further explanation.

Introduction: This essay will discuss globalisation in order to determine if it needs to adapt for the 21st century as compared with previous years.

Body: Show both sides of globalisation (once defined), the pros and cons; show both sides of this topic.

Conclusion: Overall, it is suggested that globalisation, as practiced in previous years, now needs to adopt more culture-sensitive and environment-friendly practices for the next century.

29

As you can see, the above model first sets out the assignment's intentions, investigating the subject from both sides and then arrives at the overall conclusion, which is fittingly placed in the conclusion.

A good argument sentence should not simply tell the reader what your assessment is doing, whether an essay or exam. It needs to explain *why*. As you can see, the formula above is giving both aspects: *This essay will discuss globalisation . . .* (this is the 'what'), *. . . in order to determine if it needs to adapt for the 21st century as compared with previous years* (this is the 'why'). By adding the 'why' aspect to your argument sentence, you are – once again – justifying the importance of your overall assessment. And once again, this takes some critical thinking on your part. Exactly why *is* your assessment focus important to discuss? You could of course say that the lecturer set the assignment anyway and it's the same for everyone in the class. Perhaps the assignment instructions as a result already tell you the validity of the subject under discussion. Or you may find yourself given several choices for your assessment topic, if not the freedom to create your own. No matter what the situation, however, you should always think of your argument sentence as a two-part construction: WHAT your assessment is going to focus on + WHY this focus is important. Now, some disciplines might ask you to construct an argument sentence at the start of your assessment which does indeed reflect the word 'argument' in a strict sense: *This essay argues that we must create more green cities in order to prevent a further environmental crisis*. Therefore, it is important that you discuss this with your individual lecturers in order to be clear from the start what is being asked of you. However, if you conceptualise the need for a WHAT and WHY as part of your argument sentence, then this is a good start.

Going further, it will depend also on *who* you're writing for, not just *where* you're writing (e.g. whether you find yourself in the UK, Germany or the USA). Assessments within the Hard Sciences, for example, such as physics and chemistry, often test hypotheses and so often make overt argumentation a feature of their work. In this case, your assessment will have an argument running throughout which will refer to 'argument' in a more strict sense (e.g. *If plants are watered with a 10% detergent solution, their growth will be negatively affected*; Helmenstine, 2019). In the Social Sciences, such as psychology and sociology, a statement of intentions is perhaps more common as the Social Sciences deal largely with human behaviour and phenomena. This is somewhat more unpredictable than the natural phenomena found within the Hard Sciences, and so it is somewhat impractical to suggest facts within Social Science research. Of course, this is not absolute, and hypotheses can be found in the Social Sciences (and statements of intentions can be found in the Hard Sciences by all means), but not to 'prove' anything per se, but more to *suggest* ideas and outcomes. Consider the following arguments:

Education: It is argued that if we apply a visual pedagogic approach to the group of primary school students, their understanding of the subject can be facilitated and, in turn, scores will be raised compared with those *from the control group.*

Education, while a field and not so much a subject as such, is clearly not reflective of the Hard Sciences. And yet the argument sentence above is taking an argumentative stance by using a hypothesis-based approach. Much more necessary detail would need to be provided, such as the age group of the students, what subject is being studied and what specific types of visuals will be included in the pedagogic approach. But on the basis of the above sentence, it is clear that hypotheses do have a place outside the Hard Sciences. But while the Hard Sciences are largely dedicated to facts and verifiable proof, this is less the case within the Social Sciences. Even if the students who receive a visual pedagogic approach do indeed learn better and get higher scores than the control group who do not receive such instruction, we clearly cannot generalise such results to *all* primary school students. In this case, even if the hypothesis turns out to be true, this does not 'prove' anything per se; it merely means that it was correct in this particular study and is supported by the study's evidence. But that's as far as it goes. There may be many other factors which could have contributed to the results, factors which go beyond the use of a visual pedagogic approach (e.g. the students' interest in the subject being taught in the first place). Such is the complex nature of conducting research with human participants, as there can be a great many factors which combine to produce a certain set of results.

In the end, no book can explain everything that will work for all disciplines in universities across the world, and for this reason, I strongly suggest that you talk to your lecturers about your assessments if in any doubt. This is perhaps an obvious piece of advice, but I'm thinking more in terms of quite specific aspects of your assessment, beyond the broader concerns such as how to understand the assessment question (which this book will discuss in Chapter Four). Such specific concerns may well include *the kind of argument you need to construct for your assessment's introduction* (whether part of your essay's introduction or within the first slide of your PowerPoint presentation) and *whether or not it's OK to use 'I'*; these are but two examples.

So, to sum up: your assessment's argument is seen on two levels. One, it refers to the sentence in which you encapsulate the content of what your assessment is all about – the main point/purpose and if you like, the 'gist' of your assessment. This can be a statement of intentions, thus taking a 'wait and see' approach, or a hypothesis-driven argument, if not an overt argument per se. Second, the argument refers to the much broader level of making sure that your focus is consistent and unified. In simple terms, this means that whatever the main point of your assessment is – as stated in the argument sentence – you have to make sure that **each and every sentence connects with, relates to and supports the said argument sentence**. This will create a unified focus, which is very important, so that none of your writing/speaking strays from the argument sentence and the specific focus that is implied within this one key sentence. While an effective argument sentence can ideally stand alone in terms of making sense on its own without the rest of the introduction, it's fine to have an implied argument. Let's have a look, then, at some good arguments from different disciplines – 'good' purely on an objective level, in that they summarise the purpose of the assessment in clear terms and involve examples of both direct and implied arguments.

Sociology

Assignment brief: Here we have an assignment that asks you to critically evaluate the Nordic model of gender equality in terms of its successes, but also ways in which such success has been called into question.

This essay will discuss the Nordic model of gender equality in Norway, Sweden and Denmark, to outline the shared reasons for its success, but also to approach the subject critically in order to determine if this model can nonetheless still be considered successful in the current times.

Physics

Assignment brief: The argument below may well derive from an assignment brief which asks students to explore String Theory in terms of allowing students to choose a particular approach regarding the theory's recent 'comeback'.

The report discusses the theoretical background of String Theory and makes a case for its resurgence in recent times to be a potential candidate for the Theory of Quantum gravity by addressing its former shortcomings and experimental methods.

Source: UKEssays. (2020e, May 18). *To what extent does string theory present a possibility of a unified theory of quantum gravity?* https://www.ukessays.com/essays/physics/to-what-extent-does-string-theory-present-a-possibility-of-a-unified-theory-of-quantum-gravity.php. Accessed on 12 November 2020.

Linguistics

Assignment brief: An essay which requires students to decide on the more plausible of the two main theories of language acquisition could easily produce an argument sentence as the one below.

The purpose of this essay is to investigate child language acquisition (CLA), in order to determine whether nature or nurture is the more credible explanation for CLA.

Literature

Assignment brief: The instructions that created the argument below could easily have asked students to discuss any aspect of the play *Othello* in conjunction with applying a particular theoretical aspect to the discussion; this is broad of course and could involve several theoretical approaches, such as feminism, Marxism and indeed, critical race theory.

This essay will discuss the central characters in Othello based on critical race theory, in order to highlight how this centuries-old tale is quite reflective of modern-day society and race relations.

Psychology

Assignment brief: The assignment instructions could well have asked students to explore the concept of altruism, in terms of whether this exists or not in society based primarily on an understanding of its definition.

The main aim of this essay is to consider the assertion that every action is a selfish one and thus true altruism does not exist.

Source: UKEssays. (2020k, June 1). *True altruism does not exist*. https://www.ukessays.com/essays/psychology/true-altruism-does-not-exist.php. Accessed on 12 November 2020.

Biology

Assignment brief: Here the student might have been asked to discuss the pros and cons of liquid based cytology in relation to its use within screenings for cervical cancer, with the expectation that the student will arrive at his/her final opinion on the matter within the conclusion.

In recent years a new way of screening the cervical samples has been developed. This is referred to as liquid based cytology rather than conventional cytology. However, there has been considerable debate over the costs and benefits of the new technology, as will be examined below.

Source: UKEssays. (2020g, June 1). *Example biology essay – 2:1 level*. https://www.ukessays.com/essays/biology/example-biology-essay.php. Accessed on 12 November 2020.

The argument 'sentence' directly above may appear to be more than just one sentence, but in actuality it's not. The final sentence is the essay's overall argument, but I have provided the two sentences prior in order to give necessary background, because otherwise, the reference to 'the new technology' would not be understood. Otherwise, the final sentence makes clear the rationale and purpose for the overall essay. The writer is setting up the WHAT (the use of liquid-based cytology in cervical sample screenings) and the WHY (due to the debates surrounding this technology's costs and benefits, more exploration is needed). While the argument above is perhaps less explicit than the others that preceded it, it is still effective precisely because the WHY can be found, albeit within the context of several sentences. This is an example of what I refer to as an implied argument, which still works as well as a directly stated argument sentence.

I again suggest that you take this up with your lecturers, however. Even within a given discipline, there can be much variation in terms of not only what you write, but how you write – this may influence the type of argument sentence that you construct, as well as broader concerns such as the style of writing. For example, within the subject of geography, there is both physical and human geography, with the former more reflective of the Hard Sciences and the latter more reflective of the Social Sciences (e.g. sociology). Within biology, some aspects can also at times reflect a more 'pure' scientific approach, such as the study of the human body, while at times, it can cross over into a more human-based focus, thus approaching sociology and cultural anthropology. Moreover, some essays within the same discipline might be more 'traditional' in focus, such as investigating an issue, while others might adopt a much more informal and personal approach, such as reflective essays. Much like a Russian *matryoshka* doll, there are layers within layers within layers even with an otherwise 'singular' discipline. So bear this in mind for each and every essay assessment in particular.

How to achieve a coherent structure

Like 'criticality', coherence is also a broad, rather abstract word. Yet it is also mentioned in feedback sometimes from your lecturers, and ties in with your essay's structure. To maintain a coherent structure in your essay writing requires you to think critically as you will have to decide on the topics for inclusion, the best order to present them in and exploring them in analytical depth of course. Having a coherent structure is not entirely irrelevant to exam assessments or oral presentations either, but given the amount of time often afforded to preparing your essay before the submission date, the suggestion is that with more time to prepare, there is also more time to get the structure right. So what is coherence exactly? You know what it means in a general sense, but for assessment purposes at university, it has some very specific properties which, like academic writing overall, can be likened to boxes that need to be ticked. Academic writing is actually quite predictable, and the more you can get in the habit of literally ticking the boxes, the more systematic and easier essay writing can be. But for any type of assessment, more so those that involve writing perhaps, coherence means the following.

First, ensure that the body paragraphs of your essay – those that come in between the introduction and conclusion – **focus on just one topic at a time**. This is age-old advice in writing classes, but it's there for a reason. And the inverse is true: if your paragraphs have two or more topics at a time, this is *in*coherent writing. Second, **ensure that every topic relates to your essay's argument sentence** so that not even a few stray sentences are otherwise unrelated or irrelevant. Third, **make sure that the order of the topics moves in a logical sequence**. Determining what is a 'logical' sequence/order can be based on going in chronological order if discussing the historical development(s) of a certain subject, or simply moving from broad to narrow in terms of the topics' content. Finally, you also need to make sure that **each body paragraph has a topic sentence** which, like your argument sentence, has both a topic (the WHAT) and a point to make about it (the WHY). Much more will be said about structure in Chapters Five and Six, from 1,500-word essays to 80,000-word PhD theses. But for now, this chapter will give you a brief but informative summary.

To continue, if your essay (but again, you can apply this to exams/oral presentation slides) is discussing the development of a certain theory in psychology, then it makes sense to start from its origins and chart its progression up until the present day. If you're discussing the Me Too Movement, then it might be a good idea (but by no means the *only* good idea) to begin in the 1960s with the second-wave feminist movement, and then chart its evolution through the decades that followed up until the present day regarding high-profile individuals being brought to justice. You get the idea. The inherent aspect of criticality here is once again initiated by asking, 'what does this mean to me?' Here, 'this' can refer to your assessment's overall focus, whether a sociocultural movement, the global spread of a virus or a prominent director's film output. In this way, you are asking yourself potentially many questions pertaining in this case to **what topics are most important to focus on** and **in what order** and as I mentioned earlier *whose* work should be included, thus linking to diversity within your subject area. To answer these questions – and others – you need, of course, to think critically. Potential questions might involve the following:

- What are the key historical aspects and/or development of this subject?
- Who are the more prominent authors/researchers within the subject area, who would be conspicuous by their absence?

- But are there authors whose work is indeed available but has been neglected and not promoted or disseminated as much as those within the canon – how can I access these?
- What are the more prominent/groundbreaking studies within this subject area?
- What do *I* want the reader to know about?
- What topics are most relevant to my argument sentence anyway?
- Likewise, what aspects of this subject might need to be left out of my assessment (e.g. due to a lack of time if giving an oral presentation, taking an exam or based on the word count for an essay)?
- Do certain topics need to have more discussion than others, but without making the assessment seem biased by focusing on one topic much more than another?
- Though a micro-level concern, would your essay benefit from having subheadings to announce the different topics (even for short essays)?

Once again, we can see through the bullet points above how being critical is about actively thinking about a given subject, leading to interpretation, but not always about making an overt argument. In fact, mind mapping, which is a commonly-used technique to generate ideas for your assessments or a class discussion, is a prime example of critical thinking, but an example that perhaps is not always considered as reflecting critical thinking largely due to it not involving an explicit argument.

And if your topics move from broad to narrow as another way to understand a logical progression of topics, then this means that you'll need to think critically again – in this case, deciding what the starting point is for your subject, before you end up with the most narrow and relevant point of discussion. Think of this progression in terms of an inverted triangle (Figure 3.1) to give you a helpful visual.

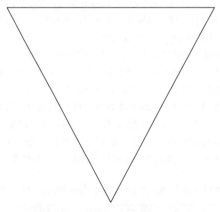

Figure 3.1   Essay topics moving from broad to narrow

If your assessment is discussing the use of language in media ads, then you need to have a think as to where you might want to begin the discussion – this is relevant to a 2,000-word essay and even more so to an 80,000-word PhD thesis when you'll have much more room to discuss things. Below are some potential ideas as to the starting point, midpoint(s), and end point, with the end point being the most relevant, narrow, and focused with regard to your assessment's argument:

Starting point: Advertisement in general in terms of its power and purpose.

Midpoint: The use of language (in general) to persuade.

End point: The use of written language in ads to persuade the audience.

The example above is, once again, merely one example amongst many others you can think of probably. Once you've decided on the topics to discuss, then you can think critically regarding the titles you want to use, assuming you're going to use subheading titles. For average length essays, say up to 2,500 or 3,000 words, subheadings are usually not necessary, but check with your lecturer on this. For longer essays, especially those that are research-based, subheadings are pretty much standard to begin with, as they help your reader to navigate what can be an essay that is many thousands of words long.

To conclude this section, I leave you with an essay skeleton, though this could apply just as well to an exam question and its subsequent structure of your answer to the question, as well as applying to an oral presentation and how you want to divide it up in terms of how you present it, both orally and in terms of written language on visual aids. Thus, by having a clear argument sentence from the start and ensuring that each and every sentence that follows in your assessment relates to and connects with the argument sentence, then you will have **a unified focus** and **a coherent structure** – but don't forget the additional considerations referred to earlier to maintain coherence!

A good way to conceptualise the skeleton of your assessment is to break it down as follows: INTRODUCTION – BODY – CONCLUSION. The skeleton below is based on an essay which focuses on the cultural impact of the selfie, taken from an anthropology essay.

Introduction

- First provide some background information on the subject.
- Then use the background information to lead into your argument sentence: *This essay will examine the cultural and societal aspects that are incorporated into selfies with references to anthropological theories as well as examples from my personal experience (referencing my attached photos before the bibliography).*

37

Topic One

Stuart Hall and representation

Topic Two

Erving Goffman and his work on the relationship between culture and imagery – this has three components which are subdivided into topics Three, Four and Five.

Topic Three

Dramaturgy

Topic Four

Individuality through the medium of the selfie

Topic Five

Visual tropes

Conclusion

- Arrive at your overall opinion on the matter, having explored the subject first in the body.
- Recap your main points.
- Don't provide any new topics at this point.
- Perhaps end with a 'closing thought' – an effective final sentence (e.g. a question, prediction, statistic, and so on).

Source: UKEssays. (2020b, May 18). *Cultural and societal impacts of the selfie*. https://www.ukessays.com/essays/anthropology/cultural-and-societal-impacts-of-the-selfie.php. Accessed on 12 November 2020.

Points to critically consider, again as part of a visual representation of what your note taking could look like:

- Does the argument sentence have a WHY, and not just the WHAT?

  o The WHY aspect of the argument sentence, once again, can be implied via the overall background information provided, and need not always be presented explicitly as part of the argument sentence. In the essay on which this skeleton is based, the WHY was indeed made clear and is captured in the following sentence taken from the background information within the Introduction.

- ○ 'Producing this type of photo is such a straightforward process, but there is certainly a more complex individual and cultural understanding behind the purpose of these visual expressions'.
- ○ In other words, the writer is focusing on the selfie in order to explain to the reader the deeper cultural and individual aspects that many of us might not have considered previously; thus, there is a gap in knowledge, however small, that is being filled. Thus, the WHAT + WHY are intact!

- Are the topics relevant to the focus on the cultural significance of the selfie?

  - ○ While the overall subject – let alone the topics that delve into it – may not be familiar to all the readers of this book, it is clear from having looked at the essay that the writer makes the relevance of the topics to the overall argument very clear.
  - ○ Certainly, key terms such as *culture, imagery* and *representation* all have a part to play in the discussion.

- Do the topics move in a logical sequence?

  - ○ Well, the work of Hall comes after the work of Goffman in terms of when their work was produced, so it could be said that it would be logical to begin with a focus on Goffman and *then* Hall to produce a kind of 'chronological coherence'.
  - ○ On the other hand, given that the work of Goffman is the dominant focus within the essay, then from another point of view, it makes sense to focus on this *after* discussing Hall.
  - ○ In this manner, Hall's work – though important in its own right – serves in part to introduce the more extensive focus on Goffman.

You can see, from what is just a partial list of considerations above, just how critical *critical thinking* can be. Again, there is much more detailed discussion of essay structure provided in Chapter Five, which will go over much of this chapter's content but in even more explicit and illustrative detail. For now, however, the purpose of this chapter has been to help get you started before you begin constructing your next assessment. Now that you understand argument and structure, and how they interrelate, let's move on to another skill on which you will be judged for your assessments: knowledge and understanding.

Knowledge and understanding

I begin with a brief discussion in relation to these two key words before discussing the implications for both.

Knowledge: This is where your insights come into focus, and this offers you the chance to reveal how much you know. Again, the more you go beyond what you were told in class, the better. Use the knowledge given to you/acquired by you (e.g. as part of textbook reading/lecture content) and then take it to the next level – offer your original insights/ideas/opinions and so on by asking yourself what the content of textbooks/lectures and such means to you. In other words, try to add something new to each and every assessment – add content that ideally makes the marker stop and say, 'I didn't think of that!', 'I never considered it that way before'. Even if the marker does not necessarily agree with your opinion, should you offer one, if he/she nonetheless agrees with the logic behind it and can see your train of thought that has led to your opinion, this is key.

Understanding: 'Understanding' is to knowledge what a tap is to water. Understanding is how you confirm that your knowledge base is present, accurate and sound. If your assessments are largely made up of content from lecture handouts, for example, then this demonstrates a certain amount of knowledge, but it doesn't reveal how much you actually understand it. That is because it is a cut and paste, to an extent, of someone else's knowledge (e.g. the lecturer, the author, etc.). Once again, you really start to make your knowledge base work for you the minute you show your interpretation of it – this in turn shows your understanding. As I have stressed, and will continue to stress throughout this book, your understanding of any subject, whether academic or not, is demonstrated when you interpret the subject in question and from here reveal your insights, whether they involve opinions, illustrations or explanations (more on this in Chapter Eight).

There is not a great deal more I can discuss in this section as, simply put, you need to make sure you understand your subject! This is your responsibility and if you have any doubts at all regarding your knowledge base, consult with your lecturers. Make sure that all your doubts are addressed, questions answered and misunderstandings dealt with before you begin your assessment. So, in a broad sense, making sure your knowledge and understanding is sound begins – and ends – with making sure you understand what your subject is all about, whether it pertains to your textbook reading, lecture content, classroom discussion and so on, and whether it pertains to theory, concepts or definitions of ideas within your discipline – you get the idea.

However, there are other ways you can apply your critical thinking skills in order to demonstrate that your knowledge of the assessment subject and understanding of such is sound. One way that has already been discussed is all about illustrating broad concepts, theories, words and so on when you mention them within your assessments. As I stressed, there are five very specific benefits each and every time you provide your reader, or listener, with an illustration. Let's have another look with an excerpt from a Nursing essay. The broad word in this case, which is in need of illustration, is *nursing shortage* when applied to healthcare.

In fact, how would *you* interpret this broad reference in this specific context, whether you study Nursing or not? Whatever it means to you, think of an appropriate interpretation. Of course, you could argue that 'nursing shortage' is self-explanatory – it means a shortage of nurses so what else do you need to say? But if you stop, interpret and thus think critically, you will generate further ideas; below is a mere sample of such possibilities:

- What are the target numbers of nurses in the British National Health Service (NHS) in the first instance? This will help better understand just how short the NHS is of nurses.
- What are some specific implications (here's where an illustration would work great) of a shortage of nurses?
- Are there shortages of nurses in certain regions/hospitals more than in others? Why might this be?
- What is the cause(s) for these shortages – can this be addressed in any way? Burnout? Working conditions? Both?
- What are the effects?

You can see that there are many directions in which your critical thinking can take you. Let's see what the writer chooses to do in order to illustrate the broad reference of *nursing shortages*:

Nursing shortage affects the quality of patient care in many ways.

Thoughts: The first sentence sets up the topic under discussion for the paragraph.

For instance, the lack of nursing staff in a hospital can lead to a heavier workload for the staff nurses present, which in turn can negatively affect nursing job satisfaction and contribute to a higher turnover and again lead to shortage (Duffield and O'Brien-Pallas, 2003).

Thoughts: The second sentence gives a clear illustration, in this case an illustration of the effects and implications of the shortage in question. This illustration is also backed up by a reference to the relevant literature, a study by Duffield and O'Brien-Pallas (2003). This might lead you to question if the illustration belongs to the writer or to the literature referred to. But the fact is that a reference to literature will always add credibility anyway.

This is a logical consequence because fewer staff nurses working in a ward means that each nurse will have to cater to a higher number of patients in order to effectively care for all the inpatients, and perhaps over a longer period of time. This can lead to work-related stress and burnout and therefore degrade the quality of care that they can render, and eventually cause them to quit.

Thoughts: Sentences 3 and 4 clearly belong to the writer in terms of his/her understanding.

Source: UKEssays. (2018p, November). *Sample undergraduate 2:1 nursing essay*. https://www.ukessays.com/services/samples/2-1-nursing-essay.php. Accessed on 12 November 2020.

The writer thus sets up things very nicely in this paragraph, as follows:

Sentence 1: Topic sentence (more on topic sentences in Chapter Five)

WHAT (nursing shortage) + THE POINT TO MAKE (it affects the quality of patient care)

Sentence 2: A broad illustration and reference to the literature

Sentences 3 and 4: The writer provides a more detailed illustration with regard to the point made in Sentence 2.

So once again, strive to provide illustrations. Even for words/concepts which you might otherwise think are clear in meaning already, it is also clear that the key term of *nursing shortage* can be interpreted differently by different people. So unless you provide your interpretation for the reader, there will be a blank space in your assessment where you could have otherwise offered your take on things.

Beyond this discussion so far, there are some final points to make regarding how to approach the category of knowledge and understanding. Chapter Nine, for example, will discuss the skill of paraphrasing in detail, but for now, consider how this practice allows you to demonstrate the extent of your subject knowledge and understanding. After all, if you do not adequately understand the topic you're reading about, then your paraphrase of it will suffer – and this has happened to me in my own earlier studies.

Ultimately, demonstrating that you know what you're talking about means more than just citing what you have been told in class, what you have been provided with in lecture handouts and what you have read in books. The information gleaned from such sources is important of course, but should always be the starting point. From here, your marker will have little doubt about your knowledge and understanding the more you interpret all of the above, as this means the more you will be able to reveal your original interpretations – hence understanding – of the subject. So interpret what you read in books/journal articles/book chapters and so on. Interpret the content of your lecture notes and lecture handouts. Interpret what the lecturer says and writes on the board. Interpret what is mentioned as part of class discussion. In doing so, you demonstrate your knowledge and understanding not by telling the marker what is already known to him/her – you demonstrate your knowledge and understanding by telling the marker what *you* know (and something that he/she might not). This is key. Every academic discipline is dynamic, not static, and this means that it is always moving forward, however slowly. And to move forward, we need to have fresh perspectives on how to look at common knowledge, as well as introducing new information across the board. In Nursing, for example, shortages are perhaps nothing new. But do you have a new way to consider this? This can include anything from an original example, as discussed earlier, but perhaps a solution or even why the shortages are a particular issue at a given moment.

Again, consider now any concept that is commonly discussed within your discipline, whether psychosexual theory, evolution or postmodernism. Don't define these concepts – illustrate them:

- Concept 1: For example, . . .
- Concept 2: For example, . . .
- Concept 3: For example, . . .

To suggest a further example, can you think of a modern way to consider psychosexual theory perhaps, given the multiple influences on psychosexual development in terms of the ever-present nature of social media (e.g. selfies posted, graphic content of postings, etc.)? Is this leading to children developing sexual knowledge, whether right or wrong, at an earlier age? I do not have an answer to this question at all, and I'm not a psychologist. But I am able to nonetheless take a relatively well-understood theory and consider it from a deeper level – and I'm doing this as an outsider to psychology.

We'll now move on to a third skill on which your assessments are based: use of sources.

Use of sources

Sources is a necessarily broad word as it captures all the outside information you refer to in your assessments which provides support for your own writing. This often refers to direct quotations, a paraphrase or a summary of someone else's research. But in terms of the actual sources themselves from which you obtain quotes and such, this is largely tied to academic textbooks, journal articles, book chapters and reports (e.g. such as those issued by the government). However, there is no reason why you can't go further afield and, in doing so, obtain information from websites, newspapers and magazines. Granted, books and journals are perhaps the mainstay of academic research, but if you find some particularly timely and relevant information in a newspaper article with which to help support your points, then by all means use that.

And again, consider the authors whose work, ideas and perspectives you refer to. This might be relevant in some disciplines more than in others, such as sociology for example, in which societal movements (e.g. Me Too, Black Lives Matter) are the topic of much academic discussion and assessment nowadays. As such, authors whose work is particularly relevant to such areas, and especially authors who have lived experiences with such movements (e.g. a black British individual who's been published on Black Lives Matter), would indeed be appropriate as a source of information for an assessment.

When writing an essay, there is an expectation to use quotes and paraphrase throughout and show evidence that you have indeed done some background reading. When giving an oral presentation, this same evidence is expected, largely displayed as part of the visual aid you might use to accompany your talk such as PowerPoint slides. As for exams, I would suggest that broad references to researchers – thus summaries of previous research – are perhaps more the norm (e.g. *Smith's theory of X means that . . .*). If you use direct quotes in an exam, this is fine in itself, but it means more pressure on you to memorise verbatim text. Moreover – and this is just my personal opinion – it might give the impression that you are memorising information to the extent of not providing more of your own. Parrot learning. This need not be the case, but what I'm getting at (again!) is not simply cutting and pasting the information you've been given in class/read about and using that for the most part to demonstrate your understanding. Instead, use it as a means to then reveal your own original understanding.

Chapter Nine will go into detail about how to use quotes, paraphrase and summaries of the literature, but for now, I want to give you one specific piece of advice, as part of a summary of how to use sources. I would consider this a golden rule when using sources in your assessments. And the advice is this: make the sources you use, whatever form they take, work for you – **do something with them**. This means not just referring to a source and then leaving it – interpret it and then provide your interpretation. As interpretation is the bedrock of being critical, I present in Chapter Eight four ways in which you can, in fact, *interpret interpretation*. This is not tied solely to what you do with any sources you use, but it is largely a part of your source use.

For now, as a taster of things to come, and yet something to start considering from this point on, I provide an illustration of what I mean. Provided is an essay sample from the discipline of business. First, the quote, in this case embedded in a larger sentence:

Knowledge transfers and the process of sharing knowledge can be defined as "the exchange of knowledge between and among individuals, and within and among teams, organisational units, and organisations. This exchange may be focused or unfocused, but it usually does not have a clear a priori objective" (Schwartz (2006) cited in Paulin & Suneson, 2015 p. 82).

Now, what to do with this? As always, begin with interpretation. Below are some potential interpretations and I should point out that interpreting something, in this case a direct quote, does not only mean giving your opinion about it. It can also refer to deciding what the best approach is for the quote. In other words, do you want to agree with it? Disagree? Provide an illustration? Let's have a look at some possible avenues:

- As is so vital with illustration, you could start with broad words in the quote. For example, do you need to illustrate 'organisational units'? Do you feel it necessary to illustrate 'focused' and 'unfocused'? Might you combine the two terms and provide an illustration of a focused/unfocused exchange within an organisational unit?
- Do you feel it necessary to perhaps explain why the lack of 'a clear a priori objective' is a feature of knowledge transfers?
- Do you want to perhaps go a bit broad in your focus, essentially 'backing up' and first explaining to the reader the significance or relevance of knowledge transfers in today's society?
- Do you feel a need to explain the scope of knowledge transfers in the first place? For example, is this practice tied solely to business per se, or does it apply further afield (e.g. in professions such as medicine, teaching or acting)?

These are merely four possibilities and there could be many more to consider the more you analyse the quote. Let's now analyse the completed paragraph and see what the writer chose to do with the quote:

Knowledge transfers and the process of sharing knowledge can be defined as "the exchange of knowledge between and among individuals, and within and among teams, organisational units, and organisations. This exchange may be focused or unfocused, but it usually does not have a clear a priori objective" (Schwartz (2006) cited in Paulin & Suneson, 2015 p. 82). This definition noted captures the different levels at which transfers may take place and captures the extent to which these may be either formal or informal with challenges coupled with each form.

Thoughts: The sentence directly above essentially interprets the quote by paraphrasing it – providing the same basic content as the quote, but still adding something new in the process: a reference to challenges (which the quote did *not* mention).

Drawing on this definition, there is a need to think about the context within which knowledge emerges and how such knowledge transfers can be facilitated, drawing in particular on challenges which may occur in the Chinese business environment which is notably different to that of the West.

Thoughts: The sentence above then refers to the quote as a means to set up a problem – this is a good example of the aforementioned need to problematise subject areas as part of your primary research. The problem in this case is considering the cultural implications of knowledge transfers, here involving China and Western countries. In addition, the writer is also perhaps implying – however subtly – that the content of the quote is perhaps too broad a definition, one that does not take into consideration the complexities of different cultures when discussing knowledge transfers.

A focus on the differences within the Chinese market is important and provides a core rationale for this research due to the increasingly powerful political and economic nature of China.

Thoughts: This final sentence serves to provide a strong rationale for the overall essay. If this were your actual dissertation I would strongly recommend more than just a sentence for your rationale, but for a regular essay (i.e. that which doesn't involve primary research) it is sufficient (though not necessarily required).

Source: UKEssays. (2018h, November). *Sample undergraduate 2:1 business dissertation*. https://www.ukessays.com/services/samples/2-1-business-disser tation.php. Accessed on 14 November 2020.

So, with just one example which involves the use of just one single quote, what did the writer do exactly with the quote? How did the writer make the quote work for himself/herself? To answer this, I too need to apply critical reading to the paragraph above, in order to truly appreciate the writer's strategy via the quote. Here it is, at least as I see things – you may disagree and that's fine of course as that shows you're being critical!

- The writer uses the quote in Sentences 1 and 2 to set the scene – in this case, to simply provide an objective definition of knowledge transfers to thus provide a background of what is to follow.
- Beyond this, the quote is used as a means to then problematise things by identifying a gap that is otherwise not suggested by the quote – in this case, the need to consider how the same knowledge needs to be considered as part of cross-cultural exchanges.
- So overall, the quote's purpose is to **define** and **make an argument**; these are but two uses of quotes.

I am not saying that each and every reference to a source, whether a quote, paraphrase or summary of previous research, needs to be addressed in some way. In fact, when a quote is used to support your own views directly, then very often this is sufficient usage of the quote in that it has already done its job – in this case, provided backup for your own views. What I am saying though is try to be more mindful about your use of sources, not just in terms of where they derive from (e.g. books, journals), who said them and what purpose they serve (e.g. to support a view or define a concept), but in simple terms of **what you make of them** – how do you interpret them and do you think your interpretation is needed in conjunction with a given source use?

Some final points to consider for your use of sources are more practical ones. Basically, while I can't give you an exact number of books/journal articles and so on that you should consult, quote from and read for each assessment, it is important to show evidence that you have consulted the relevant literature. It's fair to say that the longer the word count for an essay, the longer the references page (if of course your department uses a references page for its essays, as some will use footnotes – more on this later in this chapter). Asking yourself how many quotes you should have in your essay and how many references to sources you should have in your references page is like asking how long a piece of string is. Thus, determining how many quotes to use, how many summaries of previous literature to refer to and how many books you should refer to is indeed an area in which critical thinking must be deployed. No one can tell you in an absolute sense, unless some lecturers do specify a number. What I will say is this: ask yourself when you read through your essay before submission if you feel you have enough references to the literature **to help make your points more convincing**. If at any time you find yourself making assertions and claims, for example, then it makes sense to follow them with a reference to the literature. One such example is below:

> It is clear that more must be done to address the need for eco-cities in this century (Jones, 2006; Davis, 2008; Berisha, 2012).

You should also make sure that the literature you refer to is not too out of date, though if a groundbreaking study was conducted decades ago and is still routinely cited, then this clearly would *not* be out of date. By all means, ask your lecturer for suggestions in terms of recommended reading, the key texts and 'key players' within a given discipline (e.g. Chomsky for sociolinguistics, Goffman for sociology, etc.), to include of course names which have perhaps been neglected or excluded from the canon of literature and who may well represent otherwise missing perspectives from the overall conversation. If you rely on the reading materials that are on the core reading list, then you can't go far wrong if you refer to these; they're placed on the core reading list for a reason. But be adventurous and go beyond the core reading list and look at the materials on the recommended reading list, should there be one for your course. Better yet – look for additional sources of reading materials on the subject your assessment is based on, more relevant for essays of course as you have time to prepare for them. You never know – a Google search might just bring up a newly-published journal article that your lecturer doesn't know about and which really targets your subject area well.

Try to focus more on books and journal articles in the main – if your references page is made up of websites, it can give the impression of not making more of an effort to engage with books (many of which, along with journal articles, can be found online anyway). It might, put bluntly, look like you've taken the easy way out. But certainly don't shy away from websites that are trusted, notably those representing education and the government (usually with **gov.ak** and **ac.uk** as part of their website address). So, it's a case of being both discriminatory *and* adventurous in your choice of literature, but in the end, it's really about **what you do with the literature**, as I have stressed in this section.

I finish by presenting a list of points to consider in the form of questions to ask yourself, as part of your 'use of sources':

- Do I use a mixture of sources in terms of their dates of publication, or are most of them from some time ago and/or possibly out of date (by 'out of date', I simply mean publications that reflect discarded/rejected ideas in a discipline, or at least ideas that have since been revised/reinterpreted substantially)?
- On the other hand, am I using sources that reflect the 'big names' within a given subject area and/or well-known studies; such studies, even if they have long since been reconsidered in terms of their findings/data, would still be important to mention briefly perhaps, but as I have stressed – it's also important to bring new voices to the discussion, ones that represent perspectives on a given subject that are just starting to be shared, even though they have long been in existence.
- The two points above combine and can lead to additional related questions:
  - If discussing the evolution/progression of a given subject, how much detail should I provide?
  - Should I indeed include references to studies which may now even seem controversial in modern society?
  - Who authored such (now controversial) studies?
  - Can I use such studies to show my critical understanding by discussing them in terms of applying a modern lens to the time in which they were conducted? In doing so, I can bring in references to authors whose perspectives reveal a more current understanding of events, such as those related to history.
  - Do I rely more on books/journal articles instead of an overreliance on websites?
  - Are the websites I use trustworthy, or do I rely too much on, say, Wikipedia?
  - Do I use sources to support any strong statements or claims I make?

- o   Do I go beyond merely relying on the recommended reading list?
- o   Likewise, do I refer to a variety of authors, and not over-rely on one author throughout?
- o   And do I actually *do* something with the sources I refer to?

Feel free to think critically right here and now and consider additional areas regarding your use of sources. One thing I do want to say is to not feel too over-whelmed at the sheer number of points that could come up (as shown above) when you think critically and start to unpack something (whether how you're going to use sources or how to construct your argument sentence). Rather, take confidence knowing that once you begin to think critically – and ideally have pen and paper at the ready – the ideas that come will indeed flow like water at times and the process can actually be quite 'organic'. Once again, this is all part of the process of mind mapping. No, it won't always be easy – a point I had made earlier – but it will get easier with practice.

Analysis

Analysis is the dominant focus of this book, given that it is another way to con-sider criticality. After all, you can't really analyse a text, or anything else, unless you're being critical. Think about it: if you merely look at a painting, you might not appreciate the particular use of colour, shading, brush strokes and the placement of objects in fore-, mid- and background. Clearly, analysis would capture this and that is why analysis – of a painting, film, meal or even an academic text – requires more time. It takes only a few seconds to look at the Mona Lisa, but much more time to analyse it in order to appreciate the nuances of Da Vinci's style and ulti-mately, perhaps, to then provide an answer to questions such as 'what does this mean?' 'Who is she?' 'Why is she smiling?' and so on and so on . . .

Let's recap what has been discussed so far in terms of ways to show your analytical skills, though in no particular order:

- Illustrating broad words/concepts/terms and so on.
- Doing something with the quotes you use, as we've just discussed.
- Problematising the topic that you are being assessed on, especially important for dissertations.
- Related to the bullet point above, providing a rationale for your dissertation's focus.
- Justifying your methodological choices.
- Justifying your choices of literature, in terms of the authors/studies/theories you include.
- Identifying, and then choosing, the more relevant and important literature to include in your assessments, which may well include the work of authors who present views on society which have until recently been largely excluded.

- Identifying, and then choosing, which literature to perhaps *leave out.*
- Identifying a clear sense of purpose for your argument sentence in terms of the WHAT and the WHY.
- Deciding on the progression of topics within the body of your essay/exam/oral presentation; what topic comes first, second, third and so on? Why? What is the rationale for both the topics you choose *and* the order in which they are presented?
- Ensuring that not a single sentence in your assessment, whether spoken or written, is remotely irrelevant to your argument sentence, so that each sentence creates an overall unified focus.

To be honest, then, much of the content of analysis has been covered already, with more to come of course. Analysis/criticality is demonstrated when you explain why you used interviews and not questionnaires; analysis/criticality is demonstrated when you explain why you have focused on a relatively obscure publication as part of the sources you refer to; analysis/criticality is demonstrated when you use one word over another (e.g. *the problem has been* **made worse** versus *the problem has been* **exacerbated**); and yes, analysis/criticality is demonstrated when you make an argument. In many ways, analysis is everywhere. Again, it is not tied just to analysing your sources of information, such as that contained within a textbook. Analysis also involves deciding how to approach the literature, deciding what is a better word choice to use at a given moment in your assessment, pondering the effects on the reader of said word choice and so on.

Ironically perhaps, I will close this section here, despite the overall focus on analysis. This is because you have already learned a lot about this skill, I would hope, but simply wrapped up in different names, such as **interpret, unpack, justify, problematise, explain, illustrate** and so on. Learn these skills, practice them and learn to spot the many ways in which being critical/analysing can be seen. I now move on to the final score band which is a means to show your critical thinking on a more micro level – the language you use.

Presentation and language

Chapter Ten will focus on the use of cautious language for your assessments, as part of **hedging**, and the implications for hedging in different disciplines. Chapter Ten will also discuss very productive expressions used within academic contexts, as well as the kinds of clichéd expressions and terms to avoid. While much could be said of grammar as part of this section's title, this is not a specific focus here. This is because, in keeping with the book's focus on being critical, there are linguistic considerations which tie in more with the focus on criticality. These will now be presented and discussed.

Phrasal verbs, italics and scare quotes

The three topics in this section title represent areas where your critical thinking skills will come into play, because don't forget – critical thinking is not just something you do when you're reading your textbooks *before* you start writing your assessment. You also need to think critically *as* you write, in order to interpret what you think is the best style you can produce in your assessments. And of course, just when you think your essay or slides are completed, you need to have one last read through to make sure they are as good as they can be – this also requires a critical eye.

Phrasal Verbs

Phrasal verbs are two-part verbs made up of a verb plus a preposition or another word. We use them in everyday life and there are many to choose from, often having multiple meanings even for a single phrasal verb. Examples include *go out*, *come in*, *turn off*, *stand up*, *carry out*, *cave in*, *give up* and so on. However, they can lead to a somewhat spoken style of communication for your academic assessments. This may be ideal, actually, if giving an oral presentation, in which you would not want to sound overly formal. But for academic essays, given the comparative 'permanence' of the words as they represent written language, it's best to rely less on phrasal verbs and, instead, opt for what is often a single word, and more formal, counterpart. Also, by replacing a two-part verb with a single word, it can save on the word count for your essays. Let's now compare (see Table 3.2).

Table 3.2 Phrasal verbs and formal word choices

Phrasal Verb	More Formal Word Choice
Carry out	Conduct
Look into	Research/investigate
Find out	Discover
Back up	Support
Go back	Return

As just a quick example, compare the two writing samples below:

Sample 1

The research was carried out by the team, with the sole purpose of looking into the effects of daily watching of television on the knowledge acquisition of infants. Following our analysis of the results, we found out that it is a complex mix of factors that contribute to children's gains, or losses, in this area.

Sample 2

The research was conducted by the team, with the sole purpose of investigating the effects of daily watching of television on the knowledge acquisition of infants. Following our analysis of the results, we discovered that it is a complex mix of factors that contribute to children's gains, or losses, in this area.

There's more to write of course, but the second writing sample arguably reads better (but this does not mean that Sample 1 is in any way 'bad' writing). Sample 2 involves a more formal tone – but by no means overly formal – and communicates more professionally. Don't worry about this level of style, however, until you have first considered the larger issues, such as having a clear statement of purpose as your argument, a unified and consistent focus, coherent structure and providing adequate illustration for your points.

Italics

Moving on to italics, you'd be surprised at how this device does not merely emphasise a given word or phrase within your writing – whether essay, exam or slides. It does more than this. Italics can also reveal your personal feelings on the matter – thus showing a link to criticality precisely because by first analysing the subject under discussion, you have then deemed a particular aspect of it worthy of emphasis. Have a look below at the two sentences, one without and then one with italics:

Unlike their Anglo-American counterparts, Mexican-American immigrant children are poor.

Unlike their Anglo-American counterparts, Mexican-American immigrant children *are* poor.

The second sentence comes from a student's essay which I still recall from 20 years ago. The student was Mexican-American and was writing about her childhood. How do you interpret the use of italics here? It's not just you as the student who has to apply a critical eye to your assessments; indeed, your marker will do the same. It is by being critical regarding your assessments that you can expect to get higher scores and lecturers need to be critical when reading your assessments in order to truly appreciate what you're saying and, as a result, give a fair score.

Can the mere act of tilting a word/phrase on its side really make a difference? Yes, it can. By emphasising the word *are*, it was the student's way of voicing her opinion. I had asked her this after class and she confirmed as much. Her use of italics allowed her to basically express her opinion, and reveal her ethnic identity in the process, with the opinion being, 'I really know what poverty is, based on my ethnic background'. While some readers might not completely agree with the proposition contained with the sentence above, as there are certainly many poor Anglo-American children too, the voicing of her opinion is nonetheless done clearly, subtly and backed up within her overall essay's content.

Scare Quotes

I now move on to so-called 'scare quotes' (as I have just used), which refer to single quote marks placed around a word(s). Like italics, less is more. An essay which has italics/scare quotes on every page is a bit excessive and the effect is ruined. A little goes a long way (indeed, the student referenced above only used italics once in her essay). Scare quotes can be deployed for three reasons, with examples offered below:

> When reading back our essays, our written language can sometimes be 'cringe-worthy'.
>
> Each one of us has his or her own unique 'linguistic fingerprints'.
>
> Since childhood, there has been great emphasis placed on how I 'should' speak.

Even divorced from their context of a completed essay, you can still get an idea as to why the quotes are being used and what purpose they serve. The first example comes from an essay focused on writing and how the process of reviewing one's writing as part of proofreading can sometimes be uncomfortable, as errors are discovered. A more formal word choice instead of 'cringe-worthy' might have been, well, *uncomfortable*. However, the use of an informal word choice is arguably a better means to cut to the chase and deliver a stronger meaning, with the scare quotes essentially used to acknowledge this momentary break from more 'academic' word choices.

The second use of scare quotes serves essentially to take ownership of what is, to the writer's best knowledge perhaps, the creation of a new word or expression. I myself have done this on many occasions, using scare quotes for expressions such as 'linguistic homelessness'. The quotes, then, do more than merely emphasise; they also serve to express a more unique choice of expression and alert the reader to this.

The final example is the written equivalent of using scare quotes with our fingers, as part of spoken discourse. Here, the quotes serve to show disagreement with the notion that there should be a correct way to speak – who decides anyway? Thus, the writer is showing a degree of irony, indirectly saying, 'I don't agree with the idea that there is a correct way to speak'. It takes critical reading, as mentioned, to truly appreciate someone's writing, as these examples – and my unpacking of them – have hopefully demonstrated. But what do *you* think? To give a comparison, look at the same sentences without the quotes:

When reading back our essays, our written language can sometimes be cringe-worthy.

Each one of us has his or her own unique linguistic fingerprints.

Since childhood, there has been great emphasis placed on how I should speak.

My interpretation, and of course this is just mine (not necessarily yours), is that without the quotes, the first sentence now sounds too informal and thus, a bit inappropriate in terms of style and tone; the second example is still strong, but less so without the quotes as it's no longer highlighting what I think is an effective metaphor and taking ownership for it; and the final example is no longer making an argument after all.

Considering 'style' in different disciplines

Let's not forget, however, that defining what is or is not 'good' style in academic writing is largely a matter of the assessment type and the discipline in which you're being assessed. Writing a reflective journal for social work, for example, will require – as do reflective journals in general – a more liberal use of first person ('I'), as a means to communicate your personal involvement and taking responsibility for your actions, as part of what might have been a study placement, a case study with a client or acknowledging mistakes made with your methodological approach. For exams, your grammar and style will be less of a concern, precisely because you will be writing your answers under a time limit and possible pressure, and so it is unrealistic to expect a polished style, and some typos may indeed creep in. Of course, certain disciplines rely on certain types of assessment more than others, and here is where assessment-specific meets with discipline-specific. The Hard Sciences rely on practical experiments very often, which may or may not have a subsequent write-up; art students, while having to produce essays like other students, will also have to produce their own artwork for assessment; and from my days as a music student, my assessments indeed centred on performing, though I still had to write essays too. In fact, you may find that even within a given programme, you have a mixture of assessments: 'traditional' essays, reflective journals, exams, oral presentations, poster presentations, a dissertation and so on.

Nominalisations and Passive Voice

Broadly, writing in the Humanities and to an extent in the Social Sciences tends to use more first person as a means to signify the human presence behind the writing and given the interpretative nature of Humanities specifically (i.e. there being no absolutely right or wrong answer, unlike maths), using first person is a way to put one's interpretive stamp on the discussion. Interpretation is the key to being critical of course, but within fact-based disciplines such as the Hard Sciences, you're largely interpreting facts from the start. This is based on working with natural phenomena, which are more stable and predictable perhaps than human behaviour. As such, a lack of first person in this case ensures more objectivity, at least in terms of how the writing is perceived. To achieve this more impersonal tone, science writing tends to use more nominalisations in subject position and passive voice, whereas to do so for Humanities' writing would be inappropriate – it would rob a more personal style of writing by making it impersonal and abstract. Of course, no other word in the English language causes more confusion than 'I' regarding whether or not it can be used in academic writing. I have offered some generalisations about its use within different disciplines and different types of essay, but once again, it's more realistic to consult with each and every lecturer who sets each of your assessments. Unfortunately, even two lecturers from the same programme who even share an office might have divergent views about using first person in academic writing. I have come across blanket advice to not use it at all, but it is more context-specific than this and the use of first person is based on the discipline *and* the type of assessment being produced.

Getting back to nominalisations, these are noun forms of verbs and adjectives, with the following suffixes common to nominalisations in academic writing: *-ment* (*entertainment*), *-tion/-sion* (*condensation*), *-ness* (*happiness*) and *-ity* (*scarcity*). And passive voice does not remove the subject of a sentence, as some believe; it removes the person or thing responsible for the action within a sentence. See below to understand how nominalisations and passive voice work to make writing more impersonal by removing a reference to a human agent, and are thus common features of scientific writing:

> **I transcribed** the interviews (active voice, so the 'doer' of the action is emphasised).
>
> The interviews **were transcribed** (passive voice; the doer is now removed).
>
> **The transcription** of the interviews was completed (a nominalisation in subject position which again removes a need for a human agent).

The last two examples are more in keeping with the Hard Sciences as they sound more impersonal; the first example would not look out of place within the Social Sciences, however, precisely because it adds a human element via the use of 'I'.

As a final note to this section, you might be confused when spellcheck brings up your use of passive voice, usually with the suggestion of 'consider revising'. This is one example of how spellcheck is not always better than a human pair of eyes! The reason spellcheck flags passive voice sometimes is not a grammatical issue at all – it is a stylistic one. Excessive use of passive voice can indeed lead to impersonal writing, but this is what scientific writing is *sometimes* about (but not Humanities writing). However, excessive use of passive voice can lead to confusion about who is doing what, and as such, the implication is that putting the doer back in subject position can clarify matters. See below:

> The interviews were conducted and then transcribed. Themes were discovered based on subsequent analysis of the interviews. The themes were set up as part of the different sections within the discussion and from here, the interpretations and answers to the research questions were provided.

Of course, it is clear that it is the writer who is responsible for the actions referred to above – the conducting, transcribing, discovering and so on. But a more 'reader-friendly' version, from a Humanities/Social Sciences perspective, would perhaps read thus:

> The interviews were conducted and then transcribed. I discovered themes based on my subsequent analysis of the interviews. I then set up the themes as part of the different sections within the discussion and from here, the interpretations and answers to the research questions were provided.

The sample above uses a mix of passive and active voice, and you can hopefully appreciate the difference (by the way, did you spot the phrasal verb in both examples – *set up*; you could choose a replacement, such as *established*).

Figures of speech

A brief mention within this section on presentation and language is based on the use of metaphors and figures of speech in general, which can certainly make your writing vivid. A well-placed metaphor in the Humanities (e.g. music, art) can help to make a personal interpretation come to life and become more concrete for the reader, and metaphors can be used to good effect in the Social Sciences too (e.g. psychology, sociology) to conceptualise societal issues and problems. But in the Hard Sciences, figures of speech make the writing less precise and, for this reason, are normally avoided, as scientific writing is all about factual precision; writing in the Humanities and Social Sciences is not. Here are some examples:

> Art: The colours in Monet's painting merge into **a drunken rainbow** (metaphor).

> Literature: In Dante's Inferno, the fallen angels are trapped in **a sea of fire** (metaphor).

> Sociology: We might consider the phenomena of inequality in education as partly based on the family one is born into, as a kind of **societal toss of the dice** (analogy).

> Physics: Molecules in a gas move **like the wind** (simile).

The first three examples help to make the writer's point clear and illustrative; the final example does nothing other than confuse the reader. Just how fast *do* molecules in a gas move? We need more precision than the simile provided, and instead need a relevant formula for calculation.

Verb Tense

A very brief section here, but important to note. While you may think of verb tense as a mere grammatical topic, you need to remember that the grammatical choices you make will have *rhetorical effects*. For example, consider the use of present tense below in writing samples from Physics and Literature, respectively:

Water **expands** when the temperature goes from **4°C to 0°C**.

Othello is **deceived** by Iago.

The Hard Sciences use present tense to state facts, with present tense in this case symbolising an ever-present and habitual aspect. In other words, as water will always expand at a certain temperature, then present tense serves to address this predictability. Thus, *the water expanded when the temperature went from 4 to 3 degrees Celsius* would be a grammatically competent sentence for the physics community, but stylistically strange. This is because the use of past tense would suggest that the expansion was somewhat of a one-off occurrence, when it is in fact habitual.

Likewise, it doesn't matter that Shakespeare wrote his works hundreds of years ago – the fact is that each time someone reads his work, it will become present in that particular moment again and again. As such, Othello is being deceived by Iago for the remainder of time, and not just at a literary moment in time.

Some of these stylistic considerations might already be intuitive to you if you have done a lot of writing in your discipline at this point. But it's always good to know the rationale behind the choices made within discipline-specific writing. There are many other considerations for verb tense when writing your dissertation or thesis – these will be covered in detail in Chapter Six.

Summary

Now that you are armed with a detailed overview of the subject of criticality, to include what this means for the areas in which your assessments will be scored, the next chapter makes clear how criticality is seen on three interrelated levels: reading – thinking – writing.

4

The Connection Between Critical Reading, Thinking and Writing

As I touched on earlier, being critical can be realised on three levels: reading, thinking and writing. As an example, to prepare for your assessment, you need to critically read the relevant reading material and then process it all as part of critical thinking and then finally transfer your thoughts to the page, as part of critical writing. Critical writing assumes an essay or exam assessment, and if your assessment is an oral presentation of some kind, then critical speaking will, of course, be the final destination of your previous critical reading and thinking. An oral presentation though will often involve some evidence of critical writing too, based on an accompanying handout or slides you use as part of your presentation. Actually, after the critical writing stage, there is technically a fourth aspect – critical reading yet again. In this case, the critical reading is manifest on two levels: first, you need to read through your essay, answers to the exam questions, slides and so on to make sure it all looks perfect before submission or before delivering your oral performance. On another level, the critical reading will be done by the marker who then reads your essay/exam, and this might even involve critical listening, if you are delivering an oral presentation. Only by being critical when reviewing your assessments can the marker give an accurate score. Thus, all four skills – *reading, writing, listening* and *speaking* – are all subject to criticality at university.

However, while criticality can be seen on these three interrelated levels of *reading – thinking – writing (or speaking)* – and has been suggested above to be a linear process, it does not always work in such a predictable and systematic manner. As a reminder, I had pointed out earlier that sometimes you just don't know when inspiration is going to strike. In other words, on occasion you might find yourself bypassing the critical reading stage and jumping straight to critical thinking. This can happen before you've even started to read any textbooks, and instead, just by pondering the subject alone, you can be seemingly 'led' to a critical understanding of it. From here, you can even go to the critical writing stage, in as much as you might find yourself mentally 'writing' your eventual essay, planning your overall argument, thinking of a brilliant topic to cover and even finding a unique way to approach the subject. Nonetheless, the approach within this chapter is to indeed begin with critical reading as this will form the backbone of much of your understanding, including weekly readings set by your lecturer to self-guided reading in preparation for your eventual assessment.

To get things started, let's start at the beginning. Very often, this is seen with critically reading the assessment instructions. Because if you merely read the instructions, it is likely that some important detail and/or understanding will get missed in the assessment. Critically read the instructions for your assessment, and you will already ensure that you are on the right track from the start, as opposed to potentially falling at the first hurdle.

Understanding the assessment instructions

With regard to, say, essay assessments, you will of course have the assessment instructions in advance of your submission date. This will give you much time to ponder them and truly reach an informed understanding as to what is expected of you. For an exam, you will only have a short time to read the question and then address it, as part of an overall time limit (unless it's a seen exam, of course). But for both, it's the same – *critically read*, don't just read.

Now some lecturers will provide you with detailed information from the start in terms of what they want you to do for your essay assessments. In other words, they will do the unpacking for you, by means of telling you how you should conceptualise the subject, what topics to focus on, how many references to use and so on. Some students might appreciate this approach, whereas others might ironically find it harder to get started when faced with so much information at one time. Either way, you can expect to have the opposite experience, in which the assessment questions are captured in a few sentences only, leaving you to do the rest. Obviously, if you have any questions about the assessment along the way as you interpret the instructions piece by piece, you should ask your lecturer. And don't forget that not all assessments are presented as questions per se – some can be delivered as a statement. But the approach is the same, either way.

Now let's make a start at understanding the need to read critically, focused on just a single sentence that is the basis for, let's assume, a 2,000-word essay.

Why did the UK lose its status as a world power after the Second World War?

Source: UKEssays. (n.d.-b). *History essay questions.* https://www.ukessays. com/essay-questions/history/. Accessed on 14 November 2020.

OK, the first thing to do is to highlight the key words. Here's where your critical thinking begins as you need to first determine which words *are* key. From here, interpret what the key words *mean* to then arrive at the ultimate goal – to interpret the question/instructions overall in order to understand what you are being asked to do exactly. In this way, the bullet points below are essentially an illustration of note taking once again, and your notes – whether an interpretation of assignment instructions or textbook reading – are the window into your critical reading ability.

Key Words

Why?

This word alone tells us that the instructions are not merely in the form of a ques-tion; this one word tells us that we are expected to answer a question. This means:

- We need to determine what is being asked – in this case, we are expected to address the question, showing our understanding of why the UK lost its status as a world power after World War II.
- In other words, the overall purpose of the question is not to make an overt argument, but to explain; our explanation, however, will allow for personal opinions to be offered, a case of 'here are the facts as *I* see them'. This approach is also reflective of the aca-demic discipline of history, which is largely focused on personal interpretation of his-torical facts.
- Indeed, the question is one used for history students, and history, to a large extent, deals with facts. In this case, we can say that it is a fact that the UK lost its world power status and so we're not being asked to argue against this. However, there is room made as to *why* this happened, so once again, this shows us how facts can be inter-preted and this means that an argument will be part of the essay, albeit an indirect one, and not necessarily the main focus of the essay.

The UK

So we need to focus on England, Scotland, Wales and Northern Ireland, and not just one of those countries and not just Britain. Again, this might seem obvious and so you may wonder if I'm simply over-analysing at this point – if so, consider the following, however:

- It might be an easy mistake to make if at any point in the essay 'the UK' is referred to as, say, Britain. They're not the same, but people arguably refer to 'Britain' more in everyday reference than 'the UK' – so we need to keep the terminology consistent throughout.
- Moreover, as the UK is the focus, then we are expected to cover the four countries within. When discussing aspects of power loss that applied to the UK as a whole, state as much, but if there were differences in this loss of global status between England and Wales, for example, then this needs to be made clear.
- Indeed, has the UK ever really been as uniform as the question might even suggest? Here is where you can start to problematise – did people within the various UK countries, for example, have different experiences, attitudes and beliefs following the war, as part of this loss of global status – might this be relevant to your essay?
- In reference to the bullet point directly above, some of your critical thoughts need not, nor will they always, make it into the final assessment – part of being critical, as I have mentioned already, is deciding what goes in **and** what gets thrown out.

Lose

Again, at first glance this word seems simple enough. Indeed it is, if you're just reading. But for critical reading, you need to do more than just define it – you need to go further and *define it in the specific context of the assessment question*. Consider the following:

- For a country to 'lose' its status, then what does this mean exactly?

    o Did it commit actions that led to the loss, whatever was 'lost' in the first place?
    o If so, would this not suggest the country's leaders/government were to blame somehow?
    o Or were there forces beyond the UK's control that led to it losing its status (e.g. the aftermath of a brutal war, perhaps acting as a catalyst, or one of them at least, for the loss of world power)?

World Power

The UK was indeed a world power at one point in history, seen with the British Empire. Here, your critical thinking of 'world power', once again initiated by interpreting what this expression means, could lead to some of the following critical thoughts:

- Do you think it might be a good idea to explain the extent (and illustrate it) of the UK's previous status as a world power?
- For example, what are some clear examples of how the UK was a world power? Remember again **the importance of illustrating broad words** – how do you interpret 'power' when applied to a country, in fact?

- How do you interpret 'world', for that matter? In other words, what countries around the world reflected the UK's global power status? Give clear illustrations of (a) what power means in this context, (b) examples of how it could be seen and (c) what countries were involved.
- Or, do we disregard the above bullet entirely? After all, the question did not explicitly tell you to address the points in the bullet directly above, did it?
- On the other hand, the instructions for your assessments do not always spell every little detail out for you, and some points will be implied; as such, you need to adopt a particularly critical approach by **reading between the lines.**
- Simply put, do you think your essay would be stronger if indeed you addressed points (a) to (c) in the third bullet point? Why or why not?

Also to (Possibly) Consider . . .

- We can't ignore the word 'status' either!
- So at what point in history exactly *did* the UK have this particular status as a world power? When did it begin approximately?
- When did it end? There might not be an end point as such, but the question strongly suggests that 1945 was 'the beginning of the end'.
- So will you include a time period for the UK's status as a world power in your essay, and if so, will you need to justify the inclusion of the starting point (e.g. what events triggered the official status of the UK as a world power?)?
- This raises a second question – the essay is focused on the loss of the UK's power status, so how much coverage, if any, do you think you need to provide regarding the days when the UK's world power status was otherwise alive and well? Is this necessary background information or not?
- Finally, do we want to look at the UK's status as a world power retrospectively; would it be a good idea to include established criticisms of the British Empire and colonialism that came into particular focus during protests against racism and racial inequality in 2020, as well as discussing actions such as tearing down statues of slave traders?
- Even 'good idea' needs to be read critically – in this case, 'good idea' simply means would it be relevant to mention the British Empire from a more modern-day perspective or does the question not really suggest this aspect at all?
- This means that if you do adopt this focus, it could be seen as irrelevant to the question; or might it be seen as a brilliant example of being critical after all, and the perfect end point for the essay? You need to decide!

Essay skeleton on the Second World War

This is presented within the question as the catalyst for the beginning of the end of the UK's status as a world power.

- So just how significant was the end of the war as an influence on the UK losing its status?
- Amidst the celebrations of the end of the war, what were the after-effects that nonetheless contributed to the UK losing its status – for example, the rise of new world powers, loss of UK economic power and so on.
- For a 2,000-word essay, how many topics do you think are sufficient, in this case topics that largely relate to reasons for this loss of status?
- As I mentioned, it's always better to go deep, than wide – so three topics explained in great detail (i.e. analysed) might work better than four or five topics that have comparatively less detail and depth to them.
- Remember – thinking critically is not just tied to analysing texts or assignment questions; deciding how many topics to have, what order to present them in and so on also involves critical thinking!

So, from critically reading a mere sentence, the bullet points above represent critical thinking that is delivered as a result. It would probably have taken you less than 3 seconds to simply *read* the assessment question above; how long does it take to read it *critically*, however?

Now, in terms of critical writing – the final delivery in many cases – there are of course several ways to do this. Even if everyone in class is assigned the same question for assessment purposes, the same question will be approached in many different ways. As long as these different approaches conform to the skills required as previously discussed, then this is fine. Chapter Five will go further, but for now, I provide a potential essay skeleton based on the critical thinking above (see Figure 4.1). I provide just a skeleton illustration at this point and not a completed essay for two reasons. First, this is in keeping with an otherwise step-by-step and systematic approach in which I want to discuss things one at a time. Second, Chapter Five will dig that bit deeper in terms of an even fuller explanation and illustration of argument, structure and criticality, and it's best to analyse completed essays once you have all this extra information you need at hand.

Figure 4.1 just being a skeleton, it only provides the bare bones of what is to come. But this is nonetheless very revealing in itself, and you can get some idea at least as to what aspects of the critical thinking will feature in the proposed essay, and what aspects will not. From an essay skeleton, you are now in a position to start to develop it and provide sentences, paragraphs and then the finished essay to submit. Also worthy of mention is the fact that the three-paragraph essay is a visual guide for students in writing classes very often. Some have criticised it for giving a false impression that essays will only consist of three body paragraphs, as well as an introduction and conclusion of course. Clearly, however, no one is suggesting any essay is usually that short. I did mention that three topics might be sufficient for a 2,000-word essay, as a means to

INTRODUCTION

Background

- Provide some basic facts and statistics regarding the British Empire to first set the scene – its origins, its influence around the world, its economic power and the spread of the English language.
- Then this could segue into a sudden mention of a reversal of fortune, referencing the end of World War II (WWII) as the catalyst that set in motion the end of the Empire.
- Finish with an appropriate argument sentence, such as *this essay discusses the loss of status as a world power for the UK following World War II, in order to catalogue the various factors that led to this.*

↓

TOPIC 1

A focus on the economic devastation brought about by WWII and how this impacted on the British Empire

- This could be discussed in terms of a contrast between how things were now developing in terms of a loss of power, with how they had been when the UK was at its economic peak – and how this economic devastation was felt, particularly in post-war UK as well as in its colonies perhaps.
- For example, with a pressing need to rebuild British cities (well, UK cities specifically – look at the question!), this led to the UK questioning whether or not sustaining an overseas empire was viable.
- There was a shortage of goods and labour in post-war UK, further complicating matters.

↓

TOPIC 2

The rise of United States and the Soviet Union which were hostile to British imperialism

- This topic could unpack the emergence of these new world powers and how they came to be, thus indirectly explaining how the previous British Empire had to make way for them – but what did this mean in real terms? Again, illustrations will be needed!
- As one potential illustration, you could refer to the Suez Canal crisis in 1956, in which the USA condemned the UK's decision to invade Egypt; the UK had to cede authority to the USA – this is but one example of a new power to reckon with, as well as a reason in itself for the UK's loss of world power status.

↓

TOPIC 3

There was no longer a justification for colonisation, and the racist ideologies that accompany this

- The Allies had fought against countries which perpetuated an ideology of extreme nationalism, which made it difficult for the UK to justify its own colonialism in countries around the world, such as India.
- This also ties in with a rising anti-colonialist movement, in which countries sought their freedom, such as India in 1947.

↓

CONCLUSION

Begin with an overall conclusion/opinion – as if to say, 'I've looked at the evidence, and here's what it all means to me!'

- This could be worded thus: 'This essay has discussed the fall of the British Empire following WWII, illustrating that a combination of factors, and not just one, all worked together to bring about its decline – a loss of power on several fronts: economic, military and ideological.'
- Recap the main topics – perhaps a quick illustration of the three areas in which power was lost.
- Finish with a closing thought – you could indeed refer to the current decolonisation movement and tie that in with the subject – how about *as we can see with current movements regarding decolonisation, we are still fighting to rid the world of the legacy of imperialism.*

Figure 4.1 Essay skeleton

ensure sufficient analytical depth without going over the word count (though universities generally allow you to be above or below the word count by 10%). However, having three topics for your body paragraphs does not necessarily mean only having three body paragraphs as such. Indeed, in a desire to go deep, you might find in some of your essays that each topic might need to have two paragraphs to fully discuss it, and thus, three topics can actually equate to six paragraphs – more on this in the next chapter.

I now present an additional set of assessment instructions from art. Once again, you will have no more than a sentence to read critically and think critically.

Discuss the role of the artist in Early Modern Spain.

Source: UKEssays. (n.d.-a). *Art essay questions.* https://www.ukessays.com/essay-questions/art/. Accessed on 17 November 2020.

Consider the key words within the instructions above and interpret them in the context of the discipline (e.g. what is an 'artist' in the discipline of art – does this key word mean something different than it would to a layperson?). Space is provided for you to jot down your interpretations of the key words, though you can just as easily type them as part of a Word document:

Discuss

_____

_____

_____

The Role

_____

_____

_____

The Artist

_____

_____

_____

Early Modern Spain

_____

_____

_____

Here are some of my own thoughts:

The Role – because this word is both singular **and** uses the definite article ('the role' and not 'a role'), it strongly suggests (to me) that there was a very clear and specific role indeed for Spanish artists during this time period. Of course, we could also suggest that the word 'the' is being used in a generic way, which would not point to just one role as such. For example, consider **the whale** *is a mammal* (generic) and **the whale** *hit my boat* (specific). However, I think it's more to do with my first interpretation, but if in doubt, consult the lecturer! On the other hand, 'the artist' is clearly a generic reference and really means 'artists' in general and not just one.

I have provided a brief example of my interpretation, but simply as an illustration and not as an example of how *you* should interpret. The next stage would be to decide the overall purpose of the assessment (e.g. To argue? To explain?). Again, taking your interpretation of the key words overall, by putting it all together, this should help you understand what you are being asked to do. My interpretation is that the essay is asking you to primarily explain, at a particular moment in Spanish history, what the main role of the artists were. Though this might involve some degree of argumentation – you may, for example, wish to argue that some artists were more influential than others and explain why – this is largely about explanation. It's as if you're educating someone who knows little about the topic – imagine the role of a tour guide who is explaining something of interest whether in a museum, historical ruins and so on. This is largely what you are doing here.

Feedback From Teachers

We've largely focused on the need to critically read the texts which your assessments will refer to, the need to critically read your assessments before submission (including using the last 10 minutes of an exam to check everything!) and the fact your lecturers will critically read your assessments in order to give a fair final score.

Another area of critical reading involves reading the feedback from your lecturers for your assessments. I know from my own experience that once essays are submitted online, some students don't even access them – this means they don't look at the essay after it's submitted, and so they neither know the score nor the rationale for it (via my overall feedback and comments on the essay itself). This is a missed opportunity for students to truly engage with the feedback and their progress overall, instead of submitting their essays and forgetting about them.

Clearly, I am in no position to presume I can speak for all lecturers with regard to the kind of feedback they might provide. Some of your lecturers' feedback might be encouraging, even for low scores, while other lecturers might be more blunt in their comments. But in terms of content, there is a certain predictability to lecturer feedback, if only because they are judging your assessments using largely the same score bands (if not the same terms for the score bands, as I had pointed out). What now follows is a sample of hypothetical, but realistic, feedback that you might come across – all of which ties in with what we've discussed so far in the book.

Incoherent/rambling structure

Do you recall from the previous chapter what an incoherent structure might include? Well, it's the exact opposite of maintaining a coherent structure. So, if your lecturer deems that your writing is incoherent, it could be based on some, or all, of the following issues:

- Trying to discuss more than one topic in any of your body paragraphs.
- Moving from topic to topic in a rather illogical sequence (e.g. from narrow to broad).
- Discussing a topic which is otherwise irrelevant to the overall focus – perhaps you have an irrelevant topic sandwiched between two topics that are otherwise very relevant.
- More in keeping with a 'rambling' structure perhaps, does your essay or assignment move in and out of topics in quick succession (akin to the issues as part of the first bullet point), but without any attempt to illustrate or support the points made for each topic – in other words, your essay reads like a stream of consciousness without support made for your points, instead of maintaining a logical and coherent structure (i.e. one topic only per body paragraph, logical progression of topics within each body paragraph, clear relevance of each topic to the argument sentence).

So if any of your previous assignments involved feedback such as that above, it's largely down to issues at the level of the body paragraphs. Here's where your focus should be in terms of making improvements for future assignments.

Lack of a Central Focus

The issue inherent with the comment above is initially tied to the argument sentence, or lack thereof. If your introduction just provides background information to the reader but nothing else, then this can lead to comments from the marker such as *argument?* In other words, *what is your point exactly?* Likewise, if you tell the reader the subject of your assessment, notably an essay, but neglect to tell them the purpose of *why* you're writing about the subject (even as part of an implied argument, as discussed), then this too can lead to a lack of a clear focus. In other words, if you tell the reader your essay will discuss 'nutrition as part of schoolchildren's meals', this doesn't really give us a central focus, or if it does, then it is simply not precise enough. What is the point you wish to make? Make it!

Related to this, a lack of a central focus might also be tied to issues within the body of your assessment. Even if you have a brilliant argument sentence, if your topics which follow do not relate to it clearly enough, are quite broad throughout and/or simply don't support the content of your argument sentence, then this too can equate to a lack of a central focus.

Unconvincing Rationale

This is a comment largely reserved for dissertations and theses, which represent extended writing projects in which you must provide a rationale – a justification – for the research you are undertaking. A paragraph or two is sufficient, though write three if you feel it necessary (and yes, deciding on how many paragraphs to write for your rationale will require you to think critically!). But what makes a rationale unconvincing anyway? It could be tied to going against the advice for what makes a rationale convincing. Consider the following:

- Is the rationale comprised of just personal reasons for conducting the research, such as a personal interest in the subject area? As I mentioned, this is fine within the Social Sciences (not so much in the Hard Sciences perhaps), but it should only be part of the rationale, not all of it – use a personal interest to then lead into more objective reasoning, such as considering the benefits of your research to the subject area in general – could it lead to change? Is the gap worth filling, if you're filling a gap? Explain why – don't leave it to the reader to understand the details of what's in your head – you need to explain this yourself.
- Conversely, are you overstating the need for your research? Chapter Ten will discuss the need to use critical language in your assessments, such as being cautious in your claims. But if you make bold statements from the start, this will never be convincing as a rationale, or as anything else. So declaring that 'there is no previous research in this area' is a bit dubious. Perhaps it's a case of 'there is little previous research in this area'.

That sounds more realistic and, as a result, more trustworthy. But you still need to do more. Tell the reader what the previous studies on this subject have to say and then tell the reader what your study proposes to do that they did not (and again, why this coverage is important).

You Need to Say/Tell Me More About . . .

A classic example of a lack of illustration, one of the major weaknesses of students' assessments. One clear way to get feedback such as this is to refer to broad words and concepts but not provide concrete illustration to follow. As I mentioned, the use of broad terms is not a problem in itself and is, in fact, unavoidable. It only becomes a problem when you don't provide illustrations – of your own – with which to then make things clear for the reader, by showing that you know what you're talking about. So get in the habit of identifying broad words once they're written down and don't move on until you've given the word its own illustration, unless you feel of course that it really doesn't require one. If so, that's perfectly fine.

Don't Over-Rely on Web-Based Sources

This is self-explanatory. Your references page, if not the essay itself, will make it clear where your sources derive from. I see far too many essays which rely on websites too much and many websites used which, while not by any means 'untrustworthy', simply do not have the weight of, say, a website backed by something more official, such as the government, a leading organisation (e.g. the British Council, OFSTED, the WHO, etc.) or a university. If more than half of your sources are websites, even 'official' ones, it's time to rethink this a bit. This doesn't mean you have to take away some of the website sources, but just add some book or journal article sources. As I mentioned, these too can often be found in e-formats online.

You Need to Back Up Your Broad Assertions and Claims

This is definitely an issue which Chapter Ten will address, but for now bear in mind that if you make opinions sound like facts, then you will need to back them up by referencing the relevant literature and hedging your claims. Consider adding an illustration too. Making bold assertions is a common issue with students' writing, and it will make the writing sound unconvincing and even come across as rather immature. So as a test, you need to ask yourself if each statement you make is indeed a fact; if not, use language to reflect this uncertainty. For now, I close with two brief examples – decide which sounds more suitably 'academic':

Travel agencies are no longer relevant in the 21st-century

Travel agencies are arguably less relevant in the 21st-century than before

You can see, and appreciate, the difference, and the need for hedging is so important that I have chosen to focus on this for its own chapter.

To summarise this section, then, take the time to read through the feedback carefully – **critically** – for each and every assessment. If you have any questions, ask your lecturer. This will help you to understand the feedback even more and avoid making similar mistakes for future assessments and, by the same token, do the same things again which helped you to get a high score. But by and large, problems with **focus, coherence, illustration** and **credibility of claims made** are common areas in which students' assessments lose points, so be on the lookout for any issues in these areas in particular before you submit, or deliver, your assessment.

Assessment samples: Read, think and write

This section will now present three samples of academic writing taken from a common source of academic reading – journal articles. The articles represent three disciplines – Environmental Sciences, Art and Sociology. The purpose of this is to again present a systematic focus on the link between reading – thinking – and writing. For the first example, I will provide all three aspects. Having read through the journal sample myself, I will then present my thoughts and then use these thoughts to produce a sample of academic writing, as part of an essay response to my reading. The second example will do the same, albeit leaving out the writing part and leaving you to do this for yourself. The final example will then present you with a final sample of academic reading and leave it to you to provide your own critical thoughts and subsequent critical writing on the matter. Even though the disciplines reflected in the following three journal articles may not reflect your own area of study, look at it this way: if you can think critically about a subject that is not your own – and you can – how much easier will it be when you read texts that are focused on your own academic discipline?

For the first sample, let us imagine that you have been asked to write an essay based on the current coronavirus, specifically from the perspective of how this has changed lifestyles and what this means for societies in the future. A proposed title will help to clarify more: 'exploring personal freedoms in a time of government-imposed lockdown'. This title alone can help to generate some critical thinking, given the need to (a) identify the key words, (b) explore what they mean in this context, and (c) put it all together.

Sample 1

We begin with critical reading of a sample of text from the *Journal of Environmental Sciences*. While you should of course plan to read this sample yourself, I have done so already and will provide evidence of my subsequent critical thinking beneath the journal sample. The title of the full article is 'Changes in Air Pollution During COVID-19 Lockdown in Spain: A Multi-City Study'. The article is authored by Álvaro Briz-Redón, Carolina Belenguer-Sapiña and Ángel Serrano-Aroca (2020).

> This pandemic has forced behavioral changes in our society in contradiction to the common routines which could provide a useful insight into more sustainable supply and production patterns (Sarkis et al., 2020). The importance of reducing air pollution is understood on account of its well-known impact on climate change and its influence on health due to increased morbidity and mortality (Manisalidis et al., 2020; Xiao et al., 2018). Previous studies suggested that ambient air pollutants are risk factors for respiratory infections (Becker and Soukup, 1999; Horne et al., 2018; Xie et al., 2019; Xu et al., 2016) such as COVID-19. And even though there are contradictory opinions on the transmission of SARS-CoV-2, it seems that people can acquire this coronavirus through the air (Morawska and Cao, 2020) due to its stability in aerosols (van Doremalen et al., 2020) and the fact that the gas cloud and its payload of pathogen-bearing droplets of all sizes can travel 7–8 m (Bourouiba, 2020; Morawska and Cao, 2020). Also, a significant proportion of confirmed cases have recently been associated with air pollution in 120 Chinese cities (Zhu et al., 2020).
>
> Source: Briz-Redón, A., Belenguer-Sapiña, C., & Serrano-Aroca, A. (2020). Changes in air pollution during COVID-19 lockdown in Spain: A multi-city study. *Journal of Environmental Sciences, 101,* 16–26. https://doi.org/10.1016/j.jes.20230.07.029.

Critical Thinking

I chose the sample at random, from within the article's introduction. Before I present my critical thoughts on the sample, a few points are in order. First, my thoughts are indeed truly reflective of reading and are not in any way contrived. I first gave a quick skim read and from there read the same text carefully in order to try and extract anything in particular that I believe is worthy of writing down as evidence of being critical. In other words, my critical thinking is as authentic as it can be. Second, if I were to read the same sample again after, say, a day or two (or perhaps even after an hour or two), I might well end up with a very different reading (or I might not). Such is the nature of our reading – we can see things from one reading to the next that weren't picked up on the first time. This does not apply only to academic reading of course – how many times have we perhaps read a piece of fiction such as a favourite novel and each reading is slightly different? Nothing to worry about of course – it's simply a reflection of the nature of reading and how we come to it differently each time.

- The backdrop of this article is the ongoing coronavirus, specifically the lockdown that has been imposed in many countries.
- I immediately found myself honing in on the first sentence and the words 'This pandemic has forced behavioral changes in our society'. This in turn got me thinking about the ways in which lockdown has indeed been resisted by some – many people have flouted the rules even during the early days of lockdown here in the UK and, even now, refuse to wear face masks.
- Now the problematisation: this ties in with ways in which a government cannot necessarily police its citizens when they choose to break the rules; some people are willing to get sick perhaps for what they see as a right to meet friends, ignore social distancing and do what they want in general.
- This then makes me question the extent to which civil liberties sometimes need to be curtailed for a greater good – in this case, to protect the population.
- My overall focus, then, that derives from this brief sample has nothing to do with the main content of this journal sample, which is actually focused on air pollution and the possibility of the virus being spread through the air; instead, my reading is focused on a larger issue regarding 'forced' behavioural changes on a society and the fact that some people cannot be forced and refuse to change their behaviour (and this focus also ties in with the title of the essay that I had provided).

Now, it might seem surprising, to some of you at least, that my reading, at face value, does not particularly reference the coronavirus that much. But the thing about reading critically is that you never know what you're going to get. Sometimes just a few words might spark our interest, as is the case with my reading here. Also, if we assume that the focus I have been tasked to write about is based within environmental sciences, then this will influence my writing style. This is a discipline that focuses on sociology too, such as the interactions between societies and their environments. Thus, I would be on track if I chose to focus less on the biological aspects or the purely 'environmental' aspects and focus instead on the societal aspects. However, it would also make sense to not lose track of the 'environmental' aspect of this discipline, and so retain some link in my essay to societal influence on the environment, via human behaviour. All of this consideration clearly takes some additional critical thinking on my part, in order to essentially locate the main point/purpose of my essay. In other words, what is the angle going to be within my essay that fits within the context of environmental science and the coronavirus? This needs to be placed within the argument sentence, of course.

Also, even though my response below is based on the reading of just one key text, you can clearly see references to other authors. This is indicative of the ways in which the key text and my understanding of it then leads to the need to search out other literature which helps to support the points I wish to make. In this way, just one text can lead to the search for, and use of, many additional academic texts.

OK, I've decided to take a shot at writing the introduction paragraph and the first body paragraph of an essay on my chosen subject, a subject inspired by the critical reading of just one paragraph from one journal article. Yes, realistically I might probably do a bit more reading before I start to commit finger to keyboard, but there's no reason why I can't start now.

Critical Writing

Essay draft on coronavirus and human behaviour

> The global spread of the coronavirus has resulted in more than 500,000 deaths worldwide at present (www.who.int). In order to combat the virus, especially without a vaccine currently available, governments around the world have tried to find ways to keep their populations safe, in terms of reducing the number of new infections and subsequent deaths. However, this has played out differently in various countries, as world governments fight the virus in ways that can be very different. Sweden, for example, did not impose a lockdown, the UK did and South Korea, initially at least, was able to address the threat without the need for a lockdown in the first instance (www.nature.com). One aspect of the virus, however, that arguably unites all countries is the fact that it is the people themselves who need to pull together and take the necessary precautions, irrespective of government advice. We know, for example, that social distancing is one important aspect of fighting the virus (Matrajt and Leung, 2020; Milne and Xie, 2020). But it has also been seen how some individuals, sometimes large groups in fact, have chosen to essentially disobey government directives, if not common sense, and congregate in large groups of social gatherings, refuse to wear face masks and in essence, continue to live life 'as normal'. This essay will thus explore the dissonance between governmental directives and perceived personal freedom, in order to reveal something of the challenges that countries might face in times of national health crises.
>
> Human behaviour can often have an effect for good or bad during crises such as the current coronavirus. Certainly, there is evidence that human behaviour has led to environmental issues (Schneider, Gruman and Coutts, 2012). In terms of the current coronavirus, there is evidence that human behaviour is therefore an important factor in controlling the spread of the virus (Cole, 2020;

Gentili and Cristea, 2020). In fact, the WHO outbreak communication planning guide explains that behavioural changes can reduce the spread by up to 80%. It might be argued that this is a societal 'chicken and egg' situation in that coronavirus has affected human behaviour, including increased anxiety and xenophobia (Robson, 2020), but human behaviour can potentially affect coronavirus. This then raises the question: what kinds of human behaviour are able to both exacerbate, and improve, the situation? Das, Medley and Michie (2020) point to safety practices, such as maintaining social distancing and of course hand washing. While obvious perhaps, these practices are advocated for a reason and yet Cole (2020) discusses this from a broader perspective – that based on human compassion. This strongly suggests that if our concrete actions are governed by a deeper reason – consideration for our fellow human beings – then perhaps these actions can become more ingrained in society.

Deconstruction of the Writing: Introduction

Having now read my own sample critically, thus taking us back to the critical reading stage, what do you think? What are your thoughts? Even if this is not representative of your discipline, do you otherwise think the introduction above does what it should do (and more on this in the next chapter)? While still collecting your own thoughts, here are mine:

Sentences 1 and 2:

These combine to provide some broad background, essentially a reminder of the dangers of this virus and largely tell us what we already know. Not to be redundant, but instead to explain to us the larger backdrop from which the essay derives. The support for the claim in Sentence 1 adds credibility, as well as alerting the reader that I have actually done some reading on the subject. Having got the reader's attention (hopefully!), I move on to Sentence 3 which introduces a new aspect.

Sentence 3:

Given the word 'however' to begin this sentence, the reader will automatically know that a new idea will be introduced. In this case, it's nothing particularly argumentative, but nonetheless an important factor related to how different governments have responded to this threat.

Sentences 4, 5 and 6:

These sentences continue to 'tell the story' and take a narrower focus, by making an argument of sorts, suggesting that it is the people who need to take responsibility and not just their government, in this case by adopting safety measures. The reference to relevant literature also serves to back up my points and the literature is of course up to date, given that studies regarding coronavirus are being published as we speak.

Sentence 7:

Herein lies the crux of my point – essentially, evidence that I have hopefully problematised the subject in terms of highlighting the reluctance of some individuals to go against the required safety measures.

Sentence 8:

This sentence functions of course as the argument sentence, which builds on the content of Sentence 7 and then makes a point from it, on which the essay will be built. In many ways, the best piece of evidence of critical writing within your introduction is indeed how you conceptualise the subject under discussion via your argument sentence. This is even more relevant when you are given a choice of subjects to write about for an essay assessment.

Deconstruction of the Writing: Body Paragraph 1

Sentence 1:

This functions as the topic sentence (more on this in the next chapter), and as such, it is written so that it tells you the WHAT, which in this case is human behaviour. However, a point still needs to be made, and in this case, the point is simple: human behaviour can have an effect on health crises, here the coronavirus. At this stage, my own initial thought would be as follows: does the topic within the topic sentence relate to the argument sentence in the introduction? Clearly, it does. Also take note of the fact I use cautious language; the topic sentence states that human behaviour *can* have an effect, as opposed to *will/does* have an effect. This in turn shows a lack of absolute certainty, which in turn shows that I am carefully considering my propositions and content here.

Sentence 2:

This goes broad, briefly stating that human behaviour can be a factor involved with environmental issues. Support is added to give some credibility. You could of course argue that Sentence 2 makes a rather 'obvious' point and so, is the support needed courtesy of the reference to Schneider, Gruman and Coutts? Well, support is always welcome, even if it links to statements which might otherwise seem 'obvious' (though avoid intuitive statements at all costs; see Chapter Ten). However, not all people are necessarily convinced of the effects of human behaviour on the environment, at least not as far as climate change is concerned. Some have argued that climate change is a natural process that is cyclical, with or without human activity. As you can see, I'm critically reading – thus analysing – my own work. In doing so, I have produced a whole paragraph's worth of discussion for just one sentence.

Sentences 3 and 4:

These move to a more narrow, and relevant, focus on coronavirus, once again backed up by references to current research as well as support from the WHO itself. Again, this helps to make the writing credible by aligning assertive statements with evidence for said statements, and this reflects a degree of criticality.

Sentence 5:

This takes the content of the paragraph thus far and presents an interpretation in that it also brings in the point that human behaviour is affected by the virus, as well as the virus being affected by human behaviour. I also coin an expression – hence, the use of scare quotes. Now, whether or not you personally like the expression of 'societal chicken and egg' situation, I would ask you to evaluate it on a more objective level. That is, do you feel the coining of phrases, at least as used here, would be appropriate for the discipline of environmental sciences? I cannot answer that as such, but I am making a guess that given this discipline's involvement with, and focus on, human societies, this might in turn allow for a more 'human touch' to the writing. Or I may be out of my depth entirely. But it is precisely because such questions are being raised that we know that criticality is being put to use – we're not leaving anything to chance. I again use cautious language in regard to this evaluation of the societal situation, by explaining that *it might be argued*. Clearly, this also means that it might *not* be argued too! And this level of caution in my writing shows that I am critically considering the statements I make.

On a micro level, consider the order of items in this sentence:

It might be argued that this is a societal 'chicken and egg' situation in that coronavirus has affected human behaviour, including increased anxiety and xenophobia (Robson, 2020), but human behaviour can potentially affect coronavirus.

You can see how the potential for human behaviour to affect coronavirus comes second, after first mentioning how the virus affects human behaviour. Not a big deal perhaps, but by placing the main focus of this essay second here, it allows it to be that bit more relevant to the reader, possibly, and more recent in their processing of the information in Sentence 5.

Also, by giving an illustration – and support for the illustration – of the broad claim of 'coronavirus has affected human behaviour', this helps to make the writing concrete. Consider the following, without the illustration and support:

> It might be argued that this is a societal 'chicken and egg' situation in that coronavirus has affected human behaviour, but human behaviour can potentially affect coronavirus.

While the example directly above is not necessarily weak, it stands to reason that the insertion of an example helps to make it stronger. Even stronger is the inclusion of support for said illustration, as I have also done. The original text again:

> It might be argued that this is a societal 'chicken and egg' situation in that coronavirus has affected human behaviour, including increased anxiety and xenophobia (Robson, 2020), but human behaviour can potentially affect coronavirus.

Basically, my job in this writing sample is to make sure I'm following my own advice, especially around the importance of illustrating broad concepts.

Sentence 6:

This sentence serves to ask a question that perhaps the reader is considering – 'just what kind of human behaviour are we talking about?' Clearly, no one can second guess their reader in terms of what readers may or may not think as they read through the essay and how they might respond. On the other hand, I can guarantee a few things and one of them is that the more you don't do as suggested, this will cause problems for the reader and, potentially, your assessment's score. Thus, to use broad references such as 'human behaviour' but not provide an illustration – especially when this is such a key concept within the essay – will make the writing abstract.

Sentences 7 and 8:

This provides two concrete and clear-cut illustrations for the reader and, once again, links them to research. While we could argue that social distancing and hand washing are hardly surprising examples of human behaviour that could have an effect on the coronavirus, there are two things to consider (which the writing makes clear).

First, obvious though the examples might be (especially given the number of times we might have heard about them in public safety announcements), I link them to a relevant academic article, thus making the point that the examples are indeed backed up by the experts. Second, by acknowledging in my own writing that the examples may indeed not sound particularly groundbreaking in Sentence 8 (i.e. *While obvious perhaps . . .*), this helps to ideally win a bit of trust from the reader, in so much as I do not pretend that the information is necessarily new. Again, this shows that I have done some thinking with regard to what I write and how it might be perceived by the reader. However, the 'obvious' advice is still as important as ever, hence the link to a published article. Moreover, I take the research of Das, Medley and Michie and link it to the research of Cole in Sentence 8, and in making this connection, I subtly imply in Sentence 7 that hand washing, for example, is a product of something deeper, something internal – compassion; this is Cole's own implied point which I have picked up on.

Sentence 9:

I mentioned the need to comment on the references to outside sources. As you can see, while I have chosen not to use a direct quote, I have nonetheless referred to several studies. And in this sentence, I interpret the article by Cole, by means of focusing on what I interpret to be the most important aspect of her article. This rounds off my first body paragraph. The next body paragraph could continue the same topic, which is perfectly fine. Or, it might start a brand new topic – again, more on this in the next chapter.

I've done most of the work so far, in terms of critically reading an excerpt from an article, critically thinking about it, producing evidence of my critical thinking in the writing and then going back to the critical reading stage to analyse the content of my writing. But hopefully, you've been doing some critical thinking of your own alongside mine and have your own insights. These can include lots of things, such as honing in on the parts of the reading sample that speak to you, to deciding for yourself if my own writing is appropriate for the discipline it represents. Indeed, there are many considerations.

In order to sharpen your own critical skills, the next sample, as mentioned, will go as far as the critical thinking stage – again, by sharing my critical thoughts – but then leave you to complete the picture with some critical writing of your own.

Sample 2

The sample below comes from an article published in the journal *The International Journal of Arts Education*. The particular article that I have selected is titled 'Art Critique as Social Pedagogy' by Brian Harlan (2020). The sample chosen consists of the abstract for the article, and I have chosen the abstract for two reasons. First, abstracts to journal articles, largely consisting of a one-paragraph summary, can be ideal when you are browsing potential literature because abstracts tell you everything you need to know in a short space of time. This is because they focus on the important aspects of the article: what is under study/being investigated, why, how was the study conducted (if applicable), what are the main results and crucially, what can the results tell us? Given this level of information, it makes sense to rely on abstracts, partly at least, as a means to determine if a given journal article might be worth reading or not. Determining a journal article's 'worth' is a purely objective matter and pertains largely to judging its relevance for your assessment. If of course you have reason to doubt the credibility of the journal, then that is another matter. I would recommend, in fact, that you Google 'predatory journals' to see the ones you might wish to avoid for both your literature search and also for future papers of your own. A second reason why I have chosen to focus on an abstract is because you will more than likely have to write one yourself, as part of a research project such as an undergraduate dissertation. Chapter Six will cover this in detail with regard to the foundations of abstract writing, but it's a good idea to get critical with abstract *reading* now.

But to leave you with something of direct relevance, how about you approach the critical writing by first interpreting an essay question based on the abstract's content and a suggested title which follows:

Essay question: Discuss the use of art critique in groups in terms of how this practice can influence individual learning.

A proposed title: The ways in which art critique as a group function can affect the learning of the individual.

With the above information, can you start to formulate an approach? Or, read the abstract first and then revisit the instructions and proposed title.

Abstract

Learning feels to us like a process managed by our will. From a personal perspective, learning seems like an individual act, largely the result of our own cognitive ability. Yet, how much of what we know has actually been achieved alone, and are our actions directed only through internal deliberation? This article argues that although knowledge is mediated by our intellect, almost none of what we know is obtained through individual effort alone. We are awash in our social environment and therefore it is impossible to separate learning that results from individual cognition and learning that results from social influence. A signature pedagogy within the visual arts, group critique, draws its effectiveness from the social nature of learning. In fact, the social nature of learning is important as we design any pedagogical strategy, and art critique provides an example of a transferable process that can be exported to other disciplines. Furthermore, what is revealed through an understanding of social learning provides reflection and commentary on human nature as well. If learning is predominately social, for instance, this must have an impact not only on how we interact in the classroom, but how we relate to one another in society as well.

Source: Harlan, B. (2020). Art critique as social pedagogy. *International Journal of Arts Education*, *15*(1), 1–10. https://doi.org/10.18848/2326-9944/CGP/v15i01/1-10.

Critical Thinking

- Implied by the abstract, perhaps some of our learning – to include views, opinions and such – derives from others who we wish to emulate.
- This can clearly relate, for example, to picking up certain knowledge even from sources as 'innocent' as a stray conversation we overhear.
- This can tie in with picking up on various prejudices, based on 'societal learning'.
- Of course, my thinking here is perhaps straying somewhat from the immediate context of not just art per se, but a focus on learning in a more 'official' environment, such as a classroom.
- On the other hand, is the content of my first three bullet points entirely legitimate and appropriate, based on my interpretation of 'social learning'? I am asking myself this question as much as I am asking you as the reader.
- As I am a teacher, of course, the final sentence also 'speaks to me', given its reference to the classroom as an example of social learning.
- As such, this creates for me additional considerations, based on my interpretation and understanding of what is effectively 'the implications of social learning in the classroom' (even this summary has been arrived at through my own understanding and interpretation of the basic point of this abstract).
- How might a single comment from a student as part of class discussion influence another student, for good or bad?
- Likewise, how might my own comments in relation to the class material influence students?
- Should this social learning aspect be theorised as part of class discussion, or is it something best left as an otherwise organic process, which might very often exist 'below the learner's radar'?
- Of course, we're talking art, not linguistics! But I could apply this to my own subject – for example, having a group of students evaluate a given accent to see how they in turn evaluate the speaker.
- This reflects the potential for focus groups – a clear example of social learning (I think!) – to influence the ideas of the various group members (certainly if one person does most of the speaking).

You are now being asked to write a short (or long) response to the critical thoughts provided; of course, you can provide your own thoughts and use those instead. The evidence of critical thinking that I have generated may not be of particular relevance to an essay focused on the use of groups for art critique. However, the very nature of critically reading a text is that it can be a very organic process, one that is often not dictated by your desires or goals but influenced, instead (though not always), by something beyond this. What I mean is if you approach a text and tell yourself 'I am going to read this text in order to get some concrete ideas about subject X', you might sometimes find yourself interpreting the text based on all kinds of previous influences, those that might cause you to interpret the text in a way that goes somewhat beyond the immediate focus on the subject. For this reason, the first three bullets of mine represent a broader focus than that of art critique and its use as part of social learning. On the other hand, these bullets do indeed tie in with social learning as a whole. Whether or not their content can be related directly to an essay focused on art critique as part of social learning is another matter. But don't forget – being critical also means not just gathering thoughts in the first instance, but then deciding which of those thoughts to retain and which to discard. Clearly, I have other thoughts as part of the above list which are more directly relevant to a focus on group learning in an educational sense.

Following your response to all this, apply an analysis of each sentence as I did for Sample 1. This can be useful as a means to ensure that each sentence leads into the next and comes together to form a coherent whole. While I won't be available to see the finished product, this is something you can share with a classmate, or perhaps your lecturer – more so if you have access to writing classes and/or a writing centre at your university.

And I say again that as part of your academic reading, you will no doubt come across more than just a single article and a few paragraphs within. You know this already. But by starting out step by step, as I have previously stated, it allows you to approach the subject of being critical gradually, one step at a time. But again – be open to whatever comes your way as part of your critical reading. How you read a text in the morning might be different from how you read the same text after dinner (or it may not). And you might find yourself generating different and new ideas with each read (or you may not). Likewise, even if you were to read an entire academic textbook from cover to cover, some chapters will stand out to you more than others. Not just because some chapters might be more relevant than others but also because some will simply engage you more than others. And within a given chapter, it might well be a specific word or phrase within a specific section that truly shouts out to you, and as a result, critical thinking is generated.

Critical Writing

Here you can record your written response to the critical thoughts I created, the critical thoughts that you yourself came up with or both. Alternatively, you could create, in note form, what overall direction you might take if an introduction paragraph were to be written on the subject. What might be a strong opening for an introduction? How would you construct your argument sentence? The way you approach the writing stage is entirely up to you of course, but try to at least jot down some notes which can reflect your inner thoughts beyond what has been recorded as part of the bullet points.

Sample 3

The final text comes from the *British Journal of Sociology*, with the article titled 'Hollywood Experts: A Field Analysis of Knowledge Production in American Entertainment Television' by Arsenii Khitrov (2020). The text comprises the introduction section to the article. Before you start to read it (critically!), consider how you might start to apply your knowledge of introductions in terms of what features you expect to find. For example, is there sufficient background? Is there a clear sense of WHAT and WHY, whether stated directly or implied throughout the introduction? Given that this represents original research, there should also be a clear rationale – a justification for the value of this kind of research and the specific direction it takes in this paper. In fact, for some of your assessments you may well be asked to read a journal article, but not as the basis for your own assessment. Instead, the purpose will be for you to read it critically in order to subsequently critique it by explaining its strengths and weaknesses. This kind of assessment is actually very valuable, as it essentially forces you to read critically from the beginning to the end and, in so doing, get a real sense of what it means to be critical and unpack a published article from cover to cover. It's time-consuming, but worth it. You can of course take this approach now, and make your critical writing sample a critique of the introduction section's strengths and weaknesses, and of course justify and illustrate your evaluation. Or you can of course read critically as a means to gather critical thoughts on the subject and from there, use your thoughts to generate a sample of writing as if it were an essay assignment, for example. I have provided some guidance in the form of *Thoughts*, which might help you to consider some of the main functions of the text.

> How can we make sense of numerous instances of experts in politics, law enforcement, national security, military defense, public health, culture, history and other social and political issues working closely with the creators of scripted television series in the USA today?

Thoughts: For the sentence above, what effect does the question have on you as a reader, especially as an opening sentence? Also, this sentence makes a broad statement, but what follows is a concrete, specific illustration.

For example, *The West Wing*'s producers and writers collaborated with about ten consultants, including a former Press Secretary to Presidents Ronald Reagan and George H. W. Bush, a former Speechwriter and Special Advisor to Reagan, a former Press Secretary for the Clinton administration, former aides to senators, former White House Chief Economic Advisor to Clinton, former Chief of Staff to Reagan, a political columnist, and Al Gore's chief Speech writer (Crawley, 2006; McCabe, 2012).

Thoughts: Consider the effect of following a broad statement with a clear illustration – in this case, an illustration tied to a US TV show.

There were 49 credited consultants involved in the creation of the American version of *House of Cards*, including former Chief Deputy Mayor of the City of Los Angeles and the Press Secretary for Hillary Clinton's 2008 presidential campaign. These examples indicate that intense processes of knowledge production and transfer take place in Hollywood's TV production sector. Recent studies of police officers' involvement in entertainment TV production in the USA and Canada (Lam, 2014) as well as in the UK (Colbran, 2014) show that the use of professionals from outside the television world as consultants is standard practice in the Western entertainment industries. In other words, television series production is a knowledge-based industry, and this knowledge is not only knowledge of the craft of television production, but also knowledge about the world external to the craft. Moreover, this latter form of knowledge is often expert knowledge, that is, knowledge with a claim to legitimacy.

Thoughts: Consider the expression above of 'in other words'. Three useful words to use in your own writing perhaps – essentially a way to say 'here's a more clear way to express what I just said'.

In this article, I explore these knowledge production and transfer processes by answering the following research questions: why do TV makers need experts, and why and how do experts come to Hollywood? In order to answer these questions, I carry out a Bourdieusian field analysis of contemporary American television series production, which allows me to identify the social conditions that make this knowledge transfer possible, and thus to better understand "institutionalized ways of knowing things" (Jasanoff, 2004, p. 40) and the ways in which meanings and social categories come into existence, are reproduced, challenged, and altered in social space through popular culture.

I argue that the knowledge in question is a form of capital which players in the field of Hollywood TV, independent experts, the state, social movements, and research organizations use in their competitive collaboration.

Thoughts: This is the author's main point which summarises in one sentence his purpose for writing the article.

> Some of these competitive-collaborative practices are institutionalized and routinized, and this circumstance sometimes masks their competitive core. The major stake in this struggle is, for Hollywood TV, the accumulation of its symbolic capital for internal struggles and its struggles in the field of power. For the state, social movements, and research organizations, the major stake is the accumulation of symbolic capital for their struggles in the field of power. Finally, the stake for independent experts is primarily the accumulation of their economic and symbolic capital within the field of Hollywood.

> Source: Khitrov, A. (2020). Hollywood experts: A field analysis of knowledge production in American entertainment television. *British Journal of Sociology, 71*(5), 939–951. https://doi.org/10.1111/1468-4446.12775

Critical Thinking

Here you can use a bullet point approach, as I have done previously. This is useful as it allows you to make your thoughts clear by literally writing them down. This helps to make them more real. The next stage is to gather your thoughts and place them into a unified focus. This sometimes means having to retain some comments and delete others, in order to arrive at one overall focus. In other words, you may well find that your thoughts arrive at different topics that otherwise relate to the main focus, which in this case is 'knowledge production in American entertainment television'. Again, broad terms to consider – and unpack.

Critical Writing

This is where it all comes together. There is little I can add here as the whole point is to now do it for yourself. Remember, there is no singular 'right' way to do this. As long as you bear in mind the key points that have been covered so far, you will be on the right track.

Summary

In closing, you now have had a thorough introduction to what it means, and what it takes, to be critical in your academic assessments, from reading to writing and everything in between. The next chapter will take the time to go over the layout of essays, but in even more detail. For now, however, you have the skills you need to approach any text, whether academic or not, and understand the process involved with critical reading, to then generate critical thoughts and finally, a critically written, or spoken, assessment.

5

How to Structure Your Essays

This chapter expands on previous information regarding the topic of coherence, and the critical thinking that lies behind it. Specifically, here you will find information not just in terms of the body of the essay and how to construct that but also on the other two main components: the introduction and the conclusion. Thus, the entire structure of essays will be provided.

Essay structure

Many of your essays will range in length from 1,500 to 3,000 words. It is these essays that are the focus within this section, essays which, broadly speaking, do not involve primary research that involves you going out and doing your own project. This, then, will be the backbone of the kinds of essay assignments you will be asked to write. Once you get past the initial round of critical thinking tied to the assignment question itself, and have perhaps considered the literature you wish to use, you will then be able to move on to writing the essay. Let's start at the beginning – the introduction paragraph.

Introduction

While this is often referred to as an 'introduction paragraph', as I have done above, it might end up being, say, two paragraphs if your essay is longer. In other words, a 1,500-word essay really doesn't need more than a paragraph for its introduction (unless you absolutely feel otherwise); a 3,000-word essay might. Either way, all essay introductions should be written with the following in mind.

The Hook

The hook refers to the way you open your essay so as to attract your reader's attention. No, you are not writing the introduction to a piece of fiction, but there are certainly some interesting ways to start your essay. It will require critical thinking on your part to ensure that your opening sentence(s) is attention-grabbing, but in a manner that is both discipline-specific and fits the context of your specific essay in terms of its subject area. So how do you begin your essay in a way that will get the reader's attention?

Rhetorical Question

A rhetorical question is a question that does not require an answer, at least not immediately. Thus, if you ask someone 'what is your name?' – an answer is expected. If, however, you ask someone 'what is the meaning of life?' – well, this could be posed as a real question, but given the lack of concrete answers, it is probably being used to simply get people to think. And this is the beauty of rhetorical questions – if used as the opening sentence, then they will get the reader to immediately start pondering the subject contained within the question, which will of course relate to the essay subject overall. If you use a rhetorical question, however, don't answer it for the reader! It would defeat the purpose if the first sentence poses a question which is then answered in the second sentence. This is true for any use of rhetorical questions, whether they are contained as your opening sentence, final sentence or used anywhere in between. There is another important consideration, however.

Namely, does your discipline generally make use of rhetorical questions? The Humanities and Social Sciences do on occasion, and some individual disciplines in particular – consider, for example, the use of rhetorical questions within philosophy. But the Hard Sciences would rarely make use of this device, and this is because a rhetorical question is often used as an indirect statement of opinion. And if you're dealing primarily with facts, then opinions are clearly less valid (though *interpretation* of the facts is another matter, of course). For example, consider the following question: *Do we need a standard variety of language?* The question is essentially asking, 'I think it's possible that we *don't* need a standard variety of language'. This is fine within an argument essay on the subject of language use in schools, as part of a Social Science context of academic writing, but asking questions in the sciences which suggests disagreement with facts would be completely redundant.

If rhetorical questions are indeed commonly used in your discipline, then by all means put them to good use, but don't overdo it! As with many aspects of academic writing, it is difficult to quantify certain aspects (e.g. how many sentences in a paragraph, and how many rhetorical questions is too many). Use your best judgement, but remember – a little goes a long way and certainly, less is more. This is good advice for the use of rhetorical questions as well as italics, scare quotes and other stylistic devices that were discussed earlier.

I finish now with an example of a rhetorical question and how to best put it to use:

Are not human rights universal?

It is important to remember that a good hook is more than just the content of the first sentence of your essay. This is part of it, but most of all, it is about *what you do* with the content of the opening sentence. So if you begin with a question, make it a good one. But from here, decide what you will do with the sentences that follow. How will they derive from, and link with, the opening sentence? Consider the examples below:

Are not human rights universal? We need to focus on human rights as a matter of urgency, as there is ample evidence of individuals who lack such – from their choice in marriage, to religious persecution.

In the example above, the opening hook is somewhat diluted because it doesn't seem to serve much purpose other than being chosen for the opening. Compare now with the example below:

Are not human rights universal? This is a question that should not have to be posed, but given that many people lack freedoms that are otherwise considered 'basic', it is clear that more work is needed.

In the example above, you can see, and hopefully appreciate, the difference. The rhetorical question is a good choice in itself, but its usage is all the more effective as we can see how it is being used to build an effective start to the introduction. Clearly, additional sentences are needed to complete the introduction, but from merely two sentences alone you can see how much has already been accomplished.

Quote

Beginning your essay with a quote, or a reference in general to a published work/author, is more discipline-friendly across departments. This is perhaps because all disciplines will of course rely on referring to the work of previous studies, whether a quote, summary or paraphrase, and as such, this is a broad aspect of academic writing which is not tied to one discipline or another. But again – it's not just the act of using a quote as your opening sentence that makes it effective. It's what you do with it. So even a brilliant quote from a leading expert in your field is not so effective if the sentence(s) which follows doesn't seem to logically derive from the quote. Let's have a look:

> Smith (2019: 23) argues that 'the next twenty years or so of human behaviour will determine the state of the environment for the next century'. The environment is an ongoing concern, and daily news reports on global warming, deforestation and loss of animal life are but three interconnected examples.

> Smith (2019: 23) argues that 'the next twenty years or so of human behaviour will determine the state of the environment for the next century'. This is a sobering thought, especially in light of daily news reports that strongly suggest that the various environmental issues are not improving.

For both examples, I would say that they work well as the openings to an essay. However, the second example shows the relevance of the quote that bit more, by making a direct reference to it. The first example does not really do this, and so the quote's purpose is less clear, except perhaps being used just for the sake of it. However, this is not the reason to start an essay with a quote. Again, you need to do something with it. Broadly, this means commenting on it in some way in the sentence(s) that follows, but more specifically, it's about *how* you comment on it – how do you interpret the quote? In the second example above, it's clear that the writer is agreeing with the quote, at least on a subtle level, by referring to its content as 'a sobering thought'. Of course, the writer might then turn around and disagree, as part of a larger strategy.

In fact, consider the next example:

> Smith (2019: 23) argues that 'the next twenty years or so of human behaviour will determine the state of the environment for the next century'. However, . . .

Just the inclusion of the word 'however' to start Sentence 2 tells us that despite the serious nature of Smith's words, and presumably he/she being an expert, the writer is potentially going to make a counterargument. Maybe the writer does not disagree with Smith or the issues with climate change, but might not agree on the time frames given by Smith. Indeed, there are many possibilities that could be explored, and all initiated with the starting word of *however*. But you get the idea – choose your quotes wisely as your opening hook, but have an equally wise strategy in place as to what you wish to do with the quote. What is its overall purpose? Is it for you to agree with it and thus align your argument/position with that of a trusted authority? Or, do you wish to take on the views of said authority and launch your own argument? Likewise, you could use an opening quote to merely give an illustration or an explanation of it, without otherwise giving an opinion on the matter one way or the other.

You may also consider starting your essay with a proverb. This is a quote of sorts, albeit one whose author is not always known and/or lost to time. For proverbs, the rule of thumb is, as with actual quotes from academic sources, to make sure its purpose is made clear. A great opening will be weakened if what comes next is a weak follow-up. So first ensure that your hook – here, a proverb – is discipline-approved; then choose it well; and finally, make it work for you and your essay.

Statistic

The use of a statistic to open your essay can be an effective means to engage your reader, but make sure that it comes from a reputable source. This is sage advice for all your references in general, of course. Here's where discipline-specific considerations might come into play too, as statistics are perhaps more relevant to the Social Sciences, less so to Humanities. On a broad level, this is because the Humanities deal so much with personal interpretation and so statistics would seem less likely. To put it another way, is there any burning reason why the Humanities, here literature, would need to report on the percentage of high school students who interpret *Julius Caesar* in a certain way? Or do we really need to know how many art students interpret Dali's famous painting, *The Persistence of Memory*, as referring to the collapse of cosmic order? On the other hand, knowing the percentage of British males who work as house-husbands, as part of a sociology essay on the changing roles of married couples would be entirely useful and relevant. Likewise, we can better understand the importance of mental health if we have a statistic that shows how treatment for mental health problems has increased over the past few years.

Once again, remember the golden rules with regard to your choice of an opening hook:

- Is your choice reflective of your discipline's stylistic norms? If in doubt, check with your lecturer.
- Is your choice effective on its own – does it have something to say?
- Finally, do something with your choice – make it work by showing the reader how its position in the opening sentence influences the sentences that follow, and how they also relate back to the hook.

Background

The background information you provide within your introduction is best thought of perhaps, as well as the introduction overall, as conforming to an inverted triangle – a diagram I had used earlier (Figure 5.1).

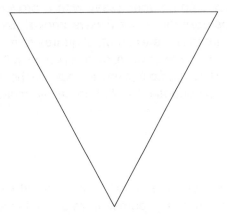

Figure 5.1   Inverted triangle: moving from broad to narrow

In other words, go from broad to narrow with the information you provide. This means that whatever the focus is within your background, start with the broadest level of information and get progressively more narrow in focus. In terms of what the content might be, this can be varied but often involves one, or more, of the following:

- Tell the reader what is known about the subject that is under discussion in your essay – give the highlights, as it were, whether the subject is decomposition rates of humans, non-verbal communication via clothing choices or the development of Armenian folk music over the past three decades.
- Possibly, but not necessarily, you could include a definition of the subject under discussion in your essay, and this could be part of the introduction. It could, in fact, function as the opening hook, given that this would tie in broadly with the use of a quote (in this case, a quote from a dictionary, or indeed from an authority within the discipline).
- You might wish to provide a brief chronology of major developments within the subject area, over a given time period.

The critical part is once again deciding what you will focus on as part of your introduction's background; again, what does 'background' mean to you in the context of your assessment's subject area? What are the most relevant points to make, albeit as part of a summary within an introduction? What do *you* think is the most important information to make as part of a background summary?

Clearly, 100 students writing an introduction to the same essay will inevitably write 100 backgrounds which, while perhaps similar in some ways in terms of what they focus on, will no doubt differ in terms of the actual content per se. This is to be expected, and thus, the choice is yours.

Whatever discipline you're writing for, I would definitely recommend that you don't begin your essay with a statement such as 'this essay will discuss . . .' or 'in this essay, I am going to discuss/debate/analyse . . .'. These expressions by themselves are by no means 'wrong' and in fact have a place within your argument sentence. The issue here, however, is that you're essentially beginning a bit too abruptly, by getting to the point (i.e. the argument) too soon. Instead, take your time and build up to it, which is the purpose of providing some background information *before* you present the reader with your argument sentence.

Essay Plan

The essay plan, by no means absolutely required, does bring a touch of coherence to your essay by alerting the reader ahead of time to the topics within your essay's body and the order in which they will appear. This can be a sentence in length, certainly no need for more than two sentences though:

> This essay will first discuss the basic tenets of Heisenberg's Uncertainty Principle, and then progress to two different interpretations of the principle; the wave mechanics and the matrix principles. The essay will then conclude with a summary of the main points covered, and final interpretation.

Admittedly, there really isn't much in the way of critical thinking involved with writing an essay plan (or whatever else you want to call it), precisely because there's no interpretation involved – it's nothing more than a statement of fact: what you will cover and in what order. It's that simple.

Argument Sentence

The argument sentence has been discussed already in detail, but a brief recap is presented now. As you know, it is imperative to ensure that you cover the WHAT and the WHY, based on having first thoroughly interpreted and unpacked the assignment instructions. Below are examples of what are two broad approaches to argument sentence writing, reflecting a more exploratory approach and then a hypothesis-driven approach:

- Exploratory approach

This essay will discuss the practice of working in study groups, to determine if this experience increases students' assignment scores.

- Hypothesis-driven approach

If students work together in study groups, they will experience an increase in their assignment scores.

In both cases, there is a clear WHAT: working in study groups. The WHY is based on a need to determine a cause and effect (if indeed there is such a relationship in the first place), albeit worded differently for the two different types of argument sentence.

Sample introduction paragraph

Now, let's see how all the above comes together. Don't just read the introduction paragraph that follows – analyse it instead. Do you think it's well-written? At this point, the answer to that question lies 100% in adopting an objective approach, one that is not tied to whether or not you think the subject matter is interesting, for example, but instead based purely on whether or not the introduction ticks the necessary boxes. Indeed, academic assessments, notably essays, are all about ticking boxes as I had mentioned – in other words, making sure that you have all the ingredients that your essay requires. Not to suggest a detached, automaton approach to your writing – make sure you are in fact fully invested in it. But instead, the tick-box approach I suggest is simply a reflection of the predictable nature of academic writing.

> This essay outlines the incidence, physiology, treatment and psychosocial effects of male breast cancer. The evidence indicating possible causes is subject to critical appraisal and gaps in current research evidence are identified. The key presenting features of male breast cancer are described, and treatment options are briefly summarised. The existing evidence investigating the psychosocial effects of male breast cancer is discussed, identifying specific issues that affect men such as the stigmatisation of experiencing a cancer normally associated with women. A conclusion summarises the salient points raised.

> Breast cancer is a rare disease in men and not included in the top twenty cancers responsible for death. Only 1 in 840 men in the UK will experience breast cancer, 55% of them aged over 75. This is reflected by low death rates in men due to the disease; in 2014 male breast cancer (MBC) caused 75 deaths (Cancer Research UK (CRUK), 2017). Macmillan (2018a) report that 10% of MBC arises from inheritance of the BRCA1 or BRCA2 genes. When combined with a family history of first degree relatives who have experienced breast

cancer, male carriers of either of these genes have a moderate risk of developing breast cancer (West of Scotland Cancer Genetics Service (WoSCGS), 2015; Ruddy and Winer, 2013).

Source: UKEssays. (2018d, November). *Sample undergraduate 1st health and social care assignment*. https://www.ukessays.com/services/samples/1st-hsc-assignment.php. Accessed on 14 November 2020.

Hook

Not really, but again – the opening is by no means 'wrong'. But consider this: your teacher might be marking 20 or more essays on the same subject, and many of them will probably begin as this one does. While I again stress that I'm not suggesting you treat your academic essays like a piece of poetic fiction, you can certainly be more inventive than the opening sentence here.

Background

Definitely, and lots of it. Points are made and assertions provided, but since both are backed up by relevant – and trustworthy – sources (e.g. Cancer Research UK), the claims are subsequently plausible. There is no doubt at all that the writer has set the scene here well, by virtue of presenting the main issues with regard to his/her essay subject – male breast cancer.

Essay Plan

Again, this is spot on. The first paragraph largely, in fact, alerts the reader to the various points that will be covered. This could have been shorter in length, however; I don't recommend, generally speaking, an entire paragraph devoted to your intentions in terms of subject area coverage, not for an average length essay which is the immediate focus here. But the information is certainly clear and leaves the reader in no doubt as to the writer's strategy in terms of the topics that will be covered in order to fully deal with the essay's subject.

Argument Sentence

There isn't a sentence per se that captures the WHAT and the WHY. However, I had explained that an argument can still work well as an implied argument. This means that as long as the reader can clearly identify your essay's argument by the time he/she finishes reading the introduction, then your job is done. Granted, it's easier to identify if you place it within a discernible sentence, but this does not mean that it still can't be identified by a combination of sentences all working together to state what your main point is. From having read the introduction, it is clear to me that the argument is as follows:

> The purpose of this essay is to discuss breast cancer in males, in order to illustrate the physiological and psychosocial aspects of a disease which is rare in males and thus, more information is needed.

A final point I want to make, however, concerns the ordering of the two paragraphs above, something that you might have considered (but don't worry if you didn't). Basically, the introduction is moving from narrow to broad. Again, this is not a mistake, but it is somewhat unconventional for an introduction. Start broad with the background, and then work your way into getting progressively more narrow, which means culminating with your essay plan and argument sentence. This is how I would rework this:

> Breast cancer is a rare disease in men and not included in the top twenty cancers responsible for death. Only 1 in 840 men in the UK will experience breast cancer, 55% of them aged over 75. This is reflected by low death rates in men due to the disease; in 2014 male breast cancer (MBC) caused 75 deaths (Cancer Research UK (CRUK), 2017). Macmillan (2018a) report that 10% of MBC arises from inheritance of the BRCA1 or BRCA2 genes. When combined with a family history of first degree relatives who have experienced breast cancer, male carriers of either of these genes have a moderate risk of developing breast cancer (West of Scotland Cancer Genetics Service (WoSCGS), 2015; Ruddy and Winer, 2013).

> This essay outlines the incidence, physiology, treatment and psychosocial effects of male breast cancer. The evidence indicating possible causes is subject to critical appraisal and gaps in current research evidence are identified. The key presenting features of male breast cancer are described, and treatment options are briefly summarised. The existing evidence investigating the psychosocial effects of male breast cancer is discussed, identifying specific issues that affect men such as the stigmatisation of experiencing a cancer normally associated with women. A conclusion summarises the salient points raised.

A simple reversal of paragraphs produces a more logical sequence, though there is room to do more by perhaps trimming some of the content of what is now Paragraph 2. Ultimately, however, this is a well-written introduction for what are, once again, purely objective reasons. It delivers what it is meant to deliver and has all the requisite items in place.

Body paragraphs

Having discussed the introduction, we now move on to the body of the essay – this consists of all the content in between the introduction and the conclusion. I begin by producing a set of bullet points which correspond to the boxes in need of ticking, in this case boxes connected with your body paragraphs.

- Does each body paragraph have a topic sentence?
    - And does each topic sentence have a point to make about the topic?
- Does each body paragraph ONLY focus on ONE topic?
- Does each topic relate back to and connect with the content of your argument (sentence)?
- Does the ordering of topics proceed in a logical sequence?

You need to ensure that you can answer all the questions above with a resounding 'YES' – these are the boxes that need to be ticked for each and every one of your body paragraphs.

Taking each point in turn, it is important to begin each body paragraph with a topic sentence which not only states the topic, but ideally offers a point about it, as I had discussed previously. Think of each body paragraph as a mini-essay, consisting of a clear point just like an argument sentence, and providing support and illustration for such. To be clear, the need to 'make a point' is based on doing more than simply saying 'this paragraph is about X'. Instead, construct your topic sentences much like your argument sentence in terms of having two parts: a topic + point. For example, *the belief that cold climates contributed to the advancement of ancient civilizations is weakened by the evidence for the Mesopotamian civilization.*

TOPIC: The belief that cold climates contributed to the advancement of ancient civilizations . . .

POINT: . . . is weakened by the evidence for the Mesopotamian civilization.

In other words, a topic sentence, if constructed critically, can often be rephrased as an argument. In the example above, the argument could be something akin to *I don't believe that cold climates helped ancient peoples to build great civilizations. Mesopotamia had a hot climate but built an advanced civilization.*

Now have a look at the sample of topic sentences below to see how *not* to write a critical topic sentence. The issue is simple: there is a topic provided in each sentence, but no point is provided about it or the point is not as clear as it could be.

Much research has been conducted about social inequality – This is OK, but 'OK' is not great. Yes, the fact that much research has been conducted is a point

97

of course, but it is quite broad. What does the research *tell* us exactly about social inequality?

A switch to green energy is now focused on – A clear topic – green energy – but no point to make.

Moving to the second point in the list of bullet points above, it is very important to stick with just one topic per body paragraph. If you don't, then your writing would be, by academic definition, incoherent. On a more concrete level, having more than one topic per paragraph can also mean that you have less to say about each topic, and this means you risk losing out on valuable critical writing. Or, it could mean that you have excessively long body paragraphs. More on both of these issues is discussed later in this section on writing your body paragraphs. For now, have a look at a body paragraph. How many discernible topics are there? How does this in turn impact on the quality of writing (and criticality)?

> Language and culture are hard to separate, as they are both interrelated. Culture is an important part of human society, and language is certainly an aspect of culture. We can also view culture as part of identity in terms of female culture, football culture and film culture. In addition, languages have developed quite recently. This is seen with text message language, which uses abbreviations (LOL) and emojis. The visual aspects of this language can say a lot.

Thoughts: The topic sentence does its job just fine. The topic is language and culture, and the point being made is that the two are connected and so perhaps cannot always be discussed as separate from each other. So far, so good. Sentence 2 offers little more than a broad, generic statement, though by itself this would be fine if it was followed by some kind of illustration of the broad words such as **culture, human society** and/or **language**. But Sentence 3 doesn't do this quite effectively. While this sentence does provide illustrations of culture within society (e.g. female culture), these illustrations don't relate to language per se, at least not as they are presented (and 'female culture' is very broad indeed). And yet, language is a clear part of the topic sentence! Sentence 5 does give a more concrete and vivid example of language, but there is no specific reference in this case to the other half of the equation – culture! The final sentence is again broad and contributes little. It makes the paragraph sound like a work in progress and not complete in itself. Moreover, there is no attempt to bring in relevant support from the literature and this, coupled with largely generic statements and little relevant illustration, and you can see how this kind of writing will lose you points, especially if all of your body paragraphs look like this one.

Furthermore, in terms of topics, how many did you find? For me, I counted five: the interconnection between language and culture, culture and human society, culture and identity, more modern language developments and the visual aspects of such (i.e. text messaging). You might not agree with my topic count and this is fine. You could argue that the five topics I referred to do not count as actual bona fide topics because they are only referenced quickly in passing, before the writer then moves on to something else. **But this is the problem!** Your body paragraphs should never move quickly from one point to another but, instead, stay the course with a full discussion dedicated to one topic at a time. Because every time you refer, however briefly, to a new topic, even if it's only a mere suggestion, you are nonetheless setting yourself up to make good on the implied promise of a more detailed discussion of said topics. Thus, cramming several topics into one body paragraph will often involve little in the way of in-depth coverage but a lot in the way of very descriptive and decidedly uncritical writing, as you have seen.

The final two points mentioned at the start of this section pertain to ensuring that each topic, and each and every sentence in fact, relates back to your argument sentence and the overall subject focus that is contained within the argument sentence. This in turn goes back to the need to ensure that the topics you choose to focus on are not only relevant (more on this later in this section) but also arranged in a logical order. Determining a logical order might be straightforward overall, but it might still need some critical consideration. Let's revisit the essay skeleton (Figure 5.2) you looked at previously, this time stripped down just to the topics (but not, at this point, written as topic sentences per se):

Once again, do you think an essay focused on the fall of the British Empire would work with the three topics in Figure 5.2? That is, are the topics relevant? And indeed, do they progress in a logical sequence? I say 'yes' to both questions. The sequence

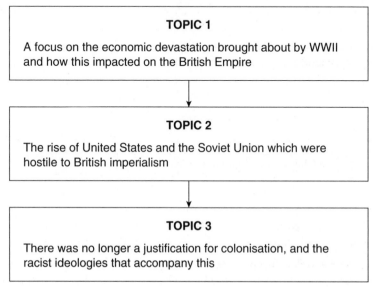

Figure 5.2 Essay skeleton 1

is logical in that Topic 1 arguably came about before Topic 2 in terms of chronology. That is, the devastation faced immediately after the war was clearly a catalyst for the beginning of the loss of the empire, with the rise of the USA and USSR being two events which were less immediate and, instead, occurred gradually over the next few years. So far, then, this represents a logical order of topics. As for Topic 3 – and let's get critical again – could we not argue that this could have been Topic 1, in fact? After all, surely one of the lessons learned from the war, and one of the reasons to fight in the first place, was that ideologies built on racist beliefs could no longer be justified from a country which had just fought against such beliefs! In this case, we are setting the scene for the content of the body by first providing a broad backdrop regarding an ethical and humanitarian reason as to why the empire started to crumble. In doing so, we are also signalling that this is perhaps the starting point not just of our essay's body but also of the beginning of the empire's end. We could also be saying that this is, for us, the most important reason, even beyond the economic devastation and resulting poverty in the UK. And don't forget – determining a logical sequence for your topics goes beyond chronology – it is also based on adopting a broad to narrow perspective in terms of the topics you choose.

In this case, there is nothing I can find in the three above topics that is inherently 'broad' or 'narrow', or that one topic is more broad/narrow than another. In cases such as this, use your critical thinking to place the topics in the order that you deem important. As such, to rearrange the body paragraph topics as in Figure 5.3 would be equally 'logical' as with the previous skeleton, but it would offer a different take on things.

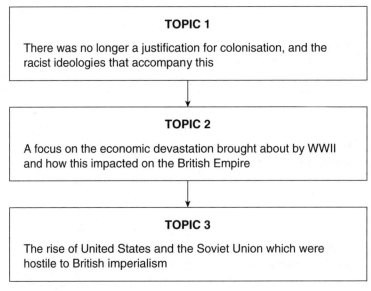

TOPIC 1

There was no longer a justification for colonisation, and the racist ideologies that accompany this

TOPIC 2

A focus on the economic devastation brought about by WWII and how this impacted on the British Empire

TOPIC 3

The rise of United States and the Soviet Union which were hostile to British imperialism

Figure 5.3 Essay skeleton 2

The topic arrangement in Figure 5.3 might indeed be the writer's conscious way of declaring his/her interest in human rights and, as such, a desire to place this first as the most important topic. On the other hand, the order can be entirely random, and yet how the reader perceives the ordering of topics is relevant. The lecturer may indeed see a focus on an end to racist ideologies chosen for the first topic as a way of signalling personal stance on the matter. All this subjectivity aside, always approach the ordering of your topics with objective criteria in mind by asking yourself this simple question: Do the topics I have chosen come in a logical order (and you must define 'logical')? If the answer is 'yes', then this is the main consideration.

How Long Should a Body Paragraph Be?

Assuming your essays adopt space and a half for the spacing between lines, then half a page is my suggestion for a paragraph's length. I find this more practical advice than to suggest a certain number of sentences, for example. Obviously, if your paragraphs (whether introduction, body or conclusion) are slightly more or less than half a page, this is fine. But if you find a paragraph is close to filling an entire page, then it's time to cut in two. If you use double spacing, then a full page or so should be OK for any given paragraph within your essay, and unless your programme of study suggests otherwise, stick with one of these two choices for your line spacing and avoid single spacing.

How Many Topics Should I Have Overall?

This is a question that might have a specific answer depending on the assignment instructions. As I had mentioned earlier, some teachers will provide you with a point-by-point discussion of the essay in terms of what to put in it. This can include the authors or theories to refer to and, possibly, the specific topics that must be included. However, it is more likely to be a case of you having to decide this for yourself. The focus in this section is on average length essays or, more broadly, those that fall outside primary research. As such, you need to decide on the number of topics that you believe are the most relevant to your essay's subject, but not to the extent that you dramatically go above the word count. You'll be surprised how quickly you can go over the word count though, and my main advice regarding the number of topics is to go for depth more than width – a point I had stressed earlier. In other words, it's better to have fewer topics to discuss but more space with which to truly discuss and analyse them than to try and cram too many topics in your essay's body and have comparatively little to say – and this is true even if you stick to the rule of one topic per paragraph. Too many topics with little to say about them will result in a rather superficial discussion in the first instance.

Remember – the whole point of being critical is to do the thinking for yourself, and in this case, asking yourself 'what does this essay mean to me?' can result in trusting your own thoughts as to how many topics is 'too many' or 'just right'. But again, 'too many' is largely based on not having enough words to truly discuss the topics in detail, which means a descriptive, rather than analytical, essay. In other words, an essay which is decidedly *un*critical, at least in some places.

What about the choice of topics? This, too, will require you to think critically. There is no doubt that there is a plethora of authors, theories and studies which are all relevant to the subject you're writing about, a sort of 'academic buffet'. As a result, it can be difficult to know where to begin, and where to end, not to mention which authors/theories/studies to choose from and discuss in your essay. As a starting point, I would suggest that you identify who the key players are within your subject – who are the main theorists and researchers, for example, who would be conspicuous by their absence in your essay? I had mentioned this before. This doesn't mean that you need to devote most of the essay to them, as this would suggest over-reliance on one particular author, which suggests a lack of engagement with wider reading overall. And this, too, would imply a somewhat uncritical approach taken, at least to your choice of references (but by extension, to the conclusions you draw, since they're mostly based on just one, and not several, authors). But don't forget to seek out authors who represent more modern views on current issues, with such authors often an authority on a given subject but whose views have been left out of the discussion perhaps. For example, with regard to Black Lives Matter, the views of black scholars and theorists are now more relevant than ever. They always were relevant of course, but the Black Lives Matter movement has brought them more into the discussion.

It really is up to you who you include, how much to include of a given author and at the broad level, what topics – and how many topics – to include overall. Many references to relevant authors and/or their previous studies might be no more than a quick summary, whereas a particularly important study might be the main point of discussion for a given body paragraph. So this is one area in which I need to leave you alone, as it were, as only you can make these kinds of decisions. You are not really on your own, of course, as your lecturers are on hand to suggest relevant literature and, even better, offer feedback on the literature/topics/authors/theories and so on that you plan to cover in your essay/assessment, so don't be afraid to ask for some of their guidance as you plan what to include in this regard.

In summary, if you attend to the following in terms of do's and don'ts, then you will already have a head start:

- Include the author(s) in your essay whose work is considered the bedrock of the specific subject you're writing about (e.g. Freud for psychosexual development, Chomsky for language acquisition, Piaget for child development), **but** consider going beyond this, especially in terms of authors whose work, and social identity(ies), connects with current societal movements.

- **Do not** over-rely on one main author – lecturers will see very quickly if the same name keeps coming up in your essay in regard to the literature that you refer to.
- Use the reading on the core reading list as an obvious starting point for the literature, and subsequent topics, that you choose, BUT . . .
- Be bold – go beyond the core reading list, and even beyond the recommended reading list, and *find your own reading* – you never know, a quick Google search of the key words associated with your assignment might bring up a brand new article.
- Don't try to put more than one topic in a body paragraph – stick with one central focus that in turn must relate to the central focus which is captured in your argument sentence.
- Is the content of your body paragraphs largely based, if not copied, from class handouts? If so, there will be little evidence of your own thoughts on the subject, and thus, the writing will be uncritical.
- And remember – to be critical, you need to have enough space to discuss your topics deeply, so this means, as a rule of thumb, having fewer chosen topics that are nonetheless discussed in more depth; this is preferable than choosing more topics which are discussed in less, if any, depth.

Also, remember that all your body paragraphs need to combine to make one overall point and not read like topics which are otherwise detached and separate from each other. To achieve this clear sense of an overall point, make sure once again that each topic clearly relates back to your argument; make sure that the first topic logically flows into the second, third and so on; and use connecting language, such as *therefore*, *however*, *on the other hand* and so on. When the reader has completed reading the body of your essay, he/she should be in no doubt as to how all the topics fit to produce a central point, whether the point is the historical development of the automobile to chart its impact on society, the significance of Korean pop music in bringing a focus on South Korea and spreading awareness of its culture, or the rise of green cities as a means to address environmental issues.

Must I Have a New Topic for Each Body Paragraph?

In short, no. The key to remember is that you need to maintain one topic per paragraph, but this does not necessarily mean one *new* topic per paragraph. If you have a new topic for each body paragraph, this might mean up to seven or eight topics for an average length essay, which in turn would strongly suggest too many topics in as much as you won't have necessary room to truly analyse them when compared with having fewer topics.

This means that if indeed you are writing about a topic which you feel needs more than just one paragraph's worth of coverage, then it's absolutely fine to discuss it across, say, two paragraphs. This will have implications for the topic sentence in the second (or more) paragraph, in that, because you're not starting a new topic, you will need to alert the reader to the fact the previous topic is still continuing. To do this, it will be sufficient to begin the topic sentence with words such as *moreover*, *to continue*, *in addition* and so forth. These words and expressions might not seem like much, but they make a big difference. In fact, get in the habit of using connecting expressions and words throughout all of your essay writing in order to show the links between ideas. Otherwise, your writing will sound choppy, which is generally not good style. The kinds of expressions and words in question can include *however*, *having said that*, *therefore*, *thus*, *on the other hand*, *on the contrary*, *furthermore* and so on.

However, even though the same topic is being covered from one paragraph to the next, it is important to introduce a new aspect of the same topic in each paragraph. For example, let's go back to Topic 2 in Figure 5.3:

> A focus on the economic devastation brought about by WWII and how this impacted on the British Empire

For this topic, the first time it is focused on could involve a discussion of explaining *the causes* of the 'economic devastation'; the next paragraph could then talk about *the effects*. One overall topic, but here subdivided into two aspects of discussion.

One critical consideration here is to ensure, as I had mentioned earlier, not to give too much focus to one topic at the expense of another. Unless you have a valid reason to discuss, say, Topic 1 for three paragraphs, and Topics 2 and 3 for just one paragraph each, the writing might come across as biased. This would be based purely on the fact that you're spending noticeably more time on one topic, which might be a particular theory, author or idea, but less time on other theories/studies and so on. Again, this is perfectly fine if it is made clear why you take this approach – again, **justify your choices** – but otherwise it might, as mentioned, come across as biased. So do bear this in mind as you otherwise want to ensure an equal focus on the various topics you discuss.

An Effective Formula for Critical Body Paragraphs

I now present a formula to ensure criticality in your body paragraphs. This is crucial as let's not forget that the bulk of your essay or assignments in general will indeed be captured in the body paragraphs, and so it stands to reason that it is here that criticality must be demonstrated.

We know that each body paragraph must start with a topic sentence, and you know the components of a good topic sentence. From here, you have choice within each and every body paragraph as to what comes next. But the ingredients that need to follow the topic sentence should include an illustration, reference of some kind to the relevant literature and a comment of some kind on said literature; these three components can come in any order following the topic sentence. Now let's look at how all this can come together nicely:

Determining what is 'good' or 'bad' language is entirely dependent on its context of usage. For example, so called 'bad' words – taboo language – can be used to signal solidarity and even show affection towards one's close friends. Likewise, excessive use of polite words and titles (*thank you, sir*) can show politeness, but can also communicate emotional distance if used with close friends or family. From these brief examples, we can suggest that word meanings and what they communicate are not fixed, but change based on the context, which includes the physical setting (e.g. a classroom), relationships between the speakers (e.g. two best friends) and even abstract concepts such as individuals' attitudes. As Smith (2018: 14) explains, 'no one can say with certainty what is or is not good language – the final determination is based on the situations in which language of all kinds is deployed'. This again suggests that our conceptions of language need not be fixed, as we might find ourselves using different types of language, from formal to informal, taboo and polite, to fit the situations we find ourselves in, and to make sure we fit in.

The topic sentence is clear in focus and its point is clear for the reader. The two sentences that follow provide an illustration of the topic, with Sentence 4 providing a brief summary of their content and, essentially, an interpretation of what they are saying. As a reminder, don't forget to provide illustrations for broad words/concepts – this is something that will perhaps be relevant for each body paragraph. The broad words provided in the topic sentence – *context of usage* – are followed by illustrations in Sentences 2 and 3, for example. Likewise, 'polite words and titles' referenced in Sentence 3, though perhaps a bit more concrete, are followed by examples (*thank you, sir*). The word 'context' used in Sentence 4 is indeed very broad and can refer to many things, and for this reason, Sentence 4 provides illustrations of some of the components of context, such as *physical setting*, with a further example provided of this, and *relationships between the speakers* is also provided with an example. Sentence 5 then provides a direct quotation, and as I have stressed, Sentence 6 does something with the quote – in this case, it agrees with the quote but also interprets it in the process, seen with the choice of language *this (again) suggests*. Clearly, if we're making a suggestion about something, it means that it could involve interpreting it in the first instance.

In summary, then, the formula as seen in the paragraph sample above is as follows:

TOPIC SENTENCE + ILLUSTRATION + QUOTE + COMMENT ON QUOTE

It could of course involve a 'mix and match' approach, such as:

TOPIC SENTENCE + QUOTE + COMMENT ON QUOTE + ILLUSTRATION

Again, feel free to play around with the components of the formula, but just remember to include them in each and every body paragraph. Look at it this way: let's say your essay has a total of eight body paragraphs, across which you're focusing on four topics (thus, perhaps two body paragraphs for each topic). Now, if you apply the formula above to each body paragraph, this means that in some form or other, each of the body paragraphs will have at least two sentences, maybe more, that offer new information. By 'new' I mean sentences which reflect your own original thinking, as seen with your illustrations and comments on the literature you refer to. This in turn means a grand total of (at least) 16 sentences throughout your essay that reveal your criticality – that's not bad at all. And this is the thing – being critical does not mean pages and pages of discussion per se. Instead, it is revealed a bit at a time in terms of a sentence here and a sentence there. The key is to do this **consistently**, from one body paragraph to the next.

Conclusion

The conclusion is where you essentially provide your overall conclusion to the reader. This means that having explored the literature in the body, you are now in a position to answer the question, 'What do I make of all this?' So you should start your conclusion with a firm declaration, which could stretch across two or three sentences, regarding what your thoughts are – your overall opinion on the matter. This can then be followed with a few sentences which recap the main points – topics – covered in the body. Then the final sentence can be thought of in terms of a 'closing thought'. Just as you want to make the opening sentence memorable, so too with the closing sentence. You could end with a question, assuming once again that this rhetorical device is permissible for your discipline. Otherwise, predictions also work well (e.g. if we don't act now, . . .), or a call to some kind of action (e.g. it is time to implement this change to policy, . . .). One thing you should **not** do, however, is bring in any new information, specifically in terms of new topics that should have otherwise been discussed in the body. It is simply too late to start a new thread of information or discussion, even if it is wholly relevant to the overall argument.

Here now is a sample conclusion. Have a look and see if the requisite boxes are there to be ticked:

This essay has shown that there are clear challenges and opportunities for technological innovation in health and social care settings, and that it is the practitioners, managers and policy makers in this area who will shape the impact that these new technological innovations have. This essay has covered some of the commonly noted challenges that technology presents in this area and has considered the opportunities that exist alongside these concerns. The concept of surveillance was then considered in depth, in particular around how discourse impacts on how technology is perceived in these settings. This discussion around discourse should remain central to technological engagement in these settings, and there is potential for technological innovation to be driven not by what is best for service users and patients, but instead by a desire to save money and promote perceived efficiency (Norrie et al, 2014). Keeping the discourse of rights at the centre of all discussions in this area will play a key role in mitigating these issues, and ensure that the vast opportunities presented by these new technological innovations are realised.

Source: UKEssays. (2018e, November). *Sample undergraduate 1st health and social care essay.* https://www.ukessays.com/services/samples/1st-hsc-essay.php. Accessed on 14 November 2020.

The opening sentence serves to offer an overview of the writer's main point. In this case, the writer is essentially saying that 'I believe that practitioners, managers and policymakers are in charge of leading technological innovation in health care' – this is the writer's main opinion, and one arrived at only through having first gone through the relevant literature and studies, as referred to in the essay's body. Bear in mind that the final conclusion that you arrive at can, in fact, have been hinted at or implied within the essay's body; it's simply that you should use the conclusion to state it explicitly. Of note also is the language used. It is fine to begin your conclusion with *in conclusion, in summary* and so on, but it is also a good idea to use language such as *this essay has discussed/demonstrated/ revealed that . . . .* Take note of the fact present perfect is used here (i.e. has discussed) as opposed to past tense (this essay discussed); more on this later, as verb tense is more than just a grammatical consideration in your writing, but it can also link with how the reader perceives your attitude towards your writing.

Sentences 2 to 4 provide an overview of the topics that have been covered, leaving the final sentence to offer a directive of sorts, essentially translated as 'we need to keep the discourse of rights at the centre of all discussions in this area'; of course, depending on how you interpret the final sentence (not in terms of its content, but in terms of its function) then you could equally consider it a prediction: 'if we keep the discourse of rights at the centre of all discussions in this area, issues will be reduced and technological innovations will be realised'. Either way, the final sentence brings the essay to a satisfactory end, as it serves to truly conclude matters, as a conclusion should do.

Essay Analysis

This section on essay writing now concludes with a completed essay for you to analyse, taken from the discipline of human resource management. My comments have been added on to the essay, highlighting the relevant aspects that have just been discussed. Rather than highlight each and every aspect of the essay that is relevant to the content thus far presented, I have chosen to highlight only a sample of the writer's work and leave it up to you to determine what else is relevant as far as good essay writing is concerned.

Introduction

Friedman (2014) comments that the 'gig economy' is a term that has attracted increasing attention in recent years, particularly so in light of a number of high-profile legal cases seeking to define precisely what working in 'the gig economy' means. A simple definition is offered by Scheiber (2015, p. 12) suggesting that the gig economy is "a labour market characterised by the prevalence of short-term contracts and/or freelance work", as opposed to permanent and/or full-time employment. Popular examples include couriers and agency workers, and according to a study commissioned by the UK Government (Gov.uk, 2018) approximately 2.8 million people in the UK – equivalent to 4.4% of the workforce – are currently directly employed in such work, either on a part-time or full-time equivalent basis.

Thoughts: The opening sentence provides a good hook, in part because it alerts us to a problem – the lack of a key definition for the term 'gig economy'.

At face value, the gig economy has been popularised as a flexible working environment, ideal for those employees seeking freedom and autonomy in their working conditions (Aloisi, 2015). Aloisi (2015) also notes, however, that the reality is rather more complicated, as whilst on the one hand the advantages of a gig economy would indeed be aligned with known employee motivational levers, in practice as the recent legal cases have shown, the gig economy is in fact far more precarious for many, meaning that they are not motivated by freedom and autonomy, but instead by 'hard' factors such as fear of not being offered more work (Manyika et al., 2016). This creates a paradox within Human Resource Management (HRM) literature. This essay seeks to shine a spotlight on this paradox, unpacking the contradictions and tensions in the literature and empirical evidence to understand how employees in the gig economy are motivated.

Thoughts: All relevant background in the first body paragraph, with the claims and statements supported by the literature. Without such support, the reader may well ask the author 'how do you know?' in response to such claims.

The Fundamentals of Employee Motivation

Thoughts: The topic above is the first main topic. It makes sense to start with this topic and clearly, the word 'fundamentals' points to the broad aspects of a topic, a starting point to set the scene. Thus, we should make this Topic 1.

The fundamental premise of employee motivation is grounded in the widely recognised work of Abraham Maslow (1943) and his Hierarchy of Human Needs. (Topic sentence – a clear topic and a point to make about it). In essence, Maslow established that grounding needs of safety and shelter must be the foundation of more advanced principles of human and employee motivation, as without basic needs being satisfied, people cannot direct their attention towards more sophisticated motivational principles. However, assuming such basic needs are satisfied, Maslow and later a clutch of other famous scholars such as McGregor (1960), Vroom (1964), Hertzberg (1968), and Hackman and Oldham (1976) examined various facets of employee motivation reaching broadly similar conclusions that people are motivated when they are appropriately rewarded and recognised for the work that they have undertaken. The detail of these various motivational theories has been carried forward to the present day and the widely established notions that the most effective way to motivate employees is via 'intrinsic' motivational levers (Lazaroiu, 2015). These include amongst others, recognition, personal autonomy, intellectually stimulating work, and flexibility to manage workload (Here the writer gives an illustration in relation to the reference to motivational levers referenced by Lazaroiu).

On paper, the gig economy offers all of these intrinsic levers, and as explained by Fernet et al. (2017), such intrinsic levers are regularly espoused as being one of the main reasons that employees elect to join the gig economy (Another clear topic sentence, which now serves to adopt a slightly more narrow focus, within the overall focus of 'the fundamentals of employee motivation'). The same scholars recognise that organisations benefit from a flexible labour workforce, meaning that they are not carrying one of the most expensive overheads – employees – on the profit and loss account, but much greater attention is always directed towards the many perceived 'benefits' to employees (Kanfer et al., 2017). Certainly, some employees within the gig economy do benefit from flexible, autonomy and intellectual stimulating work. Such employees however, are typically highly skilled, in possession of valuable knowledge or experience, and also possessed of a network of professional contacts enabling them to find such work on an ongoing basis (Steinberger, 2017). (The writer sets up a point, then suggests it only pertains to a certain group – this is clearly his/her argument. Thus, it is wise to back this up, as the writer does, with a reference to Steinberger). For employees within the gig economy lacking these transferable skills, their motivational levers are likely to be very different, much more towards the lower levels of Maslow's hierarchy. In plain terms, they work in precarious 'gig economy' employment, because there are no viable alternatives and they have no certainty of any other form of employment (Manyika et al., 2016). This represents the paradox of the gig economy, suggesting that much greater nuance and more careful interpretation of motivation within this context is necessary (Again, a summary of the writer's position to end with, demonstrating that the writer is interpreting the data).

The Paradox of the Gig Economy

Thoughts: Having explored the fundamentals and problematising such, the writer is now ready to move on to Topic 2 (with subsequent subtopics within each broad section), which focuses more specifically on the inherent paradox that he/she had hinted at within the previous topic.

The Taylor Review of 2017 sought to better understand the paradox of the gig economy, defining and examining what is understood to be 'good' work, that is to say intellectually and financially rewarding employment which is stable leading to productive and ultimately 'healthier and happier citizens' (Taylor Review, 2017). There is a wider case for 'good work' when looking beyond hard financial measures, as employees in jobs that they enjoy and in which they feel comfortable and confident are more productive and creative. Often, according to Milkman and Ott (2014), when people perceive that there is value and meaning in their work then they are more engaged, and happy and healthy employees are also less reliant on state support, suffer less ill-health, and ultimately work more. From a governmental perspective, this also offers the benefit of increased tax receipts, meaning that from all viewpoints, 'good' work is to be actively sought.

> The assumed converse 'bad work' is the rather one-sided relationship crystallised at the lower end of the gig economy, with those employees lacking the skills to negotiate longer term contracts, and instead finding themselves waiting desperately to hear if they will be working that day (Aloisi, 2015). This exploitative dynamic is demoralising and ultimately counter-productive, offering much greater benefits to the employer than the employee. Whilst UK employment levels may be at some of the highest levels for decades (Gov.uk, 2018), this topline figure masks a much higher proportion of precarious or 'bad work' with all of the associated disadvantages that this brings. As prosaically expressed by Behr (2017, p. 1), it leaves more than 1.6 million people of working age in the UK with the choice of *"crap job or no job"*. As Behr (2017, p. 1) goes on to note, *"not a very enticing choice"*, but it is a reality of the gig economy for many.

Discussion and Closing Thoughts

(The above title is another way of saying 'conclusion')

The technological advantages which have allowed the gig economy to thrive cannot easily be undone, nor indeed is anyone advocating that as the solution (Martin, 2016). (A summary of the writer's overall opinion/conclusion). However, there does need to be a careful consideration of how to establish a much higher level of 'good' work within the gig economy that protects employee rights, or at the very least rebalances the inherently unstable employment dynamic in its current form. Managed properly, flexible employment is shown in empirical research to be one of the most effective motivational levers or workplace benefits (Kelliher and Anderson, 2010). (A recap of the main points made in the body). As far back as 2004, Guest and Conway revealed in a report commissioned for that CIPD (Chartered Institute of Personnel and Development) that flexible working is the single most asked for benefit when negotiating employment contracts. Organisations that have adopted the principles of flexible working have found much greater productivity and much higher levels of employee engagement (De Menezes and Kelliher, 2017). As such, this reaffirms the recognition that on paper, flexible working is highly motivational and can certainly be characterised as one of the main indicators of 'good' work. The question therefore becomes, how can those employees at the lower end of the gig economy spectrum benefit from the same principles of 'good' flexible working as their more skilled counterparts.

Platforms that bring together those with skills for hire, and those needing work completed have mushroomed over the last decade as technology has accelerated opportunities for flexible working (Deloitte Insights, 2016). Some research suggests that certain people thrive in this flexible environment, enjoying meeting a vast range of people and having a huge variety in their working lives (Brown, 2018). The same research suggests however that these people are inherent with particular personality traits or a personal outlook meaning that they are more responsive and comfortable in a flexible environment and, are better able to adapt to the inherent uncertainty associated with flexible, gig-economy working. This suggests that alongside a tighter framework for gig working recognising the need for at least some stability in gig-work contracts, mental attitude and approach is also important. Once again however, the research in this field tentatively suggests that it is individuals with high-calibre skills and the capacity to reposition their skill set that marks them out as benefiting from the gig economy (Lemmon et al., 2016). Potentially, therefore, supporting those less inclined towards such a mindset to understand its value or perhaps even necessity in this environment could be a partial solution.

Unfortunately, however, the Taylor Review and other leading HRM scholars recognise that there is no simple fix to the arguably unstoppable growth of the gig economy principle. Unless those offering such flexible work are in some ways compelled to offer greater security and fairness, or their HRM strategies move them away from paring down their labour force to the least possible cost, then the precarious nature of the gig economy will continue. What could well become the next challenge in HRM literature is the growing dichotomy between, increasing drives for labour efficiency aligned with organisational strategy, and, recognition in that treating employees as 'resources' rather than people, is inherently dehumanising, and is ultimately leading to, in the words of Deloitte (2016, p. 1) *"contingent workforce management"* even at senior levels. It is concluded therefore, that there is also a responsibility upon the HRM profession more widely to decide for itself how good practice ought to look in terms of establishing 'good work' and also, how organisations should embrace this if they wish to have a happy, healthy, and productive but flexible workforce. (The essay ends with a closing thought, in this case consisting of a suggestion for best practice and the positive effects of implementing it).

Source: UKEssays. (2018f, November). *Sample undergraduate 1st HRM essay.* https://www.ukessays.com/services/samples/1st-hrm-essay.php. Accessed on 20 November 2020.

Summary

You have now been given a full list of the important aspects of essay writing and, more broadly, of any academic assessment really. That is, having a clear argument from the beginning, having a coherent structure, providing ample illustration for broad terms, having a clear conclusion – these are but a few things that are needed in essays, oral presentations, slides, posters and so on. The book will later discuss different types of assessments, such as presentations, but for now continues with a focus on dissertation writing.

6

How to Structure Your Dissertations

This chapter will focus on dissertation writing and, by extension, any kind of essay which requires you to conduct primary research of your own. In other words, an essay where you essentially go out and collect data of some kind to inform your research project. This can involve interviewing individuals or conducting focus groups with the public; it can involve conducting online surveys; it can involve conducting an experiment that you have set up; and indeed, your own research project need not involve people at all – some students opt to do a desk-based study, in which the focus is solely on reviewing the literature on the subject they're investigating and coming to a conclusion. But whatever you do for your own research project, there are some general points that you must bear in mind in terms of structure and content, one of which is that your dissertation/thesis/research project will be divided into chapters, each of which is outlined below in terms of its content.

Abstract

Before you construct your introduction chapter, you must write an abstract. However, the abstract might well be the last major part of your dissertation that you actually write, given that part of it must include the results of your study. So until you have your results and until they have been interpreted, this aspect of the abstract can't be written anyway. With this in mind, you might consider reading the rest of the chapter first and then coming back to this particular section later.

An abstract is a summary of the entire content of the dissertation, and often comes with a word limit. For my PhD thesis, for example, which was 95,000 words, I had no more than 500 words in which to present my abstract. In any event, I haven't ever seen an abstract that is more than one page long, to offer you a visual guide. The abstract serves to provide a background on what you have done, why you did it, how you did it and what you have found. The formula below will help you to approach abstract writing in a systematic and critical manner.

1. WHAT? The opening can serve to offer a brief background into the subject area from which your own research derives; remember, in the context of an abstract, this might not equate to more than one or two sentences. So this essentially answers the question, 'what is the subject area from which your own research project derives?

2. WHAT? You could of course skip the first 'WHAT' and get right to the point: telling the reader exactly what you're doing for your own research project, without first backgrounding it. Here, then, you're answering the question, 'what is your research project about?'

3. WHY? This equates to a brief rationale, addressing the question 'why are you conducting this research, why should we care?

4. HOW? Here you refer to your methods, explaining how you obtained the results which are then analysed.

5. WHAT? Now you're ready to inform the reader what the main results are – here, you will need to simply choose what you believe are the most important results and leave the detail for later.

6. WHAT? Finally, you need to explain to the reader what the implications are for your research – what do the main results actually *mean* for the discipline, practice, policy, society and so on?

There simply is not enough scope even in this book to detail the different types of abstracts written for different disciplines. In fact, abstract writing could conceivably be the subject of an entire book unto itself. However, if you bear the above points in mind – the WHATs, the WHY and the HOW – when you write your abstract of any kind, then your focus will be in the right place.

Here now is an abstract for you to analyse – does it attend to the requisite components of a good abstract?

Many plants in Australia have their seeds buried in order for the species to survive fires. The seeds start to germinate under the soil at certain temperatures. Seeds of *Acacia terminalis* and *Dillwynia floribunda* were examined in this experiment. It was hypothesised that the seeds need heat for the germination to start. Seeds of the two species were treated in hot and cold water and left to start germinating. *Acacia terminalis* showed a significant response in germination after the hot water treatment while *Dillwynia floribunda* did not.

Neither seed showed a response in germination after cold water treatment. The results for *Dillwynia floribunda* were unexpected but may be explained by factors such as water temperature and the length of time the seeds remained in the heated water.

Source: Uni Learning. (n.d.). *Report writing*. https://unilearning.uow.edu.au/report/2bii1.html. Accessed on 20 November 2020.

Thoughts: Sentences 1 and 2 offer a brief background into the overall subject at hand, setting up Sentence 3 to then explain what the actual study in question did. Sentence 4 offers the specific hypothesis (common in the Hard Sciences, as I had mentioned). Though there may not appear to be a clear sense of 'WHY', for the scientists reading the abstract, its presence would still be felt, implied with the content of Sentence 4. In other words, given that there is something to hypothesise about in the first instance, then this tells us, indirectly at least, that there is a gap in knowledge, otherwise why would we need a hypothesis if we are already certain about something? Sentence 5 provides a summary of the methods, with Sentences 6 and 7 explaining what the results were. The final sentence then addresses the final WHAT, by explaining what the implications are for the results mentioned prior – in this case, the implications for the results in terms of what factors contributed to them.

As you can see, an abstract is merely a snapshot of the main aspects of your research, with perhaps no more than a sentence or two for most of the requisite parts. Also, the key aspects of an abstract will need to be interpreted differently for different disciplines. As mentioned above, the need to explain the implications of your study's results will mean very different things, not only for different disciplines but also for the specific aspects of individual assignments *within* the disciplines. For example:

- SOCIOLOGY: The implications for social policy, in a study focused on social benefits payments and the need for fair distribution.
- MEDICINE: The implications for vaccination trials, in a study focused on ensuring safe vaccinations for all members of society.
- LITERATURE: The implications for a new understanding of an 'old' text, as part of a focus on modern-day perspectives, perhaps linked to social media, for readings of Shakespeare.

In fact, I challenge you to consider your own discipline and its overall goals and values, and with that in mind, what do you think would be the various implications for a given study in your field?

I will now move on to the chapters that need to be covered in your dissertation, addressing them one at a time.

Introduction

The introduction to a dissertation or even a PhD thesis largely follows that of a 1,500-word essay. You need to begin with **background information** of course, but the main difference is that you will now have more words with which to write your background. This is perhaps obvious, but given the added depth and scope that is involved with a dissertation, you will need the added words to enable you to go deep. Put it this way: for a 1,500-word essay, the background information contained within your introduction paragraph might be, say, four or five sentences; for a 12,000-word dissertation, the background information could be two full paragraphs, perhaps as many as three. Again, I can't pretend to set you a specific number of paragraphs and/or word count to use for the background – you should in fact consult with your dissertation handbook on this matter or ask your supervisor. But the main point first and foremost is to make sure that you provide all the necessary information to adequately provide an overview for your reader. Have you provided enough information to orient the reader as to what we already know within the subject area? Do you think an outsider to the subject area could make sense of things? On the other hand, save the more detailed focus for the literature review – after all, background information, no matter how long it might be, is essentially a summary of the main points, not necessarily in-depth coverage of them.

After the introduction, you should present your **rationale**. This was mentioned in Chapter One, but I will revisit it here. The rationale is the justification for your study, whether BA, MA or PhD. It is where you tell the reader why your study is valuable and needed. The rationale answers the question, 'why should we care?' I suggest placing your rationale in its own section, so that so far your introduction chapter might look like this:

1.0 Introduction

This is where you give an introduction to the actual introduction chapter itself. A paragraph will do. This is merely a suggestion, however, and not mandatory. It's sufficient to simply tell the reader the main points that will be covered within your background and then a quick mention of your own study's focus.

1.1 Background
1.2 Rationale

You can, of course, be more 'creative' with your section headings if you wish. 'Background' could be renamed as 'background to the study', and 'rationale' can be referred to as 'justification for the research'. At the early stage, however, I wouldn't worry about titles and instead focus on the big picture. That is, do you *provide* background information and a rationale? Focus on getting this right first and leave the section headings for later – section headings will be even more relevant for the literature review. But if you have a really catchy heading before you've even started to write the content, then by all means write it down before you forget!

The rationale should evolve naturally from the background, so that by the time you are coming to the end of your background section, it is made clear what the gap/issue/problem is within the subject area. Like an introduction paragraph, information within your introduction *chapter* should also progress from broad to narrow. This means that the background information in this particular section should start at whatever you deem to be the broadest level and then become progressively more narrow. At the most narrow level, this is where you can tell the reader what we *don't* know, after first telling them what is already known and understood about the subject. This then nicely invites you to come in and provide your contribution to knowledge, via the rationale to follow. As I had mentioned, it is fine to reference personal experience, certainly within the Social Sciences, as part of your rationale. If you have personal experience working as a social worker, for example, then why not reference this as part of a dissertation focused on challenges within the social work profession (that your dissertation will presumably address)? The key is not to turn a rationale into a personal declaration entirely but, instead, use any relevant personal experience as a springboard to more objective matter. For example, if you have experience teaching Special Educational Needs children, this is clearly personal experience. However, if your dissertation seeks to better define 'Special Educational Needs', in order to improve on provision for such students, then clearly your personal experience, itself part of personal and *professional* experience, has a role to play. In fact, when you're writing your own research report of any kind, be bold. You are in charge in many ways as you know the subject area you want to research, and your interests – and possible experience – in this area can be harnessed to help you write a convincing rationale and overall convincing dissertation.

The first step to creating a rationale is, as mentioned earlier, to **problematise** the subject area you wish to base your dissertation on. This is part of being critical of course and means that you have to identify an inherent issue, problem or merely a question within the subject area and exploit it. Very often, this means addressing a gap in the research. But this is still not enough! To be truly critical, you need to then explain *why* the gap needs to be filled. Let's practice (Table 6.1).

The 'WHY' is the central aspect of your rationale (i.e. *answering* the WHY is key), much as it is within your argument sentence. In an introduction chapter to a dissertation, however, there is not necessarily a statement of purpose captured in just one sentence. Instead, it is made clear throughout the rationale section, and

Table 6.1 Problematising your topic

Subject	Issue/Problem/ Question	Why Is This Important?
Mental health in children under age 11 (i.e. pre–high school)	This is becoming more common and problems are starting at younger ages	We can't afford to wait until high school as this will make the situation worse; we need an early intervention programme – as of writing, this is especially relevant given the lockdown associated with COVID-19
Visual pedagogy (e.g. using films to teach the subject matter)	Many students are very aware of, and proficient with, visual media nowadays (e.g. YouTube, social media, texting)	Given that students today have an overall ability with visual media, then surely bringing this into the classroom can be a more accessible way to facilitate classroom learning and potentially reach students better in some cases; this is important as some students do not learn best with more 'traditional' teaching methods
Children's literacy rates in primary schools	Why do girls tend to outperform boys in terms of literacy, notably reading?	This is important because we want to ensure equal opportunities for all students to perform to the best of their abilities, so it makes sense to determine what factors, if any, might be contributing to any lag in boys' literacy development

clearly, the rationale will not relegate the WHY to just one sentence as in Table 6.1 – you will need to expand. And the more WHYs you can answer as to why your study is important, the better. But the crux of the matter is shown nicely in Table 6.1 in a succinct manner.

Following the rationale, it is a good idea to then present your **research questions** – these can be part of the rationale section. Of course, you will only have research questions if you're conducting exploratory research, in which case, your goal is to answer the questions. The alternative is to conduct a hypothesis-driven study, in which case, your study rests on a prediction(s) you have made and thus you're not answering questions but, instead, you're testing to see if your prediction(s) is correct or not.

Finally, you should conclude your introduction chapter with a final paragraph which outlines the **structure of your dissertation**. Going with the ordering of sections thus far, this would be section 1.3. This section is entirely predictable, and to be honest, there's not much critical thinking needed at all. You simply need to tell the reader the order, content and purpose of the chapters that follow. Chapter two will be the literature review, chapter three the methods, chapter four the results and discussion (though these could be separate chapters if you wish) and finally, the conclusion chapter. Why tell your reader the order of chapters if this is already wholly predictable? I'm not sure to be honest, except to say that it is an academic convention, much like beginning a children's story with 'once upon a time'.

There are two critical points to mention here. First, the structure I have provided above is not a blueprint. Granted, the section content discussed here is needed – you need a rationale and background information within your introduction chapter of course. But I have seen variety within introduction chapters many times. This variety is seen in terms of adding intervening sections between the sections covered here. We might have something as below, as but one example:

1.0 Introduction
1.1 Background to the research
1.2 Context of the research
1.3 Rationale for the study
1.4 Aims and objectives
1.5 Structure of the dissertation

The added section focused on context of the research might be seen as an extension of section 1.1. The point here though is that the background section might simply provide background information, but not go beyond this. In other words, background is provided, but no mention is made of the gaps in the research. Thus, section 1.2 provides not merely the gap, but a more specific background on the specific subject area you are investigating. In this case, section 1.1 might focus on the broad subject area of modern aviation; section 1.2 then provides specific information on the more narrow area of aviation safety in the modern era. So the combination of sections 1.1 and 1.2 is just a different way to address the background information and what we already know of the subject, then followed by what we don't know within a more specific subtopic within the overall subject. As long as this kind of information is included in your introduction chapter, that's all that matters – whether you do it across one section or two.

The section on aims and objectives serves to offer a clear statement of purpose, one which evolves naturally from your rationale. But again – there's no reason why these two halves can't be part of the same section, if you prefer. It's all about making sure that your reader is left in no doubt about WHAT you're researching and WHY and beyond this, WHAT benefits the finished product can provide, whether beneficial to the discipline (but explain how, of course), society in general and so on. This will be somewhat speculative as you don't have the results yet (and if you do by the time you write your introduction, you wouldn't mention them in the introduction anyway). Students often ask what the difference is between 'aims' and 'objectives'. An aim(s) is a general statement of intent/ purpose, whereas an objective is a specific measurable goal – some kind of change/action that you wish to make happen. Thus, aims give birth to objectives.

For example, perhaps your dissertation seeks to investigate the reason for falling birth rates over the past 30 years in South Korea – this is an aim. Objectives that emanate from this are, as mentioned, measurable and specific. These could include explaining the reasons for falling birth rates, the impact on the economy via an ageing population and implications for the future in terms of jobs left to fill. There's no reason why you can't have several aims and as many objectives to follow, or one central aim with several objectives. It makes sense, however, to have a few objectives – perhaps three as a mere suggestion. Given that you are conducting academic research on a subject of your choosing, then it is important to have more than just one objective – instead, you should try to have a few in mind, as evidence of the various ways in which your work will make a difference. An example is provided shortly of an introduction to a dissertation, and this will help further to distinguish between aims and objectives.

The second point to make is that you must always **justify** your choices and decisions taken as part of your research. This is a big part of being critical. This had been mentioned earlier also, and it is a key part of your introduction in terms of your rationale. After all, a rationale is essentially a justification for your research, and some students indeed refer to it as that – as part of the section heading. Justifying the choices you make in your assessments is not meant to suggest you are doing something wrong and therefore you need to 'justify' yourself! In this case, justifying the choices you make and take is about simply explaining the thought processes and reasoning behind your choices. Otherwise, your reader won't know – as I have made clear, lecturers are not mind readers and so you need to do the talking. If you consider the structure of a dissertation in particular, then below are a sample of the more relevant places to provide a justification for your choices.

Introduction – The rationale is the most obvious item in which justification is needed, as this is the crux of why you're conducting research in the first instance.

Literature review – You may consider offering a brief justification for your choice of litera- ture, however obvious the choices might be, as well as the ordering of topics within the literature review chapter. This is not an absolute rule, as it is, once again, a case of things you *could* do, not necessarily should or must do. But the more you take the time in your assessments to explain to the reader **what you did and why you did it** – and not merely for your rationale – the better, as this is proof positive that you have indeed thought criti- cally about the subject.

Methodology – Here is where you have a lot to explain:

- What approach did you take (e.g. qualitative/quantitative)? Why?
- Who is your sample and why?
- If you are *not* conducting participant-based research, in a discipline that otherwise does (e.g. the Social Sciences), why?
- Why did you choose interviews/questionnaires/focus groups?
- Why choose thematic analysis, or any other approach, to analyse your data?

More will be provided on this in the section dedicated to the methodology chapter, but you can start to conceptualise justification more at this point. And in terms of how you provide your justification for whatever topic it pertains to, check with your supervisor/lecturer how best to go about this. But certainly for Social Science research, it is fine to spell it out for the reader as follows:

I have chosen to do X for the following reasons. First, . . ., second, . . .

The sentence above is a clear way to prepare the reader for evidence of your critical thinking on the subject by laying out reason by reason why you did what you did, whether that refers to your choice to use semi-structured interviews, refer to a theory that is otherwise regarded as out of date or apply the theory of a particular discipline (e.g. biology) to another (e.g. linguistics). As long as your reasoning is logical and clearly explained, then this is evidence of being critical, even if someone else might suggest a different approach that could have been taken.

This section now concludes with an example of an introduction chapter from a dissertation, once again with comments provided by myself regarding some of the aspects that have been under discussion.

1.1 Introduction

The aim of this study is to investigate the role of tourism in the economic development of host destinations.

Thoughts: Here is a clear aim, with background information to follow. There are also several references to the relevant literature to help support the writer's claims. Don't wait for the literature review to bring in support – you should plan to do so within the introduction chapter also as far as any claims are concerned and of course as part of the background information.

Tourism is now more dynamic and growing more than ever, with the development of new and upcoming trends which reflect the changes in tourist demand taking centre stage (Bernstein, 2013). Globalisation has enabled tourism to reach great lengths with the United Nations World Tourism Organisation [UNWTO] (2018) reporting that international tourism arrivals grew by a huge 7% in 2017, equating to 1,322 million which was accelerated by Europe, Africa, Asia and the Pacific, Middle East and the Americas. A strong indication from these travel patterns also suggest that people have also been visiting developing nations which are more apparent in Africa, Asia and the Middle East. This means that to an extent, tourists have a desire to want to explore other cultures and engage with people at these destinations. In order to investigate the aim, a qualitative approach will be taken to the study which will employ statistics gathered by the World Travel and Tourism Council [WTTC] (2018) as they are a well regarded agency in the industry.

1.2 Rationale

As portrayed by the WTTC (2018), tourism continued to have a strong consecutive year in 2017, as well as the rise in the generation of positive economic impacts for the world. A significant factor which can be derived from this is that tourism has a critical role to play in the development of economic benefits to host destinations (Banerjee et al., 2018). Economic impacts of tourism are often directed towards developing countries as well, as many academics agree that these destinations are more likely to benefit from tourism (Chou, 2013). With international tourists increasing, it is only understandable that economic impacts from tourism are also growing as well. Therefore, it is significant to assess the extent of these benefits to host nations where tourism is present and to also identify how effective these economic impacts are. (Here is just one sentence which, in the context of section 1.2 as a whole, is convincing).

The role of tourism in economic development is also closely linked with sustainability, because in order to deliver these benefits, the destination needs to have effective tourism planning in place so that income distribution is fair for example, or that there is enough opportunity available for residents to work in the industry (Ladeiras et al., 2010).

1.3 Gap in Literature

Literature often places more focus on the social and environmental impacts of tourism (King, 1993; Hillery, 2001; Gladstone, 2013). As a result, there are a limited number of case studies and articles available on the role of tourism in economic development in destinations. This may well be because social and environmental impacts are easier to measure, or simply because the effects of social and environmental impacts are more apparent than economic. Regardless of the reason, economic development is not a subject which is discussed frequently in tourism and tends to be more obvious in industries such as the financial sector, construction industry and so forth (Masoud & Hardaker, 2012). Therefore, in order to fully understand the kinds of impacts which are developed economically in destinations, both positive and negative, it is important to address them.

Thoughts: The two sentences directly above reference the gap and subsequently, an explanation as to why the gap needs to be addressed, as part of this study. While the content of section 1.3 could have been combined with 1.2, it is fine to separate them. Once again, as long as the content of these two sections is clearly present in your introduction chapter, then this is the main factor – the ways in which this information is subdivided is something you can decide later.

It is also important to understand the links between different economic impacts as well, which this study will look to do, as well as identifying how economic impacts maybe limited in developing nations. As examples, three developing destinations have been chosen based on the basis that there is a common perception that tourism benefits these countries more (Mathieson & Wall, 2006). The destinations which have been chosen are India, Kenya and Jamaica which are regarded to be developing destinations (UNWTO, 2018).

1.4 Significance of Study

This study looks to add to the existing literature of tourism impacts which has been a widely studied subject over the last two decades. As mentioned above, the significance of the study lies in the fact that there is a limited amount of information and literature on how tourism contributes to the economic development of a destination. This study will therefore aim to provide an insight into why economic development as a result of tourism matters in destinations, as well aiming to provide recommendations on how they can improve their current economic impact so that the benefits delivered to the host nation are greater. This may also prove to be useful for the countries mentioned in the study, as it will provide possible reasons as to why economic development from tourism is doing well and how they can progress further as a provider of tourism experiences.

Thoughts: The two sentences directly above are essentially about what the study's benefits could be – rather speculative as the results are yet to be presented, but it shows a critical stance for sure as the writer has essentially asked himself/herself 'what does this (i.e. the study's focus) mean to me?' in terms of its potential.

1.5 Research Aim & Objectives

The aim of this study is To Investigate the Role of Tourism in Economic Development in Host Nations. (A clear aim, which was also presented in the opening sentence). In order to address this aim effectively, the following objectives have been composed to support the study. These are as follows:

- To identify ways tourism contributes to economic development.
- To evaluate the factors which can hinder economic development in tourist destinations.

- To assess the most successful methods of tourism in facilitating economic development.
- To provide recommendations on how to accelerate economic development in tourist destinations more effectively.

Thoughts: As you can see, the objectives stem from the central aim; are specific and concrete; can suggest change in practice; and thus tie in with the rationale for the study once again, as the research clearly has something to offer. Normally, we might expect there to be research questions per se – two or three is a good number. Here, however, what might have been questions have been conceptualised as statements of objectives. Regarding your research questions, plan to present these in the introduction chapter, but if not, then definitely at the end of your literature review.

1.6 Overview of Chapters

This study consists of six chapters which aim to address the different aspects of the objectives outlined above in order to form a conclusion with recommendations which answers the research question. The study constitutes of the following chapters:

Thoughts: As you will see, what follows is quite generic and in no need of a critical approach at all, but it is nonetheless a central part of the introduction chapter to a dissertation or thesis.

Chapter 1 – Introduction: this section provides an overall introduction to the study of tourism, with a brief overview of the rationale, gap in academic literature, the significance of the study and most importantly, the aim and objectives of the study.

Chapter 2 – Literature Review: this is one of the critical sections of the study providing an overview of different theoretical concepts and frameworks in relation to tourist motivations, typologies, and types of different positive and negative economic impacts as well as tourism planning.

Chapter 3 – Methodology: this section provides the overview of the qualitative approach taken to this study by covering the research philosophy and qualitative and quantitative methods which are common in research.

Chapter 4 – Results: this section introduces the figures collected by the WTTC on economic impacts and analyses them.

Chapter 5 – Discussion: this section provides an extension of the results chapter and discusses further in-depth what the results could possibly indicate against the literature from chapter 2.

Chapter 6 – Conclusion and Recommendations: this is the last section of the study which provides an overall conclusion on the role of tourism in economic development as well as a section suggesting recommendations for the industry to further improve and accelerate economic development in the destination which they operate.

Source: UKEssays. (2018q, November). Sample undergraduate 2:1 tourism dissertation on the role of tourism in the economic development of host destinations. https://www.ukessays.com/services/samples/2-1-tourism-dissertation.php. Accessed on 21 November 2020.

Research questions

Hopefully, this introduction has given you some clear ideas, not just about dissertation writing but about your assessments in general, in terms of the need to provide illustration, support, have a clear focus and so on, which reflect so much of what has been discussed so far. One point I will make regarding research questions is that they too should follow a broad to narrow approach in terms of the order of presentation. As for the number of research questions, I have seen dissertations which had just one central question, but two or three is quite common. As I have stressed, it's better to have more depth than width. This is why a relatively small number of research questions ensures that you will have more to say about them when you provide the answers as part of your results and discussion. Below is an example of how research questions might look, in terms of having a clear focus, being specific and of course moving in a logical manner:

What are the chief characteristics of food poverty in the UK?

Thoughts: Specific to a location (the UK), which means the same issue in another country might be somewhat different, if only slightly. But by simply specifying the location, it shows criticality in that the writer (a) is not assuming 'food poverty', while perhaps a global issue, is necessarily the same from one country to the next (though there are no doubt similarities); (b) the question is broad but clear at the same time, given that 'chief characteristics' is looking for the main aspects of this issue.

What are the causes?

Thoughts: Hmmm . . . perhaps make this the first question, because the causes of any issue lead to the subsequent effects. Thus, 'causes' of food poverty lead to 'chief characteristics' and so should come first. What do you think?

What strategies can be adopted to solve this?

Thoughts: Makes sense to place this last as finding solutions to a problem can only really come into play once we've first identified the problem and its root causes.

No doubt you will find yourself refining your research questions, not to mention the questions posed to participants as part of interviews or questionnaires. This goes double for the way in which you choose to arrange the topics within your literature review, as it is quite common to have an idea in mind as to all of the above and then change and make edits as you go along. Don't forget to invite your supervisor to look at your draft chapters, to include your research and interview questions, assuming you plan to use interviews of course (clearly, you may not need to).

But in all the questions you create as part of your dissertation, from the research questions themselves to the questions you ask as part of questionnaires/interviews, bear in mind some of the general, but important, points that have been stressed:

- Move in a logical sequence from one question to the next.
- Make the questions clear – if this means having to give a quick illustration of otherwise broad words that are used in the questions as part of interviews/questionnaires, then do so; this will help the participant understand exactly what is being asked.
- BUT don't ask leading questions – questions which 'force' a certain reading, such as *don't you agree that . . .*; this is not to suggest that participants wouldn't recognise the question as leading and would still answer as they see fit, but such questions are not really ethical.

This section now continues with a focus on writing a literature review.

2. Literature Review

The literature review chapter is to a dissertation/thesis what the body is to an otherwise 'regular' essay (i.e. that which is not based on your own research project). Like the body of an essay, plan the topics to move from broad to narrow, in a logical sequence – all of this has been covered already. The difference here is that you will of course have a much higher word count and so the coverage of the various topics will be plotted section by section, not just paragraph by paragraph. Think of this like a Russian doll – go from broad to progressively more narrow in terms of the way in which you present the different parts of the literature review. This will ensure coherence, and the approach is to start with sections, then subsections.

There are three overall purposes of a literature review: first, to present information on **what we already know** within the area you are now researching; second, to not merely summarise what we know but to **interpret** it – as mentioned, this can involve agreement/disagreement, illustration, for example; and third, your literature review should also remind the reader of **what we don't know**, or simply don't know enough of. It is this unknown element that you are addressing as part of your own research, in terms of the gap you will fill. Below is a skeleton for illustrative purposes:

2.1 Introduction (again, a quick paragraph is sufficient, largely to explain to the reader – like an essay plan – what topics will be covered and in what order).

2.2 The origins of French New Wave cinema (In a dissertation focused on the cinematic movement known as the French New Wave, it would seem logical to start at the beginning – in this case, how this particular cinematic movement came to be).

   2.2.1 Post-war Existentialism
   2.2.2 Cinema verité

2.3 French New Wave (Having covered its origins first, it makes sense to then focus on the particular style of the New Wave, based on directing style and the types of narratives used).

   2.3.1 Directing style
   2.3.2 Narrative themes

2.4 Public reception (Then we move to a focus regarding how the public viewed the New Wave when it was at its peak in French cinema).

2.5 Legacy of the French New Wave (A legacy points to the effects of something, or some-one, after it is no longer around/alive; again, it is purely logical to end with this, but only after first having covered the birth and reception of the New Wave).

2.6 Summary – A brief paragraph to follow which wraps up what you have just discussed, in terms of providing a summary of the main points, before then announcing what is to follow – the methodology chapter.

I now present you with the skeleton of a literature review taken from Finance. Regardless of the content of each topic area, contained within each section/subsection, do you think that the structure below is coherent?

2. Literature Review

   2.1. Overview of Financial Innovation (Clearly, an 'overview' belongs at the start!).

   2.2. Evolution of Innovative Financial Instruments (This key word of evolution also sug-gests background information of the relevant topic and so it needs to come sooner, rather than later. In fact, this illustrates the importance of choosing your heading titles carefully, so that they give a definitive idea of what the content is and, as seen here, where such content should be placed within a given chapter.

   2.3. Types of Innovative Financial Instruments and Associated Risks (We've read about the background of such, so it makes sense to now give some specific examples).

2.3.1. Shares

2.3.2. Bonds

2.3.3. Funds

2.3.4. Derivatives

2.3.5. Mortgage Backed Securities

Thoughts: I can't personally find any inherent logic to the order in which these five topics above are presented, and so it's fine to present them as they are here, or in any other order for that matter.

2.4. The Role and Utility of Innovative Financial Instruments in the Global Economy.

Thoughts: Now we arrive at the most narrow and, presumably, most relevant topic within the literature review, the focus being firmly on the fundamentals of the overall research.

Source: UKEssays. (2018l, November). *Sample undergraduate 2:1 finance dissertation*. https://www.ukessays.com/services/samples/2-1-finance-dissertation.php. Accessed on 21 November 2020.

As a final guide, below is a body paragraph from the same essay, specifically from section 2.1. Have a look at the content and decide if you think it is well-written in terms of its overall content. For example, is there a topic sentence that ties in with the overall topic of 2.1 (i.e. overview of financial innovation)? Is there illustration of broad terms? Does the writer do something with the references he/she uses?

United Nations Development Programme (2012) stated that financial innovation increases institutional sustainability and facilitates their outreach to economically disadvantaged social segments. OECD (2014) differentiated financial innovation into three specific segments, i.e. product innovation, process innovation and innovations in financial systems and institutions. Product innovation includes the development, creation and introduction of various new financial products in diverse areas like deposits, credit, leasing, insurance, hire purchase and others. They are developed and introduced from time to time in order to respond and react to market alterations and improve marketing and operating effectiveness (Anderloni & Bongini, 2009; Schueffel & Vadana, 2015). Process innovations essentially comprise the development and introduction of different types of new business processes that can result in market expansion or greater efficiencies (Mention & Torkkeli, 2014; Anderloni & Bongini, 2009). Innovations in areas of financial systems and institutions can impact the financial sector and are connected to alterations in business structures, the development of new varieties of financial intermediaries or to alterations in the supervisory and legal framework (Mention & Torkkeli, 2014; Anderloni & Bongini, 2009).

Given that this paragraph derives from a larger section dedicated to providing background information at the broadest level regarding the literature, it does its job well. But is there still room perhaps for some illustration and 'doing something' with the literature? An actual example of product and process innovations, beyond the definitions of such (which do work well, of course), would have been an opportunity for the writer to demonstrate his/her knowledge beyond the textbook. As for the literature, its purpose here is to merely summarise the points being made by the writer, and on that level, it reads very well and certainly demonstrates that the writer has done the necessary background reading.

But with a bit of editing, the writer could have taken this just a bit further:

> Product innovation includes the development, creation and introduction of various new financial products in diverse areas like deposits, credit, leasing, insurance, hire purchase and others. They are developed and introduced from time to time in order to respond and react to market alterations and improve marketing and operating effectiveness (Anderloni & Bongini, 2009; Schueffel & Vadana, 2015). An example might include . . .

The example could then segue into a quote, which in turn could be commented on – whether a statement of (dis)agreement, another illustration or an explanation (more on all of these strategies in Chapter Eight). But this is not to say that one token paragraph can speak for the entire essay, let alone an entire literature review chapter. And what we've seen so far reads well. But one key point to remember for your literature review: **don't just summarise the literature, you must interpret it!** If your literature review, or essay in general, makes copious references to the literature in conjunction with the points it makes – as the full paragraph above does – this in itself is a sign of good writing and is, to an extent, a reflection of criticality. After all, it shows that (a) the writer knows what the key points are within the subject area; (b) the writer knows which authors/publications are relevant to the subject area; and (c) the writer has certainly done quite a bit of background reading on the subject, as opposed to making multiple statements and claims but without the necessary support of references to the literature.

However, seek to go beyond this. This is a very good way to approach the literature, but if you want to go even further then use your body paragraphs, as discussed earlier in this chapter, as a means to reveal your personal understanding that goes beyond the basic facts and figures of the subject: illustrate broad words/concepts using your own examples, and again, do something with the literature you use. Let's have one final example of just what I mean, with an excerpt taken from the literature review of a dissertation taken from the subject area of construction:

Cheung et al., (2011) maintain that there are problems with organisational culture in the industry and it is argued that this affects willingness to collaborate within the project team and across organisational boundaries, increasing the risk of delays. Arditi et al., (2017) makes a similar claim, suggesting that organisational culture can be affected by delays in construction and can also be a causal factor. For example, if there is a clan culture in an organisation then this can result in lax attitude to management's authority in terms of achieving project goals, whereas a market oriented organisation may pay too little attention to human resources which results in delays through unmotivated staff.

Thoughts: Above we see a good example of what I mean. The writer first presents the views of those in the field. But rather than present them and move on, the writer then provides an illustration, a chance to essentially say 'here is what the authors mean, based on how I understand them'.

It is submitted that the over-use of competitive procurement has an impact on delays in construction whereby clients favour cost over value, requiring contractors to submit the lowest possible price to secure work. This in turn affects the supply chain, where contractors put pressure on subcontractors to reduce the cost of work. All of which adversely affects trust, supply chain management and relationships and willingness to collaborate. These failures increase the risk of delays, and ensure that there is a viscous circle of inefficiency within the construction industry (Hartmann and Caerteling 2010; Fawcett et al., 2012; Morledge and Smith 2013).

Thoughts: In the paragraph above, the writer is presenting his/her own argument, all of which reads in a logical, flowing sequence. But it reads all the more credibly because at the end, the writer essentially backs up his/her argument by relating it to authors within the field. It's as if the writer is saying, 'this is what I believe and look, so do these experts'. This is good, critical writing.

Source: UKEssays. (2018i, November). *Sample undergraduate 2:1 construction dissertation*. https://www.ukessays.com/services/samples/2-1-construction-dissertation.php. Accessed on 22 November 2020.

The next section covers your methods chapter, explaining the most important aspects.

Methodology

There are different ways to approach methodology, often based on the discipline you're writing for. Such differences will also be reflected in how you construct and write your methodology chapter as a result. There is not enough space to discuss each and every different approach here, and so, as an oft-repeated disclaimer, it will be up to you to fine-tune your methodological approach with your supervisor, who can provide the level of detail that might be missing in this section. However, there are some general truths to consider when writing your methodology chapter, and overall dissertation, which span all disciplines.

First, and as I have made clear, justify your choices for the reader. Make it clear what approaches you have, or have not, taken, and explain why. This is a must. And it's not enough to simply refer to the literature and quote authors who declare that interviews work well to extract qualitative information, or focus groups are ideal to gather spontaneous reactions from participants. Instead – and as I have stressed – do something with the quotes! In other words, by all means quote from the relevant authors about the different ways to conduct your particular study, but go further and then explain what the quote means to you and your research – this is one example:

> Jones (2008: 75) declares that 'questionnaires can be used to potentially gather a large number of responses in a fairly short time, which might not be possible if relying on interviews'. This is a key reason in my decision to rely on questionnaires to collect data for my study, as my goal is indeed to obtain as large a number of participants as possible – ideally, 50 or more – from which I can then make generalisations, however tentative. This would not be possible, however, with the limited number of interviews that I would have been able to conduct.

As you can hopefully see, the quote is fine in and of itself. But even the best quote in the world – whatever that might be – is always going to work even better if you comment on it in some way. In the example above, the writer has chosen to explain why questionnaires were chosen for the research, based on the content of the quote. This way, the writer is relating the quote's content to the specific goals of the research and, in doing so, is further justifying why questionnaires were chosen. This does much more than simply choosing a quote and then leaving it, essentially an easy way out which is forcing the quote to do all the work which you, as the writer, must play a part in.

But at a broader level, you must think critically about the most appropriate methods for the particular research you are conducting, at the level of discipline-specific and at the more narrow level of assignment-specific. For example:

- Is your research **qualitative** or **quantitative**? Respectively, are you seeking to obtain people's opinions, feelings and attitudes on a given subject, or are you focused on numerical representations, statistics and such, which might not tell us much about people's beliefs – but this is fine if your goal is to represent numerical data.
- If you are conducting **participant-based research**, then who is your **sample**? *Why* are they your sample? What characteristics do you need in the sample in the first place?

For example, are you investigating undergraduate students' attitudes toward online learning? If so, does this include all undergraduate students, regardless of personal background (e.g. age, national origin, race/ethnicity and so on)? Why? Explain your choices.

- What method of **data collection** will you use? Interviews? Questionnaires? Focus groups? Observational research? Why?
- How will you **interpret the data**? Thematic analysis, for example, is but one method.
- Or, are you conducting a **desk-based study**, in which you will review the relevant literature in your subject area and, in doing so, come to an overall conclusion about what we know so far in the subject area.
- Is your research more science-based and thus perhaps based around a hypothesis and testing?
- How will you approach **ethics**? This might warrant its own section in the methodology chapter.
- How about the **validity** and **trustworthiness** of your study?

The bullet points above are but a mere sample of some of the considerations to think about regarding the relevant methodological approach you will need to take. You have a supervisor for your dissertation of course, and it is always best if you talk about the details of your project with him/her in the first instance, as no book can cover everything. But consider the main points that contribute to critical writing across all disciplines. First, remember to **illustrate broad concepts**, whether they relate to your literature review, methodology or any other chapter; this includes doing something with the quotes/references you use. Second, remember to **justify the choices you make**. This is going to be especially relevant for the methodology chapter, as I mentioned earlier. The more you explain why you made the choices you did, the more critical your writing. This is because it tells the reader that you have pondered, considered and truly analysed the different aspects involved with a methodology and made reasoned decisions as to your final choices.

For example:

- **Justify** why you adopted a desk-based study (and telling the reader you did this because you didn't have time to conduct participant-based research is *not* a critical approach).
- **Justify** who your sample is – be very detailed here. If you say it consists of Korean-American business owners, this raises lots of additional questions. Don't leave it to the reader to ask/answer them! Answer them ahead of time in your methodology:

  o If 'Korean-American', then this would mean Koreans who emigrated to the USA and later obtained American citizenship, or Americans by birth whose parents/ancestors are Korean.
  o Should we include both categories above or just one? What is the reason for adopting either approach?

      ○   What kinds of business? Small, medium, large? How are such defined anyway? Do the businesses have to cater mostly to the local Korean community also? Or is it just the owners who need to be Korean-American, however defined?

      ○   Is age relevant? Gender? I'm not suggesting these categories *should* be relevant, but **the more you explain, the less they complain** (as I mentioned earlier in the book).

- **Justify** how you recruited the sample. Did you have a gatekeeper who mentioned your study to the sample and, in this way, recruited them? Why use this system? Did you use posters to advertise your study? Where did you place them? Why? Did you email potential participants? Why? Don't forget – if you email participants, then this means you have their email addresses in your computer – will you delete them after you have your responses?

- **Justify** your choice of data collection. Why interviews? Why not questionnaires? Why semi-structured interviews? Why not unstructured interviews?

- **Justify** your choice of language for conducting the interviews. Perhaps your participants are not native speakers of English and you choose to interview them in their first language – which may be your own first language also. So why use their first language for the interview? What are the pros and cons? Or, why use English for the interview? What are the pros and cons?

- **Justify** all the choices where they connect with ethical issues. For example, how do you plan to keep participants anonymous? Where/how will you store the data? For how long?

- What other methodological choices and decisions might you need to consider justifying?

There is much more to consider but again, purely on the basis of displaying criticality, get in the habit of **academic justification** for all your assessed work, but notably for your dissertation. Given that this is a piece of original research for which you are solely responsible, then it means that you are in charge and are essentially left to educate *us*, the lecturers/supervisor. You must direct us from start to finish regarding your choices, from the choice of research topic in the first instance to the absolute micro-level decisions such as why you chose a certain day of the week to conduct interviews (e.g. perhaps that's your free day, so tell us). Often, papers are not published by academic journals precisely because the methods are deemed to be flawed in some way. While your dissertation will not be held to the same standards as papers for hopeful publication in an academic journal, this should nonetheless make clear that your methods need some decent unpacking.

Coherence

As with the literature review, plan to arrange the sections and topics within in a logical sequence. Again, broad to narrow often works in this regard. There are many different aspects of writing a methodology chapter in terms of its content, largely based on the discipline in which you are writing, but below I present a sample of methodology chapters by outlining the skeleton of each. Have a look at these in order to get a good sense of coherent development.

Chapter Three – Methodology (from a marketing dissertation)

3.1. Introduction, Overview and Sample
3.2. Background to Method
3.3. Role of Researcher
3.4. Data collection and Ethics of Netnography
3.5. Data Interpretation and Analysis
3.6. Limitations
3.7. Chapter Summary

Source: UKEssays. (2018m, November). *Sample undergraduate 2:1 marketing dissertation. Chapter III. Methodology.* https://www.ukessays.com/services/samples/2-1-marketing-dissertation.php#_Toc526111372. Accessed on 20 November 2020.

Chapter Three – Methodology (from an education dissertation)

3.1. Introduction
3.2. Sampling universe

    3.2.1. Recruiting the sample

3.2. Qualitative design
3.3. The use of semi-structured interviews
3.4. Thematic analysis
3.5. Ethical considerations
3.6. Summary

As you can see, there is once again a progressively more narrow movement regarding the sections of the three chapter skeletons above. I now finish this section by presenting some samples of writing which derive from methodology chapters.

Environmental sciences

It was determined that a systematic literature review would be the most appropriate methodology to apply to this research study. The aim of a systematic literature review is to identify, critically evaluate and integrate the findings of all relevant studies (Cooper, 2003). Therefore, the data which was collected was secondary in nature. A systematic literature review was selected due to the nature of the research topic. The overall aim of the study was to develop a comprehensive understanding of the socio-cultural and demographic factors influencing sanitation conditions in Ghana – therefore, the use of existing research was determined as suitable. A systematic literature review was selected as the methodology due to the potential for this methodology to include all relevant currently published research. The inclusion of all relevant research improves the accuracy and reliability of the conclusions that were drawn due to enabling the critical comparison of multiple data resources, thus increasing the potential for the identification of outlying data points/sets. This will allow for the identification of relationships, contradictions, knowledge gaps and inconsistencies in the published literature (Khan et al., 2003).

Thoughts: The sentences above all combine nicely to present the writer's rationale for the methodological approach – in this case, the decision to make the dissertation entirely literature-based.

Source: UKEssays. (2018k, November). *Sample undergraduate 2:1 environmental sciences dissertation*. https://www.ukessays.com/services/samples/2-1-environmental-science-dissertation.php. Accessed on 28 November 2020.

Medicine

After retrieval of studies from electronic database searching it is important that inclusion and exclusion criteria are applied to the results, such that irrelevant studies are dismissed and only those pertaining to the research question are considered for full eligibility (Booth et al., 2012).

The inclusion criteria defined articles published in the last two decades (1998–2018), contained within a peer-reviewed journal, primary rather than secondary research or reviews, available in English language and reporting of relevant data to the research question.

Thoughts: This provides a clear summary of what the inclusion criteria were for purposes of selecting journal articles for analysis, as part of the methodological approach taken.

This series of criteria ensures that the findings in this review are informed and comprehensive, such that any recommendations will be meaningful to current practice. In addition, peer-review helps to establish a level of validity among primary studies and only reviewing studies of English language negates the need for translation, which is time-consuming and may increase the risk of error (Cowell, 2014; Meline, 2006).

Thoughts: Further evidence of the writer being critical, seen with a conclusion drawn about the benefits of the inclusion criteria adopted. And once again, a reference is made to the literature which helps to add weight to the writer's views.

The use of exclusion criteria is also important to help refine the filtering of retrieved studies, to identify those that are most relevant to the research domain; however, no selective exclusions were applied as this can result in the exclusion of important studies (Garg, 2016). Thus, the exclusion criteria directly contrasted the inclusion criteria; articles published prior to 1988, lacking peer-review, non-primary research, not available in English language and reporting of irrelevant data to the research question.

Source: UKEssays. (2018n, November). *Sample undergraduate 2:1 medi-cine dissertation: Research question.* https://www.ukessays.com/services/samples/2-1-medicine-dissertation.php#_Toc527021272. Accessed on 21 November 2020.

To finish this section, I reiterate the need to work closely with your supervisor regarding the process of planning, writing and revising your dissertation, as that's what supervisors are for. There are a lot of considerations when planning a methodological approach, let alone carrying it out, and to get to the heart of which approach is most appropriate – for both the overall discipline and the specific goals of your dissertation – bear the broad information provided here in mind. But beyond this, seek out help from your supervisor, as this is some-thing that many students don't always do. Remember – they are there to help, but don't wait until the last minute to share dissertation drafts with them if the deadline is looming, and ask any and all questions as they come. No question is too 'big' or too 'small' and as you have gathered by this point in the book, the more you cover all areas in your assessments, big and small, and attend to the details regarding WHAT and WHY, the more critical your writing and overall assessments will be.

Results and discussion

I begin by explaining the differences between the two areas of results and dis-cussion. Both these areas can be combined to make one chapter, with each having its own section, or you can separate them into two chapters (Table 6.2). Either way, the content of each will be different:

Table 6.2   Results and discussion sections/chapters

Results Section/Chapter	Discussion Section/Chapter
Here, you present the results only – doing so with some kind of visual aid is a good idea, such as a table or graph	Here, you interpret the results and explain to the reader what they mean in light of the research questions you have set up
The results thus focus on WHAT you have found and nothing more	The discussion focuses on what it all means; *here's my results, and here is my interpretation of them*

First, whatever results you get, don't signal that you are necessarily surprised, disappointed or indeed, delighted! This is certainly the case with exploratory research in which you set up research questions to be answered. This is because you have no idea, absolutely speaking, what results you're going to get. As such, to advertise to your reader that your results are surprising or disappointing, for example, respectively, means that you're saying 'this is not what I expected' and 'this is not what I wanted'. To suggest either would in turn suggest bias. Now, it's fine to hope for a certain set of results within exploratory research, but keep this to yourself in terms of not announcing it within your assessments.

Instead, create a more objective tone throughout by simply interpreting the results you get, because what you get is what you get. Also, don't be afraid that your results are simply not 'interesting' enough or original. **You won't get extra points, or fewer points, based on your results!** Instead, *it's how well you interpret your results that gets you points*. The interpretation can be part of a combined 'results and discussion' chapter, which is often chapter four. Or, you can separate them into chapter four (results) and chapter five (discussion), as I had mentioned. Either way, consider once again justifying your choice for either of the two approaches you take, as both make sense and both work well in their own right – but as always, by explaining to the reader why you took one approach over the other, it demonstrates that you have gone the extra mile in terms of considering your approach and overall structure.

The kind of results you get will be based on the methodological approach you took. Just as there are many ways to approach your methods, so are there many ways to present, and interpret, the subsequent results. The results will be a reflection of whether you adopted a quantitative or a qualitative approach. Or whether you adopted a hypothesis-driven approach from the start, in which case you can legitimately describe the results as, perhaps, 'surprising', since you were making predictions from the start. Given so much plurality in approaches and subsequent results, I present just a few samples here to consider. But again, remember three very important rules, which apply to your assessments overall, whether an exam, essay, dissertation, poster presentation or anything else:

- Illustrate broad words and concepts
- Justify the various choices you make
- Use cautious language, a practice known as hedging

Hedging will be covered in Chapter Ten, but for now, suffice to say, it refers to the practice of using careful language in conjunction with your claims, assertions or opinions. Words/expressions such as *perhaps, it is suggested, could* and so on work well in this regard. And while there is more to consider than just the three bullet points above, **illustrating, justifying** and **hedging** are certainly three powerful steps in the right direction regarding criticality.

Presentation of the Results Chapter

The results chapter, or results section as it might be if part of a combined results and discussion chapter, is not designed to interpret. Instead, it simply serves to present what you have and no more. This can be done with tables and graphs, some kind of visual aid to present what you have found. In participant-based research, this could take the form of tables which show the number of participants who answered the interview/questionnaire questions a certain way, or the main themes you uncovered if your research was entirely literature-based. Whatever approach you have taken as part of your methodology, the results chapter is not the time to start asking 'what does this mean to me?' Instead, consider the results chapter the answer to the question, 'what did I get?' An example is provided shortly of the results taken from a nursing dissertation.

In terms of structure, there are various options. You can present samples of participants' answers from the interview/questionnaire, housed within the dissertation's research questions. In other words, by presenting the research questions once more one at a time, provide samples of participants' answers which pertain to said questions. So imagine if one of your research questions is 'what are the influences on students' decision to study overseas?' Underneath this heading could be samples of answers to interview/questionnaire questions that were asked of your participants which relate to this particular research question. Once again, criticality is key, as you will have to be discerning and decide which samples of participants' responses should be included. Don't be surprised that much of what they had to say will end up being excluded from your dissertation, because you simply won't have room to include every detail from every participant. Your supervisor won't be looking over your shoulder

138

telling you what to do. Ask for help by all means, but here is where some independent thinking will serve you well. So it might look like this:

What are the influences on students' decision to study overseas?

Here, answer the research question via samples of participants' answers from the data collection method you used (e.g. interview); do this for each of the research questions. Perhaps you had asked participants, as part of their interview, their top three reasons for choosing to study overseas for a degree; surely the answers to that question would be ideal here as they would help answer the overall research question. Now, for the results section/chapter, it would be a good idea to provide a pie chart, for example, which shows the percentages of participants who provided certain answers (e.g. 40% answered 'prestige of the university'; 35% answered 'the university has the specific programme I need', 15% answered the question based on a desire to travel overseas, etc.). For the discussion, you must now go further and explain what these percentages mean.

- Why do you think prestige is so important for overseas universities?
- Are there certain overseas destinations that tend to be chosen (e.g. the USA)?
- Universities in students' home countries are prestigious too, so why move overseas?
- Do different reasons tend to combine amongst the participants (e.g. do students who referred to prestige also tend to report a desire to travel overseas in the first instance?)?

As you can see, to provide an adequate discussion often begins with asking questions. Also, ask yourself which responses are the most relevant and illuminating with regard to the research questions posed. Which participant responses do you personally feel are most interesting? These are questions which only you can answer, and so it is down to you to do so and select samples from participants' responses that will help to get to the heart of the matter, in this case consisting of answering your research questions. This is merely one way to arrange your results chapter of course and, again, decide how you want to present the results in consultation with your supervisor.

I now present an example of what the content of a results chapter can look like.

Trial Location and Participants

As noted, six randomised controlled trials were selected for inclusion in this systematic review (Macklin et al., 2006; Flachskampf et al., 2007; Yin et al., 2007; Kim et al., 2012; Zheng et al., 2016; Zheng et al., 2018). These studies were conducted in the United States (Macklin et al., 2006), Germany (Flachskampf et al., 2007), South Korea (Yin et al., 2007; Kim et al., 2012) and China (Zheng et al., 2016; Zheng et al., 2018). The studies included an average of 147 participants, ranging from 30 patients (Zheng et al., 2016) to 428 patients (Zheng et al., 2018).

Thoughts: A brief reminder of the main methodological choices.

3.1.2 Trial Definition of Hypertension

Each of the trials included participants with diagnosed hypertension. In most of the trials ($n=5$, 83.3%), hypertension was diagnosed when a patient's systolic blood pressure was $\geq$140mmHg, and/or their diastolic blood pressure was $\geq$90mmHg (Macklin et al., 2006; Flachskampf et al., 2007; Kim et al., 2012; Zheng et al., 2016; Zheng et al., 2018). Half of the trials ($n=3$, 50.0%) also specified an upper 'acceptable' limit on the systolic and diastolic blood pressure (Macklin et al., 2006; Kim et al., 2012; Zheng et al., 2018), perhaps to ensure the participants' safety. It is important to note that one study also included patients with pre-hypertension: a systolic blood pressure of $\geq$120mmHg and/or a diastolic blood pressure of $\geq$89mmHg (Yin et al., 2007).

Half of the trials ($n=3$, 50.0%) only included patients with essential hypertension (Yin et al., 2007; Zheng et al., 2016; Zheng et al., 2018). 'Essential hypertension' is hypertension due to an undetermined, idiopathic cause (Bolivar et al., 2013). The other three trials also included people with secondary hypertension (Macklin et al., 2006; Flachskampf et al., 2007; Kim et al., 2012).

All six of the studies selected for inclusion reported participants' average baseline systolic and diastolic blood pressures. Across all the trials, the average baseline systolic blood pressure for patients in the intervention group was 140.6mmHg, ranging from 131.0mmHg (Flachskampf et al., 2007) to 149.6mmHg (Macklin et al., 2006). The average baseline diastolic blood pressure for patients in the intervention group was 88.9mmHg, ranging from 81.0mmHg (Flachskampf et al., 2007) to 94.1mmHg (Kim et al., 2012). None of the studies reported significant differences in the baseline blood pressures between patients in the intervention and the control groups.

Thoughts: Directly above, you can see results, but there is no attempt to answer the question 'what does this mean to me?' That will come later.

Trial Acupuncture Protocols

The studies tested the effects of a variety of different types of acupuncture on hypertension. Two-thirds of the trials ($n=4$, 66.7%) tested traditional Chinese acupuncture, though Kim et al. (2012) tested traditional Korean acupuncture and Yin et al. (2007) tested modern Korean acupuncture. The studies involved accessing a variety of acupoints – from a single acupoint (Zheng et al., 2016: acupoint LR3) to up to thirty-two acupoints (Macklin et al., 2006: acupoints not specified). In half of the trials ($n=3$, 50.0%), individualised acupoints were selected for a patient after a diagnosis considering their unique physiology, underlying diagnoses and/or current physical wellbeing (Macklin et al., 2006; Flachskampf et al., 2007; Yin Zheng et al., 2018).

Thoughts: Again, numbers, figures and data pertaining to the results are presented in the paragraph above, but no attempt to interpret this as of yet.

Source: UKEssays. (2018a, November). *Sample masters merit nursing dissertation. Findings – effects of acupuncture on hypertension*. https://www.ukessays.com/ services/samples/merit-nursing-dissertation.php#_Toc14424824. Accessed on 22 November 2020.

Interpreting the Results in Your Discussion/Analysis Chapter

Here is where you have your chance to shine, because here is where you display your most critical of critical skills by interpreting your results. And here indeed is where the central question of 'what does this mean to me?' comes into play. Interpreting the results should not rely heavily on referring to the literature. Some students feel compelled to compare their results to those of similar studies, or indeed to point out how their results (and interpretation) differ from previous studies. However, the problem with this approach is, if done to excess, it creates the impression that your study's validity is largely determined by how close it approximates the findings of other studies, or how different it might be from them. Instead, interpret your results on their own merits and on occasion allow yourself to use brief references to previous literature. Your voice should indeed dominate here, seen with *your* interpretation of *your* results and, with this, how critical your interpretation truly is.

In terms of structure, there is variety in how this is executed. You can also present the research questions one at a time if you did not use this approach for the results chapter. The difference here, however, is that you will now be **interpreting** the participants' responses. Or, you can simply get straight to the point and deliver an overall discussion without reference to the research questions – with 'discussion' an appropriate section heading – by presenting samples of participants' answers, and interpreting them. It's also important to have a clear sense of **what the implications are of your research**. This is the final step in a three-part process: first, present the results; next, interpret them as part of your discussion/analysis (they mean the same thing) in order to answer your research questions; and finally, explain in detail what the answers to the research questions, seen via your interpretation of the results, *actually mean*. In simple terms, what does it all mean for policy – maybe nothing, as this might not be relevant, but consider it briefly just in case. What do the results mean for society in general? For knowledge and understanding within your discipline? Do the results forward knowledge, as they should, but how would you suggest applying this new knowledge? Applying it to classroom practice? Applying it to the government, by means of engaging with the relevant politician? As you can see, it's not enough to simply answer your research questions, no matter how well analysed they might be. You need to go to the next level and ask **how you would apply the results**, not just to the immediate context of your discipline, but beyond. This is indeed the stuff of critical thinking.

I now present an example, taken from the previous nursing dissertation:

> This review has shown that not only are the effects of acupuncture on a person's blood pressure small, these effects are also variable: although half of the trials concluded that active acupuncture is *more effective* than sham acupuncture for reducing blood pressure in people with hypertension, the other half (n=3, 50.0%) returned less-positive results (Macklin et al., 2006; Kim et al., 2012; Zheng et al., 2016).

Thoughts: Quick recap of main results above and what follows in the paragraph below, is the interpretation. This is seen with relevant language such as 'if', 'it therefore seems reasonable', 'may' – again, cautious language (if, may) housed within interpretive sentences..

> If a patient were to choose to undergo acupuncture for their hypertension, it therefore seems reasonable that a nurse recommends they continue with their prescribed anti-hypertensive medication – that is, that acupuncture is used as an adjunctive treatment. *However*, it must be emphasised that this review did not consider the effects of acupuncture alone versus acupuncture in combination with anti-hypertensive medications (though half of the trials selected for review permitted patients to take anti-hypertensive medications while receiving acupuncture [Flachskampf et al., 2007; Yin et al., 2007; Zheng et al., 2016]). As two or more anti-hypertensive medications may have a cumulative effect on lowering a person's blood pressure (Bronsert et al., 2013), it is possible that anti-hypertensives plus acupuncture may have the same effect. Further research on acupuncture in combination with anti-hypertensive medications is important to inform practice.

> Another important finding from this review is that the effects of acupuncture on hypertension are unlikely to be sustainable beyond the intervention period (Macklin et al., 2006; Flachskampf et al., 2007).

Thoughts: What follows now is once again interpretation of what has been found, partly based on speculation (if a patient were to choose . . .).

> This is problematic because essential hypertension is a chronic disease and one, therefore, which requires effective long-term management (Chen, 2012).

If a patient were to choose to undergo acupuncture for their hypertension, it therefore seems reasonable that a nurse recommends they participate in regular ongoing acupuncture sessions, rather than a single block of sessions. *However*, it must be emphasised that none of the trials selected for inclusion in this review included an intervention period of beyond 8 weeks. Further research on the effects of continuous or ongoing acupuncture sessions on hypertension is important.

Source: UKEssays. (2018a, November). *Sample masters merit nursing dissertation. Findings – effects of acupuncture on hypertension.* https://www.uk essays.com/services/samples/merit-nursing-dissertation.php#_Toc14424824. Accessed on 22 November 2020.

Conclusion

The conclusion chapter, like a conclusion paragraph, is where you start off by presenting an overview of your main findings. Not just the findings of course, but *what they mean*. So once again, you are providing a brief reminder of the answers to the research questions, based on not only how well you interpreted the results but also the implications for such. A discussion of the implications was detailed in the previous section, to be included as part of your discussion. However, some prefer to leave the discussion solely to answer the research questions and discuss the interpretation of such, then discussing the implications in the conclusion chapter. It's up to you, but make sure you have both. Or indeed, include both in the discussion and then a quick recap as part of your conclusion. This initial section of your conclusion – recap of main points/ answers to research questions/implications – might be a page and a half in length for a dissertation of, say, 12,000 to 15,000 words, but the main consideration is being critical enough to decide when you have said enough to make your point. Remember, a conclusion should not suddenly introduce a new to pic or new coverage that, while relevant, was not present in the body. It's again a case of restating your main points, but not a verbatim repeat from the discussion.

From here, plan to have two final sections, ideally with their own section headings.

Limitations

A paragraph is sufficient to cover the limitations of your research, largely based on your methodological approach. Bear in mind that there are limitations that are common to many dissertations and certainly part of specific disciplines, for which there is little you can do. For example, within the Social Sciences, it is simply not possible to generalise the results of your study to the wider community based on what might have been a small sample of participants. Nonetheless, it is a good idea to mention this otherwise obvious point, and many journal papers and articles will indeed make this clear too, and often have a statement of limitations. For example, if you conducted a study with 100 six-year-old boys and girls in the UK, whatever the subject under investigation, and whatever the results, they cannot possibly speak for all 6-year-old boys and girls in the UK. A sample of a 100 students, while impressive, is still quite small. But this is absolutely fine, as long as you interpret the results as they are, without having to try and 'prove' that they can necessarily go beyond the immediate sample.

On the other hand, perhaps the limitations might be more to do with choices you made that, in retrospect, you wish you hadn't made. Perhaps the choice of using questionnaires is now revisited, with a wish you had used interviews (or vice versa). Or perhaps, there is no issue with your decision to use questionnaires, but you now realise that there were certain additional questions that were not asked, but which could have provided further illumination. Or maybe, you wish you had incorporated an additional method of data collection, but simply did not have the time to do so. You get the idea. At this level of 'limitations', it's essentially focused on methodological limitations. Remember, acknowledging your study's limitations is not the same as declaring that you're a poor researcher or you made a mistake. Instead, it's proof positive that you are indeed being critical, precisely because you've taken the time to analyse the choices you made and, having done so, have reached a critical conclusion.

Future Research

The final section, again a paragraph should be sufficient (two if you wish), can focus on the implications of your study once more, but merely a summary reminder. From here, you should then focus on what you would do next; based on the methods used and the results acquired, what *needs* to be done next in terms of academic research? Here is where you're essentially answering the question, 'OK, based on the limitations, coupled with the need to go even deeper, what kind of study would I do next?' For example, you could mention the need to have a larger sample and/or a sample which derives from multiple locations, so not just a sample of students from one primary school, but a future study might include a sample of students from three different primary schools. Likewise, perhaps a more in-depth choice of methods, such as focus groups *and* interviews, would be adopted. You could even contextualise things that bit more and refer to a future study in terms of an MA dissertation, if you're currently completing a BA dissertation. The main point, however, is to show evidence of criticality by means of knowing how to go beyond the confines of your current study in terms of a future study.

To finish, here are some samples of the various sections to be found in conclusion chapters.

Environmental science – overview of main findings

In conclusion, it was found that sanitation services in Ghana are severely lacking among low-income populations. The lack of sanitation services is suggested to be accompanied by a lack of suitable hygiene practices, although there was insufficient focus on this aspect in the identified studies, with only a couple of studies commenting on handwashing practices as secondary observations. It was found that there is a very low prevalence of private sanitation services in the low-income areas of Ghana; additionally some studies considered areas of slightly higher income where it was still found that there was a very low prevalence of private sanitation services. The majority of individuals relied on the use of public sanitation services, defecated in the home environment bags or containers, or practised open defecation. The general perception of public sanitation services was that they were smelly, poorly managed, inconvenient and expensive, and lacked privacy.

There were found to be some indications of socio-cultural differences in the use of sanitation services. Women and children were found to be more likely to defecate in the home environment in bags or containers. For young children this was predominantly due to either a fear for their safety or the expense of public sanitation services. For women the reasons given varied, with the expense and dislike of queuing with men being the most commonly cited reasons. There was also found to be an influence of religion on the perception of sanitation services — Muslims in particular were found to have some religious restrictions on their sanitation practices, including the desire to not face Mecca when defecating and the need to use water for subsequent cleansing.

Source: UKEssays. (2018k, November). *Sample undergraduate 2:1 environmental sciences dissertation*. https://www.ukessays.com/services/samples/2-1-environmental-science-dissertation.php. Accessed on 28 November 2020.

The paragraphs above clearly recount the main findings, those that the writer deems to be most pertinent to the purpose of his/her dissertation. These findings should not represent anything new that was not already presented prior. Remember though that this is not an exercise in pointless repetition; instead, it is a case of recapping the main findings, but in a different way – same points, different words, and in summarised form. Imagine being asked the question, 'Can you give me a summary of what you found?' The response to this would indeed be akin to the content of the first few paragraphs of your conclusion chapter. However, once this summary is done, it is time to then go into the interpretation mode and make clear what all this means. Merely presenting the results, or even an interpretation of them, is insufficient, as I had mentioned. If you just do this, it can beg the question, 'so what?' Therefore, go further. Based on the results above as presented, some critical questions, which require critical answers, might be 'what can be done at the government level to address public hygiene and sanitation issues?' 'How can we address women's reluctance to use public toilets where men are present – what is the underlying issue here?' 'How can public toilet facilities be improved for all?'

Medicine – limitations

The principal limitations of this review are mostly related to factors that were external to the researcher's direct control. Firstly, the researcher is not a medically trained specialist in respiratory medicine or asthma, and nor do they have significant experience and expertise in the research field. This may have had implications for this research, such as limited scope of data analysis and discussion and inadequately informed recommendations for future practice and research. Secondly, the review is inherently limited by the studies included herein, and as noted in the critical appraisal section, many studies were subject to bias and concerns for applicability, which limits the value and use of this review to the current evidence base. Thirdly, whilst efforts were made to ensure that all relevant studies were obtained for results synthesis, it is possible that some studies were incidentally excluded from the electronic databases and also, studies of non-English language may have overall, resulted in a degree of reporting bias.

Source: UKEssays. (2018o, November). *Sample undergraduate 2:1 medicine dissertation: Strengths and limitations*. https://www.ukessays.com/services/samples/2-1-medicine-dissertation.php#_Toc527021295. Accessed on 21 November 2020.

The writer clearly points out the limitations of the research, but as a result, it makes the overall research more, not less, trustworthy. This is a clear example of what a limitations section might look like and again, contained within a single paragraph.

Education – future research

Although this dissertation attempts to relate teacher attrition to factors related to ITE, it is acknowledged that these are tentative connections and further research would be required to test the hypotheses presented. A future research area which could address the decline in the number of applicants to teacher training could include interviewing new entrants to ITE programmes in England about the factors which influenced their decision to choose their pathway and how they navigated the diversity of options. To establish any links between early career teacher attrition and the framework of professional teaching standards, it is suggested that research could be conducted into newly-qualified teachers' views of these standards during their first year of teaching, with a comparison made with how the standards featured during their training period. The use of the reflective portfolios during the training period could also provide valuable insight into how individuals view the standards, thus potentially revealing a connection between the accreditation process and subsequent teacher attrition rates. Finally, because of the increased focus in both Australia and England on practice-based routes, there is a need to collect evidence of pedagogical training within schools and compare this to the content provided by university-led courses. The transition from the training period to the first teaching position will always involve challenges, since it is a unique position. To mitigate the effects of teacher attrition in Australia and the UK, it might be that training providers need to backtrack and critically assess the elements of their training programmes that might inadvertently be making this transitional period more challenging than it ultimately needs to be.

Source: UKEssays. (2018j, November). *Sample undergraduate 2:1 education dissertation. Summary of further research areas*. https://www.ukessays.com/services/samples/2-1-education-dissertation.php#_Toc526165386. Accessed on 21 November 2020.

The section above points to the need for future research, and what that might look like, but it does this by also briefly acknowledging limitations in the current study. The paragraph above, then, essentially provides a two-in-one approach: here are some limitations with my current study, so here's how they can be addressed in a future study which addresses said limitations.

Verb Tense

Verb tense might seem like a purely grammatical consideration. However, and as we have seen earlier, the grammatical choices you make can have implications for how your writing, and attitude toward it, is interpreted by the reader. This means that your choice of verb tense can have an effect on your style. Sometimes, students will ask me which tense they should use for their dissertation. The answers I'm going to provide apply to all kinds of assessments, notably whenever references to the literature are involved (which is common to many assessments, of course).

Your literature review is largely going to use present tense to describe/define relevant concepts and theories, as well as to provide direct quotes:

> This concept **describes/refers** to the process . . .

> Smith (2009: 78) **argues/states/suggests** that . . .

The use of present tense essentially symbolises that the literature/theories/concepts and so on that you are writing about are alive and well and a permanent fixture of the discipline. Yes, the words of Smith were published more than a decade ago, but the use of present tense is suggesting that Smith's ideas are still relevant to the present moment, as you are writing your dissertation and as the lecturer is later reading your work in his/her own present moment. But if an author has passed away or his/her ideas have been rejected or revised by the author himself/herself, then past tense communicates this fact:

> This concept described/referred to the process . . ., but it has now been largely rejected.

> Smith (2009: 78) argued/stated/suggested that . . ., but revised these ideas to formulate something new.

Likewise, your introduction's setting out of your research plans should be written in present tense, even if at the point of writing your introduction the research has otherwise already been conducted and data gathered:

> This dissertation **investigates** the subject of X . . .

> The following research questions **are presented** as part of the investigation . . .

> This study **is** arguably timely for the following reasons . . .

The methods chapter largely relies on past tense, however, to reflect the work already done in connection with data collection and analysis. Thus, even if you are writing your methods chapter prior to actually collecting data (which is fine), you would still need to use past tense. Some students use future tense, as a reflection of what they're *going* to do, but past tense is indeed standard:

> I **conducted** fifteen interviews with my participants . . .

> The questionnaire responses **were interpreted** . . .

> The use of thematic analysis **was** highly relevant to the study . . .

However, when you refer to the various theories and data collection methods connected to your research, then present tense is again standard. This is because its use again serves to communicate the fact that theories have a certain 'timeless' quality:

> Semi-structured interviews **are** useful because . . .

Thematic analysis **is** often used for qualitative research . . .

Ethical approval **precedes** data collection . . .

As you can see, referring to what you actually did regarding your methodology requires past tense (even if you have not yet conducted the research as such); but referring to the various aspects of methods in general (e.g. theories, approaches, etc.) requires present tense:

The use of thematic analysis **was** highly relevant to the study because

In other words, you've already applied this analysis to your results.

Thematic analysis **is** often used for qualitative research because

This is a general statement about the benefits of thematic analysis and not just tied to your own research; therefore, present tense is used.

For the conclusion chapter – or conclusions in general – present perfect is a wise choice, at least at the start of your conclusion. Yes, you can begin a conclusion with 'in conclusion', but there are certainly more expressive ways to make your point. Anyway, let's compare the differences between past tense and present perfect – you should immediately 'feel' the difference:

This dissertation **discussed** a new approach to molecular biology, arguing that

This dissertation **has discussed** a new approach to molecular biology, arguing that

By using past tense in the first example, the writer is essentially communicating that his/her dissertation is over and done with. Finished. In some ways, this is true. Once it's been read by the lecturer/supervisor, it is indeed finished, as the writer has said all he/she wishes to and it's now too late to make changes. Furthermore, it is entirely possible that the dissertation will never be looked at again by the writer, or reader. However, your dissertation has nonetheless made a contribution to knowledge and, in doing so, said something new. Moreover, as your lecturer is reading your work in real time, then this makes your work 'alive' in that present moment. Thus, present perfect communicates this well and, in doing so, its use is also subtly indicating that your work is important and indeed 'alive and well'; past tense simply communicates that the game is over.

The reason for present perfect being used in this very specific context of your conclusion is because present perfect refers to something that started in the past but either (a) still continues in the present or (b) has some kind of effect in the present, a remnant of past action, if you like. Seen from this perspective, the use of present perfect as seen above is essentially communicating, 'My dissertation and research began some time ago and is now concluded, but it's not over!'

More information will be provided on stylistic considerations later in Chapter Ten, but bear in mind the discussion so far on passive voice, use of italics and verb tense, for example, and start to think of the effects that such language choices can have on your writing and how it is understood and interpreted by the reader.

Summary

In summary, bear in mind the specific aspects of dissertation writing discussed here, once you begin to write your dissertation. But equally importantly, remember the aspects of good academic writing that have been covered in all the chapters so far – these features are necessary in all assessments and across disciplines as they combine to show your level of criticality, which, as we have seen, can be revealed in many different ways.

7

Additional Assessments to Consider

This chapter takes the information on criticality presented thus far and applies it to assessments other than essays and exams. Specifically, this chapter will focus on oral presentations, poster presentations and reflective writing.

Oral presentations

First, let's start with the basics which don't differ from one type of assignment to the next: make sure you understand the assignment instructions and what you're being asked to do. From here, you will need to plan who does what if this is a group presentation and also decide on a timetable for literature gathering/ analysis and so on; then decide on what are the most important points you wish to make in your presentation. So far, this is nothing really new and you have probably already considered this. The next steps are also based on what has been covered already, but you need to rethink them based on the nature of an oral presentation. For example, the need to have a coherent structure does not change. But in this case, the structure will be based on information typed and presented on a PowerPoint slide and not as part of a Word document to upload. So once you're at the point where you have decided your coverage, then plot this in terms of INTRO – BODY – CONCLUSION, just as you would for an essay. With this in mind, create the content that you want to discuss as part of the oral presentation and the written content that you will show to the audience as part of the PowerPoint slides or handouts.

How much time do you have to deliver your presentation? This will impact on how much information you can cover and, likewise, how many slides you should prepare. With an essay, the word count dictates the amount of coverage you can provide; with an oral presentation, the time limit does instead. Don't forget, however, to leave some of your allotted time, perhaps 5 minutes, for questions and answers following your presentation. And in terms of the content of each slide, it's best to have less writing – but not always more visuals – and then expand on the written content of each slide as part of your oral discussion. A slide(s) which actually consists of entire body paragraphs will not be as easy to process for your audience as perhaps some bullet points or simply a series of key points – with your job to then expand on such in your speech. Don't forget – the audience should be focused more on you as the speaker and not staring most of the time at your slides. Also consider who will speak and when. For example, you might want to have someone deliver the introduction, someone to deliver Topic 1, then someone else for Topic 2 and so on. Dividing up the labour is a crucial part of oral presentations in groups; if you're doing it by yourself, then the information presented in this section is just as relevant, albeit it's all on you to do everything.

In summary, the advice for oral presentations does not really deviate from that of essays or assessments in general, in that you can have a hook (asking your audience a rhetorical, or real, question can be a great way to break the ice); you will need to have a main point to make – the argument, adequate background, a logical sequence of topics, use of connecting expressions (e.g. *moving on to my next point, as we can see . . ., on the contrary*, etc.), references to the litera-ture, a final wrap-up and so on. The difference is, of course, that you will be speaking, not writing, and the only written information is contained in a con-densed version of your slides, not as part of an essay. In this sense, the two halves of an oral presentation – WRITTEN INFORMATION (slides) + SPOKEN INFORMATION (your actual discussion) – combine to make a whole.

Some final points to consider:

- Yes, visuals are also good and can be attention-grabbing, but all the best visuals and vivid colours in the world are nothing more than window dressing if the actual written content of the slides is weak in some way: typos, grammatical errors, hard to read text or, even more importantly, inaccurate statements, misunderstandings of the literature, too much content shoved onto the slides – these issues need to be avoided and care-ful proofreading can help to do so.
- A good set of slides with a weak oral presentation, or vice versa, will lose marks; so ensure you speak clearly and at a good volume, make sufficient eye contact with your audience as opposed to reading off your slides too much and use an overall natural body language; try to have a conversation with your audience and bring them in.

Poster presentations

Regardless of how big a poster is, you are still left with just one page to capture all the key aspects of your assessment. Based on this, you will need to have more written content and all in one place of course, as opposed to being a bit more sparing with written content on slides. Also, visuals will be more important here perhaps than an oral presentation and may count for a larger percentage of the final score. In summary, then, you need to enable your poster to be eye-catching and act as its own 'visual hook', while also ensuring that the written information provided is detailed enough for onlookers to understand what you're saying.

A poster presentation is sometimes an overview of a research project you undertook, and so with that in mind, consider its counterpart to be a dissertation, and not an essay as such. Of course, a poster does not always have to reflect primary research and may well reflect secondary research, in this sense mirroring the structure of an essay. If so, think of the structure and content as you would for an essay – set up the argument; provide a summary of the most relevant literature; establish your poster's overall selling point in terms of what your content is all about. Or a poster may well reflect nothing more than an explanation of a given topic, seen with a title, definition and illustration of the topic. I will provide examples, but for now, should you be tasked with a poster based on primary research, then consider the structure below:

TITLE – INTRODUCTION – LITERATURE REVIEW – METHODS – RESULTS/ DISCUSSION – CONCLUSION – REFERENCES. Here you are presenting a summary of each section above and so it is important to include the basic aspects of each section, which are as follows, in order of presentation:

- A title which is catchy (this is true for any assessment which requires a title)
- Your RATIONALE
- A summary of what the literature has already told us about the subject
- Your chosen methods of data collection and WHY you chose them
- The findings and then a summary of the IMPLICATIONS of the findings (e.g. what does it all mean for the department you study in/society as a whole perhaps/why is it all so important – what do *you* think people should know and take away from your study?)
- A conclusion which can signpost people to what a future study would look like/involve
- A brief references section which lists only the references listed on your poster

You may ask how do I make my title 'catchy'? One method is to consider a double title, though not too long, with each title separated by a colon. The idea is to place a more informal or amusing title before the colon and the more 'serious' title after the colon. For example:

In the ear of the beholder: Understanding societal perceptions of accents

A picture speaks a thousand words: An analysis of the cinematography of the films of Martin Scorsese

Clearly, formatting is important, as it is with essays and oral presentations. This refers to using an appropriate font (e.g. Times New Roman), font size (for a poster, big enough to read clearly, but not so big that it can't fit on the poster) and layout, which includes the spacing, placement of text and visuals and how it all comes together. You should probably have access to completed posters as these might be provided by your lecturer, and these will help you get a good idea as to what your poster could, and should, look like. But I will say this: formatting, important though it clearly is, is not as substantial as the actual written content – whether this refers to the written text on your PowerPoint slides or that written on your poster. It is the *content* of the writing that is most crucial as this tells the viewers/audience what is special about your research, why it was conducted and what new information it can contribute. This is more important than the most beautiful visuals and graphics.

In summary, consider the points below:

- Focus on the content first and establish what you will/will not include.
- To this end, consider the potential content in terms of what you *must have, should have, could have* and *won't have.*
- Decide on the exact purpose of the poster in broad terms related to whether it is designed to reveal a summary of a research project or is simply being used to provide an explanation of a concept/theory/practice within your area of study.

I now present a sample poster (see Figure 7.1) to give you some clear ideas as to what your poster can look like.

Reflective writing

Reflective writing can be considered as conforming to an essay format for the most part, in terms of establishing the relevant checklist, such as argument sentence, topic sentences and so on. The chief differences, however, are based on two points. First, the style of writing is meant to be more informal and personal, and there is not the same need to refer to the literature as with a more 'traditional' essay. This is not to say that you shouldn't use literature, but that its presence is designed to add just a bit of extra support – to help explain how and why events happened the way they did as they are described in the essay. Put together, this means the following:

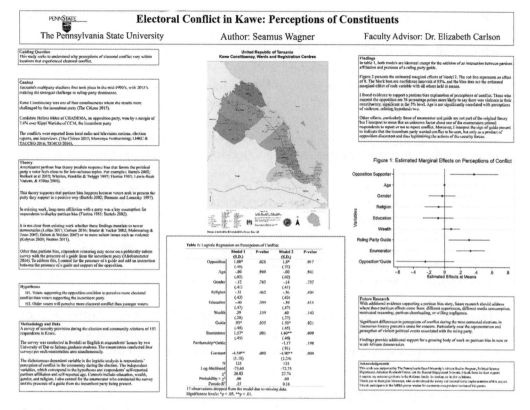

Figure 7.1   Example poster

Source: Wagner, S. (2018). *Electoral conflict in Kawe: Perceptions of constituents*. The Pennsylvania State University, https://guides.libraries.psu.edu/c.php?g=882127&p=6338035, under a Creative Commons 4.0 license. Accessed 1 December 2020.

- Your reflective essay will rely on first person.
- You write about personal experiences in relation to the assessment guidelines.
- You can use more informal language.
- It can be more emotional in terms of truly expressing your feelings on the matter.
- While structure might not be as prescriptive as a traditional essay, it makes sense to still construct your reflective essay with an intro, body, conclusion format in mind.
- This means you should still strive to have a clear argument sentence, topics for each body paragraph and a conclusion that provides your overall thoughts and feelings on the learning experience.
- And yes, you still need to be critical and not merely describe your experiences as a summary.

Let's put this all together now:

Assignment brief: Write a reflective essay which explains what you learned about working in groups as part of your group assignment.

For such an essay, you would need to do more than simply tell the reader, 'first this happened, and then this happened'. Do this by all means, but then **explain what it all means. Interpret** what happened. **Explain** how it made you feel – and *why*. Explain what you learned and *how* you learned. So describing your emotions is fine, to include using informal language (e.g. 'One of my group members never pulled his weight') and you could consider this kind of writing to be like an academic diary – more personally written like a diary, but the academic aspect pertains to the need for structure and criticality. Therefore, the sentence above in the bracket is not enough in itself and needs to go further:

> *One of my group members never pulled his weight. For example, he sometimes missed meetings and did not give a reason why and as a result, he did not contribute to the final assignment as much as the others did. This suggests that within group work, differing personalities, schedules and even work ethics can all combine to produce an imbalance in terms of individual contributions. Thus, I believe that groups should perhaps lay out expectations for individual contributions and commitments from the start.*

Thoughts: Illustration of a broad concept – 'did not pull his weight'. Interpretation of what the example tells us. Here you conclude with an overall summary of what this all means – in this case, a solution to the problem that has been identified.

I conclude with some final examples:

> *The group leader was upset, as the rest of the team did not do their share of the project that they had otherwise committed to doing.*

Thoughts: Quite descriptive, which is fine as a starting point of course, but it also includes a clear result based on the cause of not considering the rota system carefully.

> *The group leader was upset about the lack of work from the other members of the group. I suggested that we should have a quick meeting to try and identify the problem.*

Thoughts: Again, another good use of reflective writing, seen with use of 'I' describing what happened; and exploring one's own role.

> *I felt that a meeting, while obvious perhaps, was needed as a means for us all to express our opinions and get things off our chest. As a result, we found out that while all group members were indeed committed to the project, the leader had not realised, and they had not explained, that some of the tasks were too big for them to do alone. As a result, we had groups of two working on the various tasks, as part of a buddy system.*

Thoughts: All of the above, but now with the addition of a clear solution presented.

Summary

In summary, then, approach each and every assessment with the same broad criteria in mind regarding what it means to be critical. These criteria will not change, whether an essay, exam or poster. From this broad starting point, you can then move to more narrow considerations in terms of assessment type and the formatting within (e.g. PowerPoint slides vs. poster). But being critical is indeed the same throughout.

8

Four Ways to Approach Interpretation

Interpretation is key to being critical, as you know. But there are different ways to consider interpretation when you come across your academic reading. The different ways to approach your interpretation of source material have been hinted at earlier in the book, but these will now be presented in detail here. Broadly, there are four ways to approach interpretation of source texts: **agreement**, **disagreement**, **illustration** and **explanation**.

Agreement

This is simple. You read a text, whether a book, journal article or website, and you agree with the author's claims, argument or theory. As I mentioned before, however, the critical part is explaining *why* you agree. Let's take a sample text, read critically and from there, an example is provided of what agreement can look like. The sample text is taken from the *Journal of Sleep Research*, from an article titled 'Stress Vulnerability and the Effects of Moderate Daily Stress on Sleep Polysomnography and Subjective Sleepiness'. The full details of the article are provided below, along with a website link. I have deliberately chosen a subject of which I know nothing, so I'm out of my comfort zone here. But that's actually a good thing, as it forces us to think extra critically and look at it this way – a point I had made before: if you can be critical with an unfamiliar subject, how much easier when you're reading about a subject you are familiar with? To give some context, the study discussed in the journal article investigated the effects of work-based stress on sleep, recording the sleep patterns of 28 teachers.

Rather than use a different sample of text in conjunction with the four topics covered here, I have chosen to use the same text each time – this helps to show just how versatile a text can be in terms of how we can all read the same text and yet interpret it in different ways at a given moment. In fact, even the same person can read a text very differently from one moment to the next and, thus, agree with the propositions in the text one week and then a few weeks later, perhaps, find himself/herself disagreeing.

> Taken together, the results above suggest that the present results may represent a mild acute sleep disturbance due to modest work stress. The effects were less than expected considering that a time period that would maximize work stress was selected, in contrast to a previous study (Åkerstedt et al., 2007) that recorded sleep once per week and selected high and low stress sleeps post-hoc from ratings. The reason for the modest effects in the present study could be several. One may be that either the high stress level may have been too low or the low stress level too high. More severe stressors or a longer period of elevated stress may have produced larger effects. Anecdotal evidence from interaction with the participants suggest that even low stress periods contained daily effort and were certainly not periods of relaxation. It is possible that due to low power because of the small sample other effects of stress such as increased latency to REM as in the above mentioned study could have been present but not detected. At present there are no data indicating how high stress would need to be to cause a more dramatic impairment of sleep. It may also be a matter of type of stress. Work stress may, for example, involve mainly excessive amounts of work, rather than any emotional components that would cause much real worries and anticipation. The two latter seem essential for disturbed sleep (Harvey, 2002). To resolve this question will require additional studies of situations involving higher levels of threat.

> Source: Petersen, H., Kecklund, G., Nilsson, J., & Åkerstedt, T. (2012). Stress vulnerability and the effects of moderate daily stress on sleep polysomnography and subjective sleepiness. *Journal of Sleep Research, 22*(1), 50–57. https://doi.org/10.1111/j.1365-2869.2012.01034.x.

For different readers, different aspects of the text will of course stand out more than others. But have a go and pick out anything that speaks to you. Do you agree with any of this? True, the full article would provide more insights, but very often it might well be a segment of an article or book chapter that grabs our attention and becomes open to critical analysis. An example is now provided of one way that agreement can be seen.

Agreement

Petersen et al. (2012) provide evidence for the effects of work-based stress on people's sleep patterns, notably that sleep can be disrupted. This is perhaps unsurprising, given the stress encountered on the job, as it were, but added stress that continues long after the workday is finished needs to be considered. For example, worrying about returning to work the next day, based on dealing with unreasonable bosses or co-workers and having tight deadlines to meet can leave individuals sleep-deprived long after they've returned home for the day and prepare to sleep. Indeed, Petersen et al. (2012) cite the emotional aspects of work as a key factor in affecting sleep, as opposed to having a large workload per se; this in itself need not contribute to stress if individuals are truly engaged in their work, however.

Thoughts: A brief summary of what the study is about and then agreement, not signalled in an obvious way by stating 'I agree', but revealed through the expression – and example to follow – of 'this is perhaps unsurprising'. Furthermore, the writer signals agreement with the emotional aspects of work and not just workload – this is another point which the authors bring up, albeit tied to previous research (Harvey, 2002). All in all, then, the writer demonstrates agreement by (a) agreeing directly with the main aspect of the research; (b) offering an illustration of the issue, to further back up the agreement; and (c) tying in the agreement to a further point made by Petersen et al. (2012), a point not connected directly to the authors' study per se, but a point they make nonetheless in broad relation to the effects of work-related stress on sleep.

So, this is critical writing as it doesn't just agree and move on. Instead, it provides a rationale for the agreement, seen with a clear illustration of some of the causes of work-based stress and then smartly backs it all up by referring to the authors again at the end. It also finishes with a good point: a high workload within a job that someone otherwise truly enjoys need not contribute to stress, certainly not negative stress that can cause people to lose sleep at night. Thus, in agreement with Petersen et al. (2012), perhaps we need to look beyond workload per se when considering work-related stress.

Disagreement

Taken together, the results above suggest that mild acute sleep disturbance due to modest work stress is a reality. The effects were less than expected considering that a time period that would maximize work stress was selected, in contrast to a previous study (Åkerstedt et al., 2007) that recorded sleep once per week and selected high and low stress sleeps post-hoc from ratings. The reason for the modest effects in the present study could be several. One may be that either the high stress level may have been too low or the low stress level too high. More severe stressors or a longer period of elevated stress may have produced larger effects. Anecdotal evidence from interaction with the participants suggest that even low stress periods contained daily effort and were certainly not periods of relaxation. It is possible that due to low power because of the small sample other effects of stress such as increased latency to REM as in the above mentioned study could have been present but not detected. At present there are no data indicating how high stress would need to be to cause a more dramatic impairment of sleep. It may also be a matter of type of stress. Work stress may, for example, involve mainly excessive amounts of work, rather than any emotional components that would cause much real worries and anticipation. The two latter seem essential for disturbed sleep (Harvey, 2002). To resolve this question will require additional studies of situations involving higher levels of threat.

Petersen et al. (2012) conducted a study investigating the effects of work-based stress on 28 teachers, in terms of how such stress affected their sleep patterns. That stress of any kind can impact on sleep – whether quality or quantity of sleep – is perhaps unsurprising. However, the specific details might be further clarified. The results reveal that there is mild sleep disturbance in participants and problematise the topic of stress and its effects on sleep. In fact, the authors state that 'Work stress may, for example, involve mainly excessive amounts of work, rather than any emotional components that would cause much real worries and anticipation' (page 55). Thus, it makes sense to delve further into not merely a definition of work-based stress, but also what the specific source of the stress is. It is suggested that the source of the stress, as Petersen et al. (2012) allude to, can be varied and as such, this can perhaps affect sleep quality in different ways. Many of us find ourselves with a heavy workload, but this may or may not contribute to stress which in turn may not impact on sleep.

Thoughts: Again, a brief summary to set the scene, with implied agreement in Sentence 2. The start of Sentence 3, with the use of the word 'however', indicates that the writer is not in complete agreement perhaps, or will at least find a way to problematise the results of the study. In fact, the writer acknowledges that Petersen et al. (2012) themselves problematise matters – thus, the writer is skilfully questioning things by referring to the fact that the authors also do so somewhat. The writer, taking a cue from the authors, is arguing for the need to further determine stress in terms of its causes and subsequent effects, suggesting that different causes will have different effects on sleep. That the writer mentioned these differences in the paragraph that otherwise agreed with the authors' needs to be understood in terms of what the writer is choosing to do with the information. In the agreement paragraph, the writer briefly references different sources of stress, but not as a means to take on the authors' results. Rather, the writer does so to help backup his/her previous illustration.

Here, however, the writer is more prominently discussing this point in order to show a gap in the authors' research: why are the participants stressed? The writer makes the point that work-based stress is too broad a category, because there might be different factors involved with this type of stress in terms of its root causes. This, in turn, can have different effects on sleep.

The writer's disagreement is thus very critical, as it offers some insights by means of suggesting the need for a more nuanced discussion of an otherwise broad category, perhaps suggesting in turn the need for a more qualitative element to the research (e.g. asking participants why they are stressed: Workload? Deadlines? Students? Staff? Overall job dissatisfaction? Pay?). As you can hopefully see, however, 'disagreement' is itself not a singular category. In other words, the writer is not completely disagreeing with the authors. This would be quite difficult to do actually, as 'complete' disagreement might mean arguing against the methods, the findings as a result, challenging the interpretation and so on. I don't recall anyone who has ever done this, especially with an article that was otherwise judged strong enough to be published in a major journal. Thus, whether you agree or disagree, it might well be that it is not 100% of one or the other. This, in fact, would not suggest a critical approach at all, as it stands to reason that there are surely some aspects of a given study that are convincing, perhaps others less so. Therefore, you may well find yourself being persuaded by some aspects of an author's work, other aspects less so – this can be true even for a small segment of a completed article. Therefore, agreement and disagreement are not absolute categories, and they can both often apply to certain aspects of an author's work.

Illustration

Taken together, the results above suggest that the present results may represent a mild acute sleep disturbance due to modest work stress. The effects were less than expected considering that a time period that would maximize work stress was selected, in contrast to a previous study (Åkerstedt et al., 2007) that recorded sleep once per week and selected high and low stress sleeps post-hoc from ratings. The reason for the modest effects in the present study could be several. One may be that either the high stress level may have been too low or the low stress level too high. More severe stressors or a longer period of elevated stress may have produced larger effects. Anecdotal evidence from interaction with the participants suggest that even low stress periods contained daily effort and were certainly not periods of relaxation. It is possible that due to low power because of the small sample other effects of stress such as increased latency to REM as in the above mentioned study could have been present but not detected. At present there are no data indicating how high stress would need to be to cause a more dramatic impairment of sleep. It may also be a matter of type of stress. Work stress may, for example, involve mainly excessive amounts of work, rather than any emotional components that would cause much real worries and anticipation. The two latter seem essential for disturbed sleep (Harvey, 2002). To resolve this question will require additional studies of situations involving higher levels of threat.

Petersen et al.'s (2012) study on the effects of work-based stress on sleep offers insights into this phenomenon. The authors chose 28 teachers as the participants for their study, and this is a telling choice. If we consider sleep problems – based on deprivation of sleep and/or quality of such – and initiated by work-based stress, this is perhaps unsurprising. Indeed, the reasons for sleep problems caused by work-related stress can be myriad, whether caused by a huge workload set against tight deadlines, or it might not be related to the work per se but is focused more on 'emotional components' (page 55). Such might relate to a myriad of issues, from personality clashes with colleagues to insecure contracts. Indeed, during the current Covid-19 crisis, teachers in particular have been greatly affected (Bintliff, 2020), seen, for example, with absentee students who perhaps experience poverty at home and have no access to online learning in the first instance. Thus, it could be the case that teachers who are committed to their work are experiencing stress not due to a job they are not dedicated to and do not enjoy, but based on outside issues which in turn affect their work.

Thoughts: First, you may well argue that an illustration was also part of the previous paragraphs that were otherwise not focused on providing illustrations as such. This is indicative of the simple fact that you may provide an illustration in what is otherwise a chunk of your writing dedicated more specifically to agreeing/ disagreeing. There is no reason, then, why you can't have more than one strategy and you may in fact need to provide an illustration as a means to help you make your (dis)agreement more clear and convincing.

In the paragraph above, however, there is no specific agreement or disagreement, and instead, the bulk of the paragraph is dedicated to providing a longer, more detailed illustration of the issue at hand, and as such, it seems wise to consider the paragraph more focused on providing an illustration as its main purpose. Going further, it is clear that the use of teachers as participants in the study inspired the writer to focus on teachers more specifically in the illustration, even to the extent of drawing on additional research which discusses the specific stress that this group are facing during the current COVID crisis.

This shows how our mind can easily wander – in a good way – when we read our academic texts. That is, an idea can be sparked by reading a text and lead us in all kinds of directions relevant to the discussion at hand. In this case, a reference to the work of Bintliff (2020) takes us away from Petersen et al. (2012) to a relevant area. Here, the writer is drawing on a previous study involving teachers, taking just one of the main focuses (i.e. work-based stress, but not sleep issues) and applying it to a current health crisis and its effects on the participant group of teachers. This represents that critical thinking is indeed going on, and this makes the writing convincing.

Explanation

Taken together, the results above suggest that the present results may represent a mild acute sleep disturbance due to modest work stress. The effects were less than expected considering that a time period that would maximize work stress was selected, in contrast to a previous study (Åkerstedt et al., 2007) that recorded sleep once per week and selected high and low stress sleeps post-hoc from ratings. The reason for the modest effects in the present study could be several. One may be that either the high stress level may have been too low or the low stress level too high. More severe stressors or a longer period of elevated stress may have produced larger effects. Anecdotal evidence from interaction with the participants suggest that even low stress periods contained daily effort and were certainly not periods of relaxation. It is possible that due to low power because of the small sample other effects of stress such as increased latency to REM as in the above mentioned study could have been present but not detected. At present there are no data indicating how high stress would need to be to cause a more dramatic impairment of sleep. It may also be a matter of type of stress. Work stress may, for example, involve mainly excessive amounts of work, rather than any emotional components that would cause much real worries and anticipation. The two latter seem essential for disturbed sleep (Harvey, 2002). To resolve this question will require additional studies of situations involving higher levels of threat.

Petersen et al.'s (2012) study on the effects of work-based stress on sleep involves 28 teachers, and indeed reveals that stress can impact on sleep, whether quality or quantity. Two aspects of stress are clearly explained by the authors, which might of course apply to stress beyond the context of work. These two aspects which the authors reference pertain to type and level of stress. Petersen et al. (2012) make a valid point, which is that we perhaps need to have set criteria to determine where stress falls on a 'low to high' continuum, as this will have different effects on sleep. Second, in referencing type of stress, the authors are revealing that this can produce different emotional effects, which in turn can have different effects on sleep perhaps. Thus, Petersen et al. (2012) are attempting to move away from a one size fits all perspective on the broad topic of stress, in this case work-based stress, and instead investigate further what its root cause is beyond merely being 'work-based' – we need to know what the exact circumstances are within the workplace in order to better understand stress and its effects on sleep.

Bintliff, A. (2020, September 8). How COVID-19 has influenced teachers' well-being. *Psychology Today*. https://www.psychologytoday.com/intl/blog/multidimensional-aspects-adolescent-well-being/202009/how-covid-19-has-influenced-teachers-well. Accessed on 1 October 2020.

Thoughts: As you can see, explaining what you have read as an indication of criticality is essentially about saying 'here are the facts as I understand them'. You're basically retelling the content of the source material to your reader. This is actually a good way to make sure you understand what you've just read – imagine a prompt of 'now explain it to me in your own words'. The next chapter will focus on this practice – paraphrasing – as it is a clear way to make sure you understand the content of your reading, but you should also strive to bring out the information that the original text is implying beneath the surface. This is all about reading between the lines and will be revisited in the following chapter. But for now, the text above is critical because it clearly demonstrates an understanding of the original text, and more broadly, it's critical precisely because the writer has answered the question, 'what does this mean to me?' The answer lies in the writer's decision to focus on explaining the text, without, for now at least, signalling a stance in terms of agree/disagree. Moreover, the writer appears to have been motivated by the mention of stress type and level in the original text, which stood out to him/her. As you can also see, however, by acknowledging that 'Petersen et al. (2012) make a valid point', then clearly this implies a certain level of agreement, but without making this explicit or a dominant focus. Instead, the main focus within the sample is to explain personal understanding of the source.

Summary

In summary, consider interpretation of your source texts – whether an entire article, one page of text or even a single sentence – on the aforementioned four levels. Thus, the directive to 'do something' with the literature you refer to can involve any of the four areas mentioned in this chapter, or indeed more than one at a time. But the main point is indeed to answer the central prompt whenever you read your texts, or merely consider the subject matter: *what does this mean to me?* As we've seen here, this question can be understood in different ways.

9

How to Use Quotes, Paraphrase and Summarise

This chapter will focus on three other ways in which to 'do something' with the source material you read, regardless of where it derives from – book, journal article, website, newspaper and so on. The three choices available to you in this case are to use a direct quotation, a paraphrase or a summary. Ideally, your assessments, notably essays and slides as part of presentations, will incorporate a bit of each, though some disciplines rely on paraphrase more than quotes perhaps (and maybe vice versa). But by seeing how all three work, you'll then be better placed to approach the three strategies with more confidence in your academic work.

The use of reporting verbs

Before we discuss the three ways to refer to the literature you read, you should consider your use of reporting verbs. These are verbs that are often placed next to an author's name and function to reflect the author's attitude toward the subject he or she is reporting on. In other words, when you read someone else's work, you will need to determine for yourself how certain the author is of his/her propositions, claims, opinions and so on. This is part of being critical because you are interpreting not just what the author's text means to you but also the degree to which the author is certain of his/her views. Let's practice with a brief textual sample below:

> I believe that given the success demonstrated so far with the new testing system, it is safe to say that this new method is the solution we have been hoping for.

Now, if you were to use the sentence above as a direct quote, paraphrase or a summary (although it's hard to summarise the content of just one sentence!), then you have the shared need to use a verb in conjunction with the author you refer to:

Smith (2018: 34) argues that 'given the success demonstrated so far with the new testing system, it is safe to say that this new method is the solution we have been hoping for'.

I could have used other reporting verbs, such as *state, explain, suggest, imply, declare* and so on, but I instead opted for a verb which reflects a stronger stance toward the material. This is because in my reading of the original text, it seemed clear to me that the author was indeed quite certain of his/her points, and as such, verbs such as *argue* and even *conclude* reflect this stance. So do consider this carefully, in terms of AUTHOR NAME + REPORTING VERB. It is up to you which verb you use, but again, the verb you use will indicate your understanding of the strength of the author's claims and propositions. This in turn reflects your own ability to be discerning regarding the strengths and weaknesses of the literature you refer to. The use of just this one verb is important as it will have an effect on the rest of the text that follows:

Smith (2018: 34) argues that 'given the success demonstrated so far with the new testing system, it is safe to say that this new method is the solution we have been hoping for'. This level of certainty suggests that we have, at last, a clear way forward.

In the sample above, you can see how one author's certainty is being interpreted at the micro level with a verb – *argues* – and at a broader level with an interpretation that comes in the sentence that follows. It's as if the writer is saying, 'Smith is confident in his/her assertion and so this allows me to be confident in my *own* understanding of Smith's views: namely, that we have "a clear way forward"'.

So again, consider the level of certainty that authors suggest within their comments, opinions and so on and use this to select a reporting verb that is reflective of your interpretation of the author's certainty levels. This can then be used to construct the text which follows, as seen above.

Plagiarism

No book can fully explain the subject of plagiarism, and so I strongly advise you to discuss the subject with your lecturers if you have concerns. But the information that I present in this section should be sufficient to help you understand plagiarism better and know what to do to avoid it. The most obvious kind of plagiarism involves deliberately pretending that someone else's work is your own. This can mean taking a paper off the internet and pretending it's yours or paying a ghostwriting service to do the writing for you. A ghostwriting service is not illegal, as it is a business and you do get what you pay for (e.g. pay a higher fee, get a higher score). However, it is indeed unethical.

On the other hand, plagiarism is a broad term that can also be used to refer to situations in which students are not deliberately cheating at all but simply have poor use of references to other authors. To explain, imagine if you cite a great deal of direct quotes for your essay – each one will come up as part of the online plagiarism check because it recognises the quotes as material that you didn't write yourself. BUT – as long as you use the correct formatting – quotation marks, author's/authors' last name(s), year of publication and page number, there is no problem. This is **not** plagiarism at all as you have clearly identified that the quote is from someone else.

But what if extended pieces of text – say, a few words in a row, and several times throughout your essay – come up as someone else's exact words, but you have not otherwise identified the author and year of publication, as a minimum? In this case, this would constitute plagiarism whether intentional or not. If there is a minimum of such cases, then this need not be an issue. But if there is a high percentage of such text, then this could be problematic and lead to a reduced score for your essay or at the very least a warning from the marker. Generally, if a certain percentage of text as described above appears in a student's essay, this might be accepted – but check with your department on this! However, if such text is deemed to be excessive then this will be a problem indeed. Have a look at the text below as an idea of what I'm talking about, with the bolded text representing that of someone other than the student who is writing the essay:

> It is clear that **previous approaches to this subject** have not been consistent, **nor have they arrived at solid conclusions**.

Granted, this is merely one sentence and within the sentence, only 12 words are coming up as someone else's, **but** without giving credit to the author. But imagine if you have many sentences in your essay that look something like the one above. As you can imagine, this will result, little by little, in a large chunk of your essay coming up as using outside sources (which is perfectly fine), but without identifying the author of them (which is not fine). So, the way to fix this is to give the original writer of the bolded text his/her credit:

> It is clear that 'previous approaches to this subject' have not been consistent, 'nor have they arrived at solid conclusions' (Disha, 2006: 78).

You need to also remember that even if you provide the author's name and year of publication for what is otherwise a brief summary or paraphrase of someone else's work, this will not be enough if you still have large stretches of text appearing from that author that are otherwise presented as your own. So if you have several sentences that look like the one below, this is still plagiarism by definition:

> Disha (2006) states that it is clear that **previous approaches to this subject have not been consistent, nor have they arrived at solid conclusions**.

Yes, you have identified the author whose work you read, but you have not identified the bolded words as belonging to him/her. The solution? Use a direct quote, as shown above, or paraphrase (discussed in the next section).

Even an entire book dedicated to the subject of plagiarism is no substitute for discussing this subject in detail with a lecturer(s), programme director or someone else within your department. So use this brief focus on plagiarism as a guide, but by all means seek out assistance from someone in your department as the main way to learn more about plagiarism as the means to then avoid it.

Direct quotations

Much of this has been covered already, but here I will provide a bit more detail. First, you need to decide what the purpose is for the quotes you choose. Often, quotes (or as we'll see, brief references to previous research) serve to back up your own views. Thus, quotes often act as support. But they can also be used to explain various concepts/theories within your discipline; they can be used to define concepts; and they can be used as a springboard to then launch into your own argument, sometimes by disagreeing with the claim made within the chosen quote. So the critical part begins with asking yourself what kind of quote you're looking for in terms of the purpose for using it. That said, the process is not rigid and you may find yourself merely skim reading an article and a great quote appears to you that you then decide to use, without having first given any thought whatsoever as to what kind of quote you're looking for. Again, there are certain things that I can't pretend to be able to teach, and searching for quotes is one of them. In fact, given that thinking for yourself is indeed a large part of being critical, then it stands to reason that some things you just have to go out and do for yourself. And choosing quotes to use, by no means a particularly difficult task anyway, is one of them.

However, it's important not to rely on direct quotations alone and, instead, apply a mix of quotes, paraphrase and summary. Certainly, if you don't feel entirely comfortable with the use of paraphrase and summary, then an over-reliance on quotes means you are missing an opportunity to broaden your critical thinking skills – and possibly get a lower score for your use of sources – ironically because you take a comparatively easier path of using direct quotes throughout your essay and do not engage with the literature in other ways. For this reason, this chapter will provide information on other ways to engage with the literature beyond direct quotes.

For now though, let's start by looking at a text sample and, from here, choosing a quote from it to then do something with, along the lines of the content of the previous chapter.

> Scientific articles are usually thought to be impersonal, characterized by lexico-grammatical features such as nominalization and the passive voice. They are, in fact, more complicated and subtle than this simple view would suggest. A brief review of the development of scientific journal articles as a genre helps reveal how their form and style have changed over time and how textual evolution has addressed the communicative purposes of scientists as researchers and writers as well as the discourse functions of journal articles as required by the scientific-academic community. Research on the historical development of articles in journals has indicated that early scientific articles were mostly in the form of letters that scientists wrote to each other. Many of them, therefore, used first-person narrative (Swales, 1990). This was related to the fact that, at that time, human agents played the most critical role in scientific investigation, but it also reflected the attitude of personal honesty and modesty. In other words, the large number of first-person pronouns in early scientific articles helped explain early scientific reporting as peer exchanges and gave prominence to the individual scientist (page 122).

Source: Kuo, C. H. (1999). The use of personal pronouns: Role relationships in scientific journal articles. *English for Specific Purposes, 18*(2), 121–138. https://doi.org/10.1111/1468-4446.12775.

Now, is there a sentence(s) that stands out to you? Regardless of what you're looking to do with it, is there a sentence that sounds good, makes an interesting point, suggests your own views perhaps or even better, is there a sentence which you wish you had written? Answer 'yes' to any of the above, and the sentence(s) in question is a very good contender to be used as a direct quote. So let's choose one now and go from there:

> Scientific writing is often regarded perhaps as impersonal as a reflection of fact-based writing and as such, personal views – or even the use of first person – might suggest bias. This in turn could render the methods used and/or the discussion in general to be less trustworthy. In this sense, particular pronouns (e.g. I, we, they) can convey specific connotations to the

reader, depending how, and where, they are used. Kuo (1999) takes up this topic in relation to scientific journal writing specifically, and suggests that the style of writing is not necessarily rigid. Citing the history of scientific writing, Kuo explains that historically, 'human agents played the most critical role in scientific investigation . . . [and] the large number of first-person pronouns in early scientific articles helped explain early scientific reporting as peer exchanges and gave prominence to the individual scientist' (page 122). This strongly suggests that earlier generations of scientists felt that first person was entirely appropriate, arguably coupled with a connotation of sharing knowledge with one's fellow scientists, and not regarded as being suggestive of bias, subjectivity or even undue attention on the individual.

OK, let's analyse this now, and apply critical reading to a piece of (hopefully) critical writing.

First, the quote itself. Let's start with the formatting. First and foremost, always check with your department regarding their preferred formatting system and stick with that. You may have an online programme handbook anyway which makes this information clear – just ask. This is not a particularly critical endeavour, as it merely requires you to copy the formatting style as outlined in your department, or programme's, handbook. It doesn't get any simpler than that.

But on a more specific level, you will notice my use of ellipsis (. . .) and a bracket [and]. These formatting aspects pertain, as you may know, to my decision to delete text from the original quote (i.e. *but it also reflected the attitude of personal honesty and modesty. In other words*), and in order to join the two halves together to make a grammatically correct sentence, the insertion of the conjunction 'and' was needed. So the ellipsis signal text which I have chosen to remove from the author's original words and the bracket reflects the insertion of a new word in order to join things together. Now, the critical part in all of this is based on the decision to choose to delete original text in the first instance. Because when you choose the words of someone else to be placed in your own writing, you have the option of deleting parts of the quote as you deem appropriate. I chose to delete the text in Kuo's article as it came across as somewhat less relevant to the immediate focus at that point on the personal aspects of scientific writing. Therefore, by trimming a bit, the resulting quote is tighter and more to the point. This is a decision reflective of critical thinking and that is always a good thing, but if too many of your quotes involve ellipsis, it is possible that the reader might question why you have done this to excess. Again, this is not a question of 'right' or 'wrong', but more to do with practices which are conventional or simply 'less conventional'. Again, you have to decide for yourself, but the example above illustrates how quotes can be used to good effect.

There's also a brief touch of paraphrase, as I use the term 'one's fellow scientists' as another way to refer to 'peer exchanges'; in the context of the article, peers refers of course to fellow scientists, a shared identity.

Going further, the use of the quote serves to add support for the argument building up prior within the paragraph and comes in at the right time. And, as you can see, something is very much done with the quote, seen in the final sentence. In this case, the final sentence serves to explain the quote's content and the significance of it. Implied in this of course is agreement with the quote, seen with the surrounding text, and the language used in the final sentence is also tentative – as it should be (e.g. *suggests, arguably*). All in all, a good use of a good quote.

Another 'trick of the trade' regarding quotation use is to consider emphasising an aspect of the quote via italics. Usually, this might not be more than one word within the quote which you nonetheless feel needs to be emphasised. Let's use the same text from Kuo's article again to illustrate:

Scientific writing is often regarded perhaps as impersonal as a reflection of fact-based writing and as such, personal views – or even the use of first person – might suggest bias. This in turn could render the methods used and/or the discussion in general to be less trustworthy. In this sense, particular pronouns (e.g. I, we, they) can convey specific connotations to the reader, depending how, and where, they are used. Kuo (1999) takes up this topic in relation to scientific journal writing specifically, and suggests that the style of writing is not necessarily rigid. Citing the history of scientific writing, Kuo explains that historically, 'human agents played the most critical role in scientific investigation . . . [and] the large number of first-person pronouns in early scientific articles helped explain early scientific reporting as *peer* exchanges and gave prominence to the individual scientist' (page 122; my emphasis). This strongly suggests that earlier generations of scientists felt that first person was entirely appropriate, arguably with a connotation of sharing knowledge with one's fellow scientists, and not regarded as being suggestive of bias, subjectivity or even undue attention on the individual.

The difference might be subtle, but it is a difference nonetheless. By choosing to emphasise the word 'peer', I am in turn making an argument, but without shouting about it. In fact, sometimes less is indeed more – a stylistic point I have mentioned before. By emphasising this particular word, it is in turn emphasising the connotations, and not the mere definition, of this word. Connotations of this word, in my mind at least, involve camaraderie, friendship or at least a sense of equality. This is just my interpretation, of course, and you will have yours. But the use of italics still helps to create a slightly different reading of what is otherwise the same words and offers an alternative way to state something like,

'Scientists did not initially hide their personal contributions and revealed them through use of the first person, while at the same time having a sense of belonging to a group of like-minded individuals'. And the use of the words 'my emphasis' tells the reader that the emphasis was indeed my choice as the writer. If emphasis via italics appears in the original text, however, then you need only state 'original emphasis' in the bracket. But again, use italics for emphasis, whether part of a quote or simply your own text, sparingly.

There's always more than can be said about the use of direct quotes. You know they make a great way to initiate your essays and are pretty much standard within the body of an essay. But it's what you do with them that ultimately counts. This is the main piece of advice to give you in terms of being critical with your use of quotes. Quality is also more important than quantity, with quality not just a reference to the quotes you choose as such but also about, once again, what you do with the quotes you choose. Each body paragraph should not be littered with one quote after another, with little, if any, follow-up from you as the writer. Instead, a single quote followed by your take on it – agree, disagree, illustrate and/or explain – will work best. And there is no magic answer as to how many quotes you should use in your essay – this is something you will need to decide. And as we'll see in the sections to follow in this chapter, you don't need to rely simply on quotes – paraphrasing and summarising are equally valid ways to refer to the work of others, so it makes sense to have a mixture of all three.

One final critical consideration is where exactly to place your quotes within your body paragraphs. I wouldn't suggest using a quote as the topic sentence, but again, I don't say this because quotes used as topic sentences would be 'wrong'. But the issue here is that as it's up to you to signal the topic and use your own critical thinking to add a point about said topic, then using a quote to do all this for you is a bit of an easy way out. There really is no prohibition otherwise as to where in the paragraph you place your quotes. As I mentioned regarding my formula for critical body paragraphs, a quote could come second, third or beyond in terms of its sentence position. Some might say, however, not to use quotes to end a body paragraph, but I disagree. It's *how* it is used and what its content is that determines where it is a best fit. Let's see some final examples below:

Human decay involves predictable stages which are nonetheless affected by multiple factors. = TOPIC SENTENCE

Wescott (2018: 332) references the stages in terms of 'skin slippage, marbling, bloat, purge, and skeletonization', but then follows this with the admission that 'the rate at which decomposition occurs is dependent on a number of intrinsic and extrinsic factors' (ibid). QUOTE TO FOLLOW TOPIC SENTENCE

Some of the influential factors which in turn affect the rate of decay include outside temperature, body mass, age of deceased and clothing, among others.

This suggests that while human decay is predictable in terms of the process, the speed of decay is not.

A final sentence to wrap things up, in this case consisting of an interpretative summary.

Human decay involves predictable stages which are nonetheless affected by multiple factors. Some of the influential factors which in turn affect the rate of decay include outside temperature, body mass, age of deceased and clothing, among others. Wescott (2018: 332) references these stages of decay in terms of 'skin slippage, marbling, bloat, purge, and skeletonization', but indeed confirms that 'the rate at which decomposition occurs is dependent on a number of intrinsic and extrinsic factors' (ibid).

Thoughts: This time, the quote works to confirm the content of Sentence 2, essentially a way for the writer to say, 'my understanding as captured in Sentence 2 is confirmed by an expert'. Also, at an absolute micro level, the use of the word 'indeed' serves to add a bit of oomph. It's a way to emphasise that someone in the field really *does* agree with your statement in Sentence 2.

Human decay involves predictable stages which are nonetheless affected by multiple factors. Some of the influential factors which in turn affect the rate of decay include outside temperature, body mass, age of deceased and clothing, among others. This suggests that the decay of a human corpse, while predictable perhaps in terms of the various stages of decay it undergoes, is not predictable in terms of time frame for the process of decay. Indeed, Wescott (2018: 332) summarises this phenomenon first in terms of the stages of decay, such as 'skin slippage, marbling, bloat, purge, and skeletonization', but concurs that 'the rate at which decomposition occurs is dependent on a number of intrinsic and extrinsic factors' (ibid).

Thoughts: With the sentence directly above, in this case the words of an expert are being used to wrap things up; the main point for using quotes to end body paragraphs is to ask yourself if the quote truly brings this to a close, as it should; or, does it leave things up in the air, as it shouldn't? And again, don't discount the 'small' things – the use of the word 'indeed' again serves to emphasise a point and, in this case, can also serve to function as a marker of a closing statement.

Source: Wescott, D. (2018). Recent advances in forensic anthropology: Decomposition research. *Forensic Sciences Research, 3*(4), 327–342. https://doi.org/10.1080/20961790.2018.1488571.

I now continue with a focus on paraphrasing, another practice to become familiar with as part of academic assessment.

Paraphrasing

Paraphrasing involves taking the words of others and instead of quoting them directly, you rephrase/restate them. This in itself often involves a bit of summarising, so one of the critical aspects is to decide which parts of the text to include, and which parts to exclude. Again, this is up to you and you alone. The decision to paraphrase, as opposed to using a direct quote, is sometimes based on a purely practical consideration. Quotes generally aren't going to be more than a sentence or two; for longer quotes, say those that involve several lines of text, you often have to embed them – place them further into the page as I have done with the paragraph samples above. Check your programme handbook for more information on this, as it's a relatively straightforward formatting issue, and there's nothing really critical about it. Just copy what the formatting guidance tells you!

So getting back to quote length, it would be unusual to have a quote that takes half a page, though for a PhD thesis this would not look out of place (but even then, you wouldn't want to do it too much). Therefore, if you find an especially engaging piece of text that you deem is simply too long for a direct quote, but very relevant and illustrative of your assessment's subject area, then paraphrase is a wise choice in this case. But let's first determine the important things to bear in mind with paraphrase:

- Obvious perhaps, but make sure that you truly understand the source text and what it is saying; if not, your paraphrase will reflect this misunderstanding.
- Make notes as you read the literature and try not to use too much of the original source text; this way, when you use your notes as the basis for the eventual paraphrase, there shouldn't be too much of the original source text which could then lead to plagiarism – but the ideas discussed in the source text will be present.
- Therefore, consider replacing some of the key words in the original text with synonyms, BUT don't be afraid to retain some of the original text too.
- In reference to the point directly above, paraphrasing can be a bit tricky at times – if it sounds too much like the original text, then it will come across as a sloppy or careless paraphrase (and potentially plagiarised); if it's too different, it might appear to wander away too much from the meaning of the original text.
- Finally, try to read between the lines and, in doing so, make explicit the more implicit aspects of the original text – this is a very good indicator of critical reading indeed.

Let's take another paragraph of text, and this time, we're not selecting any of it for a quote per se. Instead, read it to get the overall gist of what it's saying to you; decide what aspects to retain, emphasise and leave out; choose appropriate synonyms; and finally, bring in your understanding by interpreting the original text – again, this can be seen by bringing out elements of the original text that might otherwise be implied, but not stated directly. An example is also provided for you to consider, which you can compare with your own work.

> Western diets are, however, typically high in animal protein, and these diets are spreading around the globe. A recent report for the United Kingdom (UK) (CCC, 2019) suggests that a 20% reduction in beef, lamb, and dairy consumption by 2050 – which can be seen as a relatively modest target compared to other major reports' suggested reduction targets (e.g. Lorenz-Walther et al., 2019) – would be acceptable when achieved in tandem with other decarbonising and negative emissions efforts. Whatever the appropriate scale might be: Shifting food consumption patterns to become less GHG-intensive and less wasteful certainly and decidedly matters for climate change mitigation (Tilman and Clark, 2014).
>
> Source: Reisch, L., Sunstein, C., Andor, M., Doebbe, F., Meier, J., & Haddaway, N. (2021). Mitigating climate change via food consumption and food waste: A systematic map of behavioral interventions. *Journal of Cleaner Production, 279.* https://doi.org/10.1016/j.jclepro.2020.123717.

There is a decided link between food consumption and climate change. As Reisch et al. (2021) argue, the link is specifically centred on diets high in animal protein, including meat and dairy, and the association such diets have with greenhouse gas (GHG) emissions and their contribution to climate change. Thus, as Reisch et al. conclude, a change in diet, coupled with additional endeavours regarding decarbonisation and efforts to reduce negative emissions, can work together to address the growing issue of climate change. The high UK consumption of meat, as but one example of a so-called Western diet, is one concrete example of a practice that, if reduced by 20% by 2050, can help to address the situation. Perhaps this in turn suggests that alternative diets from other regions might be considered, such as the Mediterranean diet which generally involves the consumption of less red meat and more fish, fruit and vegetables.

A few things to point out. First, some of the original word choices are retained, as very often, there is no replacement for technical words in the first instance. Thus, *climate change, GHG, emissions, animal protein* and *decarbonisation*, for example, do not really have viable synonyms in use. However, for more 'everyday' words, there are synonyms that work just fine. For example, the original text mentions that 'when achieved in tandem with other decarbonising and negative emissions efforts'; the paraphrased text changes this to 'coupled with additional endeavours regarding decarbonisation and efforts to reduce negative emissions, can work together . . .'. But as I had mentioned, if you make notes in the first instance when you do your reading, and avoid using the original text too much, then you are already on the right path to a good paraphrase. And the question to ask here is, **does this say the same thing but in a different way?** Because this is the crux of determining a good paraphrase, and as such, the answer needs to be a clear 'yes'.

Moreover, is there a sense of adding something extra, which was nonetheless embedded in the original text? Well, the paraphrased text brings out just that bit more the mention of the UK diet in terms of making its connection to a Western diet somewhat more explicit. The original text references Western diets in Sentence 1, with a reference to food consumption in the UK to follow in Sentence 2. In this sense, it's the original writer's way of essentially saying that the UK diet is an example of the larger category of Western diet. But the paraphrase makes this link more explicit, seen with the text 'The high UK consumption of meat, as but one example of a so-called Western diet'. This is not a major reveal perhaps, but it nonetheless does show how the paraphrased writing has sought to bring something out a bit more from the original. But if we look even closer, we can see a hint of disagreement, perhaps even irony. This is seen with the expression 'so-called' in reference to a Western diet. By merely adding this one phrase, it can affect the reader's perception and their understanding of the writer's attitude toward the original text. On the one hand, perhaps 'so-called' is merely addressing the fact that 'Western diet' is a term in use, as is Mediterranean diet; on the other hand, it is questioning the validity of this term in the first instance. Personally, I feel the term 'Western diet' is a bit too broad, as surely the Mediterranean diet is also subsumed under the category of Western diet, and yet, it is quite different from the one suggesting high meat and dairy consumption (this is perhaps why the Mediterranean diet is often put forward as the ideal diet to follow). So the paraphrase is (a) using synonyms where appropriate, (b) has chosen to hone in on various elements over others, and finally, (c) has brought out an otherwise background point in the original text and chosen to make it more explicit – and even mildly challenge the original text – as part of the paraphrase.

A final point to make about paraphrasing is to take care to make sure the balance is right between saying the same thing in a sufficiently different way, but not to the extent that your paraphrase bears no resemblance in meaning and content to the original text – I had mentioned this, but it bears repeating. But a more serious problem I have seen with students' work is the opposite:

paraphrase which retains far too much of the original material – to the extent that entire sentences are cited verbatim. I had already pointed this out earlier as an example of plagiarism, even though this is not plagiarism in the obvious sense of cutting and pasting an essay from the internet and presenting it as your own, or paying a ghostwriting service to do it for you. But what is otherwise careless paraphrasing will be flagged as plagiarism nonetheless, especially when the source of the original text is not even mentioned in the body of your essay. As you saw from the paraphrased example, you must provide the author's name and date of publication, but there is no need to provide a page number of course as this is not a direct quotation.

However, as a final word of caution, do bear the following in mind once again. If you identify a paraphrase with the author's name and year of publication as you are otherwise expected to do, but nonetheless have stretches of exact words from the original text, then this could pose a problem and constitute plagiarism. The reason why is simple: you're using someone else's exact words, but not identifying them as such; in this case, the 'identifier' would be the page numbers, to show the reader that the words in question are a direct quote and not merely a paraphrase:

> Voss (2017) argues that **trickle-down theory is a naïve approach to economics** and is not economically credible in terms of its intentions.

OK, you have given Voss his/her due credit in terms of telling the reader where you obtained this information on trickle-down theory. However, if the bolded text represents the original words of Voss, and not merely a paraphrase of such, then you need to identify it by means of (a) quotation marks AND (b) the page number(s). Otherwise, the bolded nine words would be understood as coming directly from you, when in fact they come directly from Voss. But as I have mentioned already, check with your department if you have any further questions or doubts – they will make sure you are left in no doubt.

Summarising

Finally, we come to the practice of summarising. Unlike a paraphrase, a summary serves to only offer the bare bones of the original text and nothing more – it essentially reduces entire chapters, even books, to the crux of what they are saying. This can be anywhere from one sentence in length to a paragraph. Going back to the abstract which is used in dissertations and theses, we can see how the text of an 80,000-word PhD is reduced to one page of text, and no more. The abstract, then, is a clear example of a summary, but not a paraphrase. A summary seeks to get to the main overall point; a paraphrase seeks to rephrase much of the content instead. While a paraphrase might seek to summarise some points of the original text, it stays with others in the same detail and, very often, summarises in the sense of simply deleting some aspects of the original text.

The first example of a summary which will definitely prove useful is what we might call a 'super summary', the shortest summary of all. This is something you will need for essays, posters and PowerPoint slides, for example, and especially for the literature review of your dissertation. It consists of multiple references to previous studies contained within a bracket, as seen below:

> The subject of X has been well covered in the literature (Johnson, 2002; Wells, 2006; Berisha, 2007; Hadikin, 2009; Davis, 2011; Kim, 2016; Lee, 2019).

Whatever subject 'X' is, the bracketed names and years might refer to books, book chapters and journal articles, all of which might combine to reach a grand total of 100,000 words, give or take. As you can see, thousands and thousands of words have been reduced now to a mere 11 words prior to the bracket. This is not to say that you can't go further, and perhaps the sentence(s) to follow might expand on what the literature has to say. But even then, it might still merely offer a summary, albeit a bit more detailed perhaps:

> The subject of X has been well covered in the literature (Johnson, 2002; Wells, 2006; Berisha, 2007; Hadikin, 2009; Davis, 2011; Kim, 2016; Lee, 2019). Key findings include a, b and c . . .

It's important to remember that a summary is somewhat relative. You can have a summary of an entire book captured in a sentence or two, and you can also write a summary of a book chapter in an entire page. It's again up to you how long, or short, your summary will be. The main point to always remember is to ensure that your summary is designed to offer nothing more than what you consider to be the source text's main point(s), unlike a paraphrase which otherwise seeks to capture the original text as a rephrased copy and indeed add something new.

We've discussed the reasons for using direct quotes and paraphrases, but why summarise? Outside of 'standard summaries', such as abstracts, and 'super summaries' as illustrated above, there is a key consideration in choosing to summarise, which again involves some critical thinking on your part. In this case, the consideration is entirely centred on the subject of your essay, or assessment in general. In other words, and as is the case for any assessment, you need to choose literature that is the most relevant to the immediate subject at hand. This doesn't have to mean focusing solely on the most well-known literature, however; as I explained before, to demonstrate criticality in your background reading, you should plan to include, but also look beyond, the items on the core reading list and seek out publications that are not, in fact, on any of the course unit's reading lists, whether core, recommended or suggested reading. But the extent to which a given reading source is relevant is pretty much based on the degree to which you might choose to quote, paraphrase or summarise. You can, of course, choose to summarise a highly relevant study, as opposed to quoting from it. Again, there truly are no 'rules' here for how many quotes versus summaries you must have, and there is no ratio such as 'for every three quotes you must have one summary'. It's not an exact science.

So you decide the relevance of the reading you do and, as such, the likelihood of incorporating some of this reading into your assessment. From here, you must then decide *how* you're going to use the source material. If indeed you decide to summarise, you then need to make a final decision: how long will the summary be? Again, it's up to you. If I were writing an essay on the subject of attitudes toward accents and how we form judgements of people based on their accent, then a name that immediately comes to mind is that of Noam Chomsky, a major American sociolinguist. There are, of course, many other sociolinguists, but Chomsky was certainly a pioneer, to the extent that his study in New York City in the 1960s is often still routinely referred to. For this reason, it would make sense to refer to this study, but in what detail and to what extent would be up to me. Some considerations, however, which you can adapt for your own assessments:

- **How many words is the assignment?** If it's an average length of 1,500 to 2,500 words for an essay assignment, then I may well decide to report on Chomsky's study in just a few sentences.
- **What is the specific subject coverage within the essay?** That is, is it focused on accent perceptions in general or just here in the UK? If the former, then perhaps a bit more detail on Chomsky's study, albeit still a summary, would be a good idea.
- But if the specific focus within the essay is just on the UK, then a study conducted in the USA might suggest a bit less coverage regarding Chomsky's study.
- On the other hand, more coverage of an American-based study on accent perception could make sense, in order for me to make a critical point such as *though Chomsky's study is set in the USA, it is argued that the attitudes toward accents in New York City broadly reflect the same issue on a global scale, to include of course the UK: the issue is accent prejudice.*

The italicised sentence above reflects some critical thinking, by means of declaring that a study set in the 1960s 3,000 miles away from the UK is just as relevant now as it ever was, regardless of national focus. As you can see, your use of references to studies and authors can be very versatile, in terms of *how* you choose to refer to previous studies, *how much* you choose to reference and ultimately, *why* you do so, based on your strategy. I remember once using a quote from the 1800s regarding attitudes to accents. But my strategy was simple: to then follow this otherwise 'old' quote with more recent quotes from the 21st century, which expressed the same views. In this manner, I was then able to turn around and basically declare to my reader, 'see, things haven't really changed in more than a hundred years, have they?' Had I not followed the older quote with more recent literature, then my marker might well have questioned my use of a quote from so long ago. True, this pertains to quotes, not summaries. But the illustration I have provided is all about the bigger picture in terms of formulating a strategy for your references to other authors to include summaries. So whether one sentence, one paragraph or somewhere in between, a summary is relative in terms of how long or short you wish to make it. It again largely depends on the specific subject area of your essay, and by specific, I don't just mean 'language and identity', 'chemical engineering' or 'stoic theory'; instead, I am referring to the more narrow subject areas that derive from these larger subject areas. And the closer the match to your subject area that a given study is, can play a part in terms of deciding how you will use it and if indeed you decide on a summary, then you can go from there to decide how long, or short, the summary is.

I now conclude this chapter with a final example of a text, from which illustrations are provided of direct quotes, paraphrase and summary.

> Discussing what is desirable in education is to enter contested terrain. Barnett (1992: 6) puts it bluntly, 'The debate over quality in higher education should be seen for what it is: a power struggle where the use of terms reflects a jockeying for position in the attempt to impose own definitions of [the aims of] higher education.' Therefore, when proposing a balance and relationship of academic and professional aims of engineering education, there is no objective or neutral position available, but we are all jockeying for positions with ideological and normative arguments.
>
> Source: Edström, K. (2018). Academic and Professional Values in Engineering Education: Engaging with History to Explore a Persistent Tension. *Engineering Studies, 10*(1), 38–65. https://doi.org/10.1080/19378629.2018. 1424860.

Quotation

At the broad level of higher education, there are indeed ideologies relating to, for example, the aims and purposes of higher education. Ideologies regarding aims and purposes can also be seen on a discipline-specific level, with

Edström (2018) discussing this at the level of the discipline of engineering. The point is made clear that 'we are all jockeying for positions with ideological and normative arguments' (p. 39). In this case, the 'we' can refer to insiders within a given discipline, as representatives of higher education and the discipline in question also. Far from maintaining what might be considered a kind of 'academic objectivity', Edström appears to be making the point that even within a given discipline, shared subject expertise does not equate to shared agreement regarding the fundamental aims and purposes of higher education.

Paraphrase

Edström (2018) reflects on a subject of contention within higher education. Citing Barnett (1992), Edström argues that there is much conflict regarding the differing views on the subject of the overall aims and purposes of higher education, **using the discipline of engineering perhaps as a stand-in for academia in general.** (This is my added extra marked in bold here merely to identify it. This 'extra' is based on my close reading of the original text. Notice the use of cautious language, however, to make my view more credible, seen with the word *perhaps*).

The main point is that there appears to be no neutral stance to be found, with academics dispensing with academic objectivity in favour of promoting their own personal values – and personal agendas perhaps – regarding the aims of higher education.

Thoughts: The term 'neutral stance' above replaces the original text of 'neutral position'. The expression 'and personal agendas perhaps' represents some 'digging' regarding the original text, but again reflecting a cautious stance with my word choice of *perhaps*.

Summary

Edström (2018) comments on the suggested lack of objectivity when applied to the aims and values of higher education, arguing that there are discrepancies in this regard due to the differing ideological positions held by academics.

Thoughts: Of course, this is just a summary in isolation. What comes before it? What comes next? By now, you hopefully feel better placed to address this, in terms of a strategy. What is your strategy here? Follow the summary with an agreement? Illustration? Both? How will you use the summary for your own purposes?

Summary

I close this chapter now, hopefully having provided clear discussion and illustration of three common strategies with regard to how you can incorporate the work of authors in your own work. As I have stressed, there is a great deal of freedom involved, from whether to use a quote or paraphrase, to whether to have a short summary or a longer summary. It's up to you, and as such, take the relative freedom afforded to you and make the choices you think work best in terms of **how, why** and **how much** with regard to your use of source material.

10

How to Use Critical Language in Your Assessments

I had referred to hedging earlier, and this chapter will now focus on it in detail. Along with the oft-mentioned skills of **illustration** and **justification**, **hedging** is in the top three of critical skills you need to develop and use in your assessments.

What is hedging?

Hedging refers to the practice of using cautious language in your assessments, especially in conjunction with your interpretations, claims, arguments, opinions and so on. Basically, whenever you make a statement which you can't assert to be a fact, hedging is needed. A simple rule is this: **don't make your opinions sound like facts!** Too many students do, and as a result, their writing is decidedly uncritical and not credible at all.

It might seem counterintuitive, but the more you show caution with your claims, and in effect show a degree of doubt, the more credibility you will have and the more trustworthy your assessment will be, whether essay, exam, poster and so on. The more you use direct and bold language, the less your statements will be taken seriously and it will not make the writing appear 'confident' at all. Likewise, hedging will not make your writing come across as unconfident either. It will instead make your work sound suitably academic.

Why do we need to hedge?

As indicated, we need to hedge to show that we are being critical, logical and reasoned in our statements and comments. If we can't absolutely prove our points, then we need to use language that reflects this. Also, another reason perhaps is to show a degree of academic modesty, if you like, as a reflection of not appearing to sound too confident in one's views, more so in the results of one's research. To do so might appear a bit arrogant. So having set the scene for what hedging is and why it is practiced, let's see examples of what it looks like.

Examples of Hedging in Action

Consider the sentence pairs below and decide which sounds better:

It has been proven that his theories are correct.

It has been suggested that his theories are valid.

This is the best way forward.

Arguably, this is the best way forward.

This is the solution to address the issue.

This could be the solution to address the issue.

The second sentence in the pairs is clearly the hedged example. Using words and expressions such as the following will work well for hedging practice:

*It is **suggested** . . ., it **could** be said . . ., **arguably**, . . ., this **might** mean that . . . , **perhaps** this is an alternative idea worth exploring . . ., her views **can** be regarded as a unique way to approach this issue . . .*

As you can see, good candidates for hedging-based language are modal verbs (*can, could, might*), words such as *perhaps/maybe* and constructions such as *it is suggested/implied*. Also, beginning a sentence with *arguably* is a very good approach. First, it immediately tells the reader that you're going to make an argument on some level, to some extent – not necessarily in terms of a long discussion about a brand new theory to consider, but perhaps simply offering your take on existing literature, theory and such. Don't forget, when you make an argument, it can be something as prominent as taking up the entire length of your essay, such as an argument against capital punishment. On the other hand, the minute you interpret someone else's words, as we have already seen, then you are making an argument. In this case, it is an argument on a smaller scale, but it is nonetheless an argument, seen via interpreting something you've read and, having done so, presented an opinion as to what it means. In this case, even if the interpretation is only delivered across a sentence or two, and not the length of the essay, it is still an argument nonetheless. And even if you agree with someone else's argument, this too means that you are making an argument in support of the original one you read.

A second point to make about this particular use and placement of the word *arguably* is that it also tells the reader that you are about to interpret the content of the previous sentence – it gives the reader advance notice. Clearly, however, there are all manner of hedging devices in terms of the linguistic choices you make, and you should plan to use a variety of them. Below are some examples, with the relevant language highlighted:

Conversely, individuals with higher scores in the MAAS are less prone to social anxiety and self-consciousness than participants with low MAAS scores (Brown and Ryan, 2003). The results therefore **indicate** that mindfulness is an effective means of treating depression because it reduces the scope for rumination (Brown and Ryan, 2003).

Source: UKEssays. (2018g, November). *Sample undergraduate 1st psychology assignment*. https://www.ukessays.com/services/samples/1st-psychology-assignment.php. Accessed on 21 November 2020.

The potential impacts of Brexit in curriculum terms are **perhaps** not to be overestimated either; whatever the new relationship between the UK and Europe, there will be changes mandated to teaching and learning across the National Curriculum to reflect the new political and geographic realities (Ulster University, 2017). An example **may** be found within the subject specialism of geography.

Source: UKEssays. (2018c, November). *Sample undergraduate 1st education report*. https://www.ukessays.com/services/samples/1st-education-report.php. Accessed on 21 November 2020.

The use of technology is also linked to an increase in childhood obesity, which is a significant public health concern in contemporary society (Rosen et al, 2013). Other concerns commonly raised include cyber bullying (Office of Communications, 2015), internet addiction (King et al, 2012) and online grooming practices (Palmer, 2015). It is important, however, that these concerns do not lead to an irrational proclivity towards technological scepticism at the expense of the benefits that new technologies **could** provide service users and patients.

Source: UKEssays. (2018e, November). *Sample undergraduate 1st health and social care essay*. https://www.ukessays.com/services/samples/1st-hsc-essay.php. Accessed on 14 November 2020.

Now, let's see these examples again, with the hedged language replaced with something more 'direct'. How does your perception change regarding the writing and, subsequently, the writer?

Conversely, individuals with higher scores in the MAAS are less prone to social anxiety and self-consciousness than participants with low MAAS scores (Brown and Ryan, 2003). The results therefore **prove** that mindfulness is an effective means of treating depression because it reduces the scope for rumination (Brown and Ryan, 2003).

The potential impacts of Brexit in curriculum terms are **definitely** not to be over-estimated either; whatever the new relationship between the UK and Europe, there will be changes mandated to teaching and learning across the National Curriculum to reflect the new political and geographic realities (Ulster University, 2017). An example **is** found within the subject specialism of geography.

The use of technology is also linked to an increase in childhood obesity, which is a significant public health concern in contemporary society (Rosen et al, 2013). Other concerns commonly raised include cyber bullying (Office of Communications, 2015), internet addiction (King et al, 2012) and online grooming practices (Palmer, 2015). It is important, however, that these concerns do not lead to an irrational proclivity towards technological scepticism at the expense of the benefits that new technologies **provide** service users and patients.

The differences may not, in fact, seem so different. After all, you're only analysing short patches of text, not an entire essay. But even the 'tiniest' mistakes or issues with your writing, whether typos or non-hedged writing, can build up and become, in essence, a big issue. Having said that, I'm not advocating non-stop hedging. If you look at the example directly above, by removing the word *could* prior to 'provide service users and patients', does it automatically mean the writing now suddenly sounds less trustworthy or somehow 'over the top'? Of course not. And herein lies, once again, one of those moments – and you'll have lots of them as you plan and construct your assessments – in which you will have to display critical thinking skills by deciding for yourself what the best approach is. In this case, the best approach is with regard to the linguistic choices you make in terms of hedging, or indeed choosing not to hedge. Understand that it is not an absolute 'one or the other' here. So if you don't choose to hedge, this does not mean that your writing will sound less academic. Rather, it's a case of choosing when there is a real need to hedge and when there really isn't. But I will say this: the number of times I have told my students that they're overdoing it with hedging I can count on one hand. But I can't recall the countless times in which I have had to tell students the opposite, as a reflection of writing which does not hedge at all, or not enough, and comes across as, frankly, immature writing.

Discipline-Specific Hedging

Hedging is common across disciplines, and as such, we can safely say that it is an academic practice in general. However, there are implications for hedging based on the discipline you study in. The implications are for the quantity of hedging that is needed, and not necessarily the specific linguistic choices you use to do this.

Humanities

The Humanities, seen with subjects such as art, music and literature, are in some ways the most interpretive of disciplines. Of course, interpretation is a key aspect of being critical and is used across disciplines in the first instance. But in this case, 'interpretive' points to something else. Here, I'm referring to the fact that the Humanities don't deal in facts, are not looking for some ultimate conception of 'truth', and as a result, all answers – interpretations – are valid, as long as they are explained clearly and supported. So whether the interpretation is based on a book, play, symphony, painting, film and so on, we will all see such creative media in different ways. And this is why, on a basic level, we can't judge someone's interpretation to be 'wrong' simply because it's different from our own.

So consider your favourite film, book or artwork on a thematic level, a level that goes beyond the mere plot, narrative or paint on the canvas, and instead goes much deeper. In terms of so much interpretation to be had, how would this then translate into writing in the Humanities? Given the inherently interpretive nature of this academic community (as I've defined interpretive), we would expect hedging to feature quite prominently indeed. Having said that, what do you make of the argument sentence below, taken from a literature essay?

> The aim of this essay is to compare and contrast the ways in which Charlotte Bronte and Jean Rhys interpret the theme of isolation to construct such characters as Rochester and Jane from the novel Jane Eyre and Antoinette from Wide Sargasso Sea.
>
> Source: UKEssays. (2020j, June 1). *Theme of isolation in Jane Eyre* https://www.ukessays.com/essays/english-literature/isolation-theme-jane-eyre-wide-sargasso-sea.php. Accessed on 22 November 2020.

The writer is discussing two literary works in terms of 'the theme of isolation'. Now, at face value, this would mean that there is only one theme, given the use of the definite article – 'the'. Or, it could be interpreted as suggesting that isolation is the central theme, one that defines these works above all else. In short, it could be read as the writer stating, or certainly suggesting, that 'this is the only theme (of importance)'. But this of course would completely go against the ethos of the literature community and the Humanities overall.

However, we also need to consider who we are writing for. On an immediate level, we're writing for, and being assessed by, our markers. But on a broader level, we're writing/constructing assessments in general for a certain academic community. So while my reading is purely reflective of my academic identity as a linguist, those within the literature community would certainly not read this key sentence the same way. Rather, it would be read by people within literature as 'I will discuss the theme *as I see it* in these two works'. In other words, the writer is not even implying that this is the 'correct' theme, or that there is a singular theme to be gleaned from the reading of these two works. Instead, he/she is simply saying, albeit indirectly, that this is his/her reading only, and of course everyone else is free to interpret the same works however they please, and indeed they will do so.

Thus, to hedge this key sentence would be seen as unnecessary and may even come across as a bit defensive:

> The aim of this essay is to compare and contrast the ways in which Charlotte Bronte and Jean Rhys interpret the **suggested** theme of isolation to construct such characters as Rochester and Jane from the novel Jane Eyre and Antoinette from Wide Sargasso Sea.

I'm not saying that the sentence above would be inferior with the addition of a hedge, but merely that it's not necessary. And this is because the community of readers understand what is being communicated in the original version. What is being communicated is clearly a hedged commitment to the student's reading of the text, though it is otherwise placed in what looks like non-hedged writing.

Some additional sentences from the same text can be seen, in which hedging has a clear role to play, however:

> **Perhaps**, Jane's social isolation is explained by the fact that this young woman is unable to accept society that has constantly pushed her away.

> Analysing the ways in which the writers present the theme of isolation to construct the characters of Rochester, Jane and Antoinette from *Jane Eyre* and *Wide Sargasso Sea*, the essay **suggests** that Bronte and Rhys provide both similar and different interpretations of this issue.

But there are many examples which might seem to run contrary to a discipline in which hedging would otherwise be an expected norm:

> Unlike Jane, Antoinette doesn't have such people in her life, thus her isolation and loneliness result in the tragic end.

Antoinette's lack of identity makes her rather helpless. Jane is simply isolated from society, but Antoinette is destroyed by society, because she is dependent on people that reject her.

The lack of social relations and solitude of Antoinette deprive her of the possibility to recognise her true self.

There are many options available to use of course regarding hedged language, and below are the same sentences with hedged insertions:

Unlike Jane, Antoinette **arguably** doesn't have such people in her life, thus her isolation and loneliness result in the tragic end.

It could be said that Antoinette's lack of identity makes her rather helpless. Jane is simply isolated from society, but Antoinette is destroyed by society, because she is dependent on people that reject her.

The lack of social relations and solitude of Antoinette **appear to** deprive her of the possibility to recognise her true self.

It would be most appropriate for someone from within literature, or perhaps the Humanities as a whole, to decide which set of sentences sound better. In this case, 'better' is not based on personal taste; instead, it is entirely based on objective criteria that relate to the disciplinary norms as expressed through language. It might be said that there is no need to hedge when making one's claims if hedging is already understood, as I had mentioned earlier in this section. Second, it could also be said that as a reflection of the more literary style of language found within fiction or poetry, this might somewhat influence the writing style of essays based on literary analysis. Indeed, I had mentioned that figures of speech are more commonly found within Humanities essays, but would feature much less prominently in the Hard Sciences, for example. This can be seen with the rather strong word choice in Sentence 2 above (in the second sample text) of *destroyed*. However, this same word in other contexts of academia might be inappropriate. But in keeping with maintaining a critical approach, I am careful not to make blanket statements and assertions. Thus, while it is generally true that figures of speech would be less commonly used in the Hard Sciences, I certainly can't say that no scientist, or student within the science community, has never had a legitimate use for a metaphor in their essay.

Also, if a character within the text expresses emotion and the author of the text – whether Shakespeare or Dickens – uses strong language such as 'destruction', 'rage' or 'hate', for example, then is it really inappropriate for the academic essay to reflect such language in its analysis of the text? Another textual example is provided: 'Both characters are furious at being unrealised by the other (99).' As the text in question found on page 99 of the original literary text references the word 'furious', this is why it might appear in the resulting essay. So know who you're writing for, and when needed, seek out the advice from insiders where necessary, such as your lecturers, advisors and supervisor.

Social Sciences

Again, know the community for whom you're writing and presenting your assessments. This also means understanding what the broad goals of the community are – what is its *raison d'être*? Admittedly, I don't have the expertise to provide such information for each and every academic discipline, but what this chapter does is provide broad information tied to the three main academic communities under which many of the disciplines fit.

In the case of the Social Sciences, much of the research is focused on participant-based studies, spanning areas such as psychology, sociology and human geography. Interpretation in this instance is focused on interpreting human behaviour, beliefs, attitudes and so on, which can be impractical to generalise to the larger population since human beings are complex. To put it another way, a study conducted twice with the same population and with the same methods might still generate different results. So while the Social Sciences do attempt to understand and inform us regarding human behaviour, the reality is that the information provided can often only be generalised at best, and then only to a certain extent (e.g. based on multiple studies, sometimes conducted over a length of time), or at least, provide some deeper insights into a smaller group as part of a particular case study. So while the Humanities do not really focus on generalisations and quantitative research approaches for the most part, the Social Sciences might often involve both a qualitative and a quantitative approach. To an extent, we want to find out more about what motivates humans and their behaviour – this requires in-depth qualitative research – while there is often a need to also understand this on a statistical level (e.g. what percentage of families are choosing to homeschool their children?).

Given what might be seen as a kind of tentative generalisation, hedging is needed in terms of playing it safe regarding the conclusions one draws regarding the results of a given study. Hedging is needed to also act as a caveat, should the interpretation of the results promise more than it can deliver, as it were – this is particularly relevant when researchers apply for funding and need to be careful as to what they will do with the money in terms of its potential benefits when applied to the study. And hedging is used for more everyday reasons – to simply avoid overly assertive statements within a community when such statements cannot be safely made anyway.

Here are some examples of hedging as used in the Social Sciences. As you read the samples, pay particular attention not just to the bolded language which reflects the hedging used but also your perceptions and understanding of the text as a result, as well as the writer's possible attitude toward the text he/she is creating:

> The urge to divide the human race into broad categories similar to the animal kingdom **seems** to be a starting point for many of the theorists in the Nineteenth Century (James, 1981, p.19) . . . Darwinism **can** be seen as a significant academic contribution to the racism paradigm.
>
> Source: UKEssays. (2020h, June 1). *Race in the 19th and 20th centuries.* https://www.ukessays.com/essays/sociology/ideas-race-century.php. Accessed on 22 November 2020.

> According to Aristotle, "excellence of character has to do with pleasures and pains" and a further **proof of this fact** is shown by the "practice of forcible correction, which takes place through pleasures and pains" (*NE* II.3, 1104b8-18). This **seems** to highlight the fact that moral development for Aristotle is clearly shaped **at least in part** by pleasures and pains and that they both play a major role in excellence of character.
>
> Source: UKEssays. (2020d, May 18). *Pleasure and pain: Aristotle's theory of moral development.* https://www.ukessays.com/essays/philosophy/pleasure-and-pain-aristotles-theory-of-moral-development.php. Accessed on 20 November 2020.

Thoughts: This doesn't sound like hedged language at all. But consider the context! The writer is not claiming anything as 'proof of fact'. Rather, he/she is reflecting on Aristotle's propositions in a hypothetical manner, thus presenting them for discussion as facts merely for argument's sake, as opposed to arguing for the propositions to be actual facts.

> **The evidence presented indicates** that early childhood abuse and neglect, which is also referred to as deprivation, **typically** has a long-term detrimental effect on the cognitive, emotional and behavioural development of children. Thompson and Tabone (2010) **suggest** that the effects of deprivation may not be immediately apparent, and therefore assessments of abused and neglected children should be undertaken through childhood and adolescence.
>
> Source: UKEssays. (2020f, June 1). *Case studies on childhood neglect.* https://www.ukessays.com/essays/psychology/childhood-neglect-its-impact-later-in-life.php. Accessed on 21 November 2020.

Thoughts: The expression *the evidence presented indicates* is a hedge, along with other commonly used expressions, especially in journal articles, such as based on the results of this study . . . This functions as a hedge precisely because it is saying that 'these results are tied solely to *this* study and *this* evidence, and thus cannot be generalised beyond the confines of the current research'.

However, let's not forget instances in which stronger language is entirely necessary. Have a look at the sentence below in which the modal verb *must*, which carries a degree of certainty, is otherwise being used merely to state the obvious. As such, no need to hedge:

> In order to explain the characteristics of imperialistic language policies, we **must** first define the concept of 'imperialism'.
>
> Source: UKEssays. (2020a, February 9). *Impact of linguistic imperialism*. https://www.ukessays.com/essays/linguistics/impact-of-linguistic-imperialism.php. Accessed on 21 November 2020.

There are instances, such as the one above, in which hedging would be fine as a choice, but unnecessary. Let's now illustrate some more examples of this, focusing on the Hard Sciences.

Hard Sciences

The Hard Sciences, such as chemistry and physics, deal by and large with facts. This is true of biology too, though the study of biology can sometimes cross over into the Social Sciences when it deals with human societies, for example, as a point of focus. Likewise, the Social Science of linguistics crosses over into hard science territory when it deals, for example, with the biological apparatus of the vocal tract and brain function to help understand how human beings make sounds as part of language and the role that the brain also plays in this. Crossing from one discipline to another can also mean crossing from one set of goals – and language use – to another.

Given the focus on facts in the Hard Sciences, then this suggests less of a need to hedge. After all, facts are facts. But there is still room to interpret facts, of course, and therefore, a need to hedge where necessary. But as I had mentioned earlier, the use of present tense in the Hard Sciences is a means to indeed indicate facts, given their predictable nature. Whereas natural phenomena, as studied within the Hard Sciences, are predictable to a large extent, human phenomena, as part of the Social Sciences, are not.

Let's see some examples of writing in the Hard Sciences, taking note of the lack of hedging in some cases against times when it is in fact wholly necessary:

> According to collision theory, **reactions occur** when the reactants hit each other with sufficient velocity and the correct orientation. For the reaction to occur, the energy of the particles **must** be greater than the activation energy of the reaction;

therefore, if the average energy of the system is increased, or if there are more reactants with sufficient energy, the rate of the reaction **will** increase.

Source: UKEssays. (2020c, May 18). *Effect of sodium hypchlorite on red food dye reaction rates.* https://www.ukessays.com/essays/chemistry/effect-of-sodium-hypchlorite-on-red-food-dye-reaction-rates.php. Accessed on 21 November 2020.

A photon emitted at an infinite distance from the black hole with speed c0 **arrives** near the horizon of the black hole with a real speed zero. And yet the local measurement of the speed of the photon carried out with a material clock and a material ruler remains c0. Study of the possible orbits of a material particle around a black hole and the **possibility** of orbits of a photon around a black hole.

Source: Pignard, O. (2020). Black holes in the theory of the dynamic medium of reference. *Physics Essays, 33*(4), 395–399. https://doi.org/10.4006/0836-1398-33.4.395.

Thoughts: The need for a hedge (*possibility*) because science doesn't know everything, or claim to for that matter. Thus, in the absence of proof and fact-based knowledge, science needs to hedge too as in this example here.

Although M-phase specific drugs are remarkable in that it **prevents** further malignant growth, the administration of combinations of drugs given intermittently **often** produces better results than more continues (sic) treatment with a single drug. The rationale is that a combination of drugs with different toxic effects and affecting different biochemical pathways has anti-tumour activity without addictive toxicity. However, a large number of antimitotic drugs are currently under development, this **implies** that microtubules are still a very worthwhile target for anticancer therapies.

Source: UKEssays. (2020i, June 1). *Structure and functions of microtubules.* https://www.ukessays.com/essays/biology/microtubules-structure-functions.php. Accessed on 20 November 2020.

Thoughts: Often, but not *always*. Thus, here we have a need to hedge, as this is not a regular, predictable occurrence each and every time. Given that the drugs are under development, this means that the results are not in – we lack conclusive evidence. Therefore, we need to hedge, as seen with the word *implies*.

We've covered examples of an important academic practice, seen across several disciplines with the larger disciplines of the Humanities, Social Sciences and Hard Sciences. I now move on to two final pieces of advice in terms of what **not** to do if you want to make your assessments sound critical.

First, avoid empty expressions, which refers to clichéd uses of language that perhaps seek to sound decisive, but actually communicate nothing in the process. Examples are presented:

Many researchers believe that . . .

It has been said/discussed/argued . . .

Almost everybody knows . . .

Hopefully, you can see the problem immediately. 'Many researchers believe' is empty because it doesn't tell us how many is 'many', let alone which researchers you're referring to. This kind of writing is a bit lazy, to be honest, as it can give the impression that the writer is trying to sound convincing, but without providing the necessary information based on having done some background reading first. This is because background reading would allow the writer to supply some names in the first instance. Likewise, the second example again begs the question *who* said/discussed/argued this (whatever 'this' refers to)? And how do you know? On the other hand, if you follow through with the missing details, then these two expressions are perfectly fine. To be clear, there is nothing wrong with them in and of themselves – the issue is whether or not they are followed with the necessary details because sometimes in students' writing, they aren't.

Many researchers believe that the approach, while controversial, has great potential (Adams, 2009; Galusha, 2013; Paley, 2017).

It has been said/discussed/argued that the results reflected a flawed methodology (Johnson, 2009; Berisha, 2010; Richmond, 2019).

However, the final example above is beyond saving and needs to be changed completely. First, it reflects a more informal style of writing, similar to a conversation; this is not really good style for academic essay writing. Second, it is far too hyperbolic – *does almost everybody truly know*? Really? Hyperbolic writing is the kind which is the polar opposite of hedged communication. Even with the attempt to hedge seen with the word *almost*, it is insufficient. In fact, if you use a hedge alongside what is otherwise a very over the top statement, the hedge won't be of use. For example, consider the sentence *it seems like a fact*. This doesn't work, but with a revamp it could – *it seems to be likely*, or *it appears that this could be true*.

There are perhaps other examples you might have seen, or even used, but consider the underlying issue with the examples provided. Regardless of what specific language you use, avoid expressions that essentially attempt to rush to provide evidence which isn't evidence of anything at all. Remember, this kind of dramatic language works absolutely fine if part of an everyday conversation, a personal blog or fiction writing, for example. But for the purposes of *academic* writing, the tone needs to be more sober. Exaggeration and otherwise 'colourful' language have no place.

The second topic of discussion here is to watch out for intuitive statements within your assessments. These are statements which, at face value, might seem true – even factual – and might come across as common sense to others. But they are not factual at all, and for this reason, you once again need to be careful and hedge. Consider the examples below of these so-called intuitive statements:

> The Royal Family would never give their children names such as Dustin, Madison or Lonny.

> It is clear that it is easier to acquire one's first language in infanthood than to learn a second language in adulthood.

> A diet of junk food and constant social media are contributing to physical and mental health issues in our children.

For every subject you can think of, there are statements like the ones above. Now, if we were having a casual conversation, far from the academic context of a classroom debate, academic essay or oral presentation with all eyes on you, then the statements above work just fine. That's because in informal, friendly and everyday contexts of communication, hyperbole, informality and exaggeration are common. They make conversations more fun and interesting. Consider expressions such as *I'd give my right arm to go there!* Clearly, you wouldn't really do this.

Another point to make is that you might be tempted to say that the expressions above are not solely based on hyperbole. They might appear to have a certain degree of credibility. After all, when it comes to children's names, the three names presented above have not appeared in royal circles for centuries, if at all, and so it is unlikely perhaps that they will appear anytime soon. The (British?) Royal Family do seem to give their children 'traditional' names, and not informal varieties of names, or names reflecting the latest trends. But this is the academic world, and as such, can you prove that the statements above are true?

Have you conducted research with all members of the current Royal Family to verify your claims? Have you interviewed infants, say 2 to 4 years old, to actually get their opinions on how easy it is to acquire their first language? Chances are, they wouldn't have a great deal to tell you. The final example does, however, have some truth perhaps. Indeed, I have no doubt that you could find journal articles which investigate the consumption of unhealthy diets and social media use amongst children, with, in some cases, detrimental effects. But I am certain that such articles would not use language like that employed in the sentence above. If they did, they wouldn't get published in the first place. The problem with the final sentence is, like the other two, it is making a sweeping statement. In the final example, a statement which may indeed have *some* truth for *some* children is being used to apply, as written, to *all* children. Clearly, not all children have ever experienced social media or even have a mobile/cell/hand phone. And by 'children', does the writer honestly mean all the children in the world? I'm sure he/she does not, but taken at face value – as the language within your academic assessments will be – this sounds like a fact. It is not. And the final sentence is also bordering on gross stereotypes, which are hardly evidence of careful, rational thought.

So, how to fix this? Simple. Hedge, illustrate and, to top it off, add some support. Or at least hedge, if nothing else:

> It is arguably the case that the Royal Family tend to give their children names considered 'traditional' such as William and Charles, and this might suggest a reluctance to use names considered more reflective of current trends such as Madison or Parker.

> It's perhaps assumed that it is easier to acquire one's first language in infant-hood than to learn a second language in adulthood. However, this can be questioned, as infants perhaps do not recall the actual acquisition process of their first language – which is not the same as conscious learning anyway as is involved with adults learning a second language.

> A diet of junk food and frequent use of social media are contributing to physi-cal and mental health issues in some children whose lifestyles are reflective of such habits.

As you can see, even before we have inserted relevant support, the hedging already makes the statements credible and encourages the reader to have trust in the writer. The second revised example even problematises the original statement, which makes it quite critical indeed. So while the revisions are still a work in progress, they are already off to a much better start.

Final exercise

It seems fitting to now close this chapter, and this book, with one last analysis. In this case, I present an essay to now analyse in detail, based on all that the book has covered. There are no other prompts provided, such as my comments, but following the essay is a series of points to remember for each and every assessment, more so those that allow time to prepare, such as essays. Consider this a tick box exercise – an analogy I have used frequently in this book – and use it not only for the final essay that follows but also for all of your own assessments that you are involved with from this point on. Again, this need not point to just essays and the way to achieve criticality involves the use of many different skills, but skills which are nonetheless quite generic and apply to all manner of assessments. True, you might not be able to take this tick box list with you to an exam, but you can certainly become more aware of what is involved by familiarising yourself with the list. And in time, addressing the various points involved with displaying criticality will become second nature.

Internet Safety in Schools

This essay addresses the topic of internet safety in terms of how it relates to school contexts. A focus is taken on compulsory education within the UK. The essay draws on governmental resources, and from work from charitable and educational sector organisations, in supporting online safety measures relevant to schools. The essay also discusses the implications of the 2018 GDPR (General Data Protection Regulations) in terms of their relevance for educational settings.

> With the pace of developments in online technology, the relationship between the operation and administration of education and convergence culture bringing the online and the offline together in ever more-complex ways, and the increasing sophistication of the uses made of technology, it is imperative that schools keep abreast of current thinking regarding internet safety (Jenkins, 2008; Hunter, 2012). Statutory guidance from the UK government with respect to schools' safety is updated regularly; the next iteration of this guidance becomes effective September 2018, replacing the current 2016 version (Department for Education, 2018; Department for Education, 2016). The guidance – entitled Keeping Children Safe in Education – discusses recruitment checks, safeguarding protocols and how to work in instances where allegations are made; an annex to the document focuses on online safety (Department for Education, 2016). Here, the potential issues which face educationalists and learners alike are summarised: these range from online radicalisation, accessing illegal or pornographic material, child sexual exploitation and the activities of sexual predators, both within and outside the school (Department for Education, 2016).

> The guidance document advocates a whole-school approach in terms of three main areas of risk and concern (Department for Education, 2016). First, that of content: "being exposed to illegal, inappropriate or harmful material [including] fake news, racist or radical and extremist news" (Department for Education, 2018, p. 92). The second area is that of contact; this is outlined not only in terms of abusive or predatory behaviour by others, but also commercial advertising. The third area is conceived of as conduct-related: "personal online

behaviour that increases the likelihood of, or causes, harm; for example making, sending and receiving explicit images, or online bullying" (Department for Education, 2018, p. 92).

An ongoing requirement is for settings to limit pupils' access to potential risk via the school's computer system through the use of appropriate filtering software and oversight via monitoring systems; while there is latitude on the nature of the systems and policies put into place so that the school can contextualise their approach to local needs, there is an expectation that settings will articulate their online safety protocols with their Prevent duty risk assessment (Department for Education, 2018; HM Government, 2016). The Prevent duty, which explains public bodies' obligations under the Counter-Terrorism and Security Act 2015 to support prevention of people being drawn towards terrorism and other forms of extremist activity, states that such bodies are "expected to ensure children are safe from terrorist and extremist material when accessing the internet in school, including by establishing appropriate levels of filtering" (HM Government, 2016, p. 12; HM Government, 2015). Furthermore, this should be supported by staff training to support school staff in identifying such risks, challenging extremist thought, and making appropriate referrals where there are concerns to be addressed (HM Government, 2016).

Filtering software should be flexible to that it can be adjusted – for age groups or other forms of differentiation where appropriate – should be easily-controllable by staff, be backed by a clear policy, and be able to identify users. Such software should operate at a network level rather than at the level of the individual device being used, and should allow reporting where problematic sites or other issues are encountered so that both system usage and new sites where there are concerns may be addressed (UK Safer Internet Centre, 2018). Furthermore, there should be an interlocking range of monitoring strategies in place. These include physical monitoring of learner online activity by staff, oversight of search terms and of sites accessed, with the capacity for internet access to be suspended immediately if an issue is encountered, and the issue of technological solutions which may, for instance, be keyword or keystroke-responsive (UK Safer Internet Centre, 2018).

Such initiatives should be contextualised to a whole-school approach which integrates positive messages about safe internet usage, the potential dangers of the internet, and clear mechanisms for pupils to voice their own concerns across the curriculum (HM Government, 2016; Rooney, 2014). Schools also need to consider their policies as regards pupils' personal access to the internet via their own mobile devices, as this will fall outside the boundaries of the school network (HM Government, 2016). The guidance documentation also offers links to education-sector agencies dealing with different aspects of online safety from purchasing of hardware and software, training packages, and on appropriate guidance on internet security protocols. While schools are encouraged to make their bespoke arrangements with respect to online safety, there are links offered to a range of organisations and charities with a remit which engages with key aspects of appropriate and safe online conduct, and its contextualisation to different curriculum areas (HM Government, 2016). Exemplar materials – including sample and customisable policies addressing online safety, acceptable use of school network facilities, and responding to an e-safety incident are available from children's charity the NSPCC; these include a self-assessment tool for schools so that an audit may be undertaken in respect of the comprehensiveness of setting policies and procedures (NSPCC, 2017). Local authorities may provide centralised support for schools who are grant-maintained, and there are multiple consultancies who can provide such support on a fee-paying basis. Furthermore, organisations such as the UK Council on Child Internet Safety offer frameworks which support positivity in pupils' online engagements, from matters related to copyright to online information management which is graduated so that it can be mapped across to different Key Stage levels of national curriculum documentation (UK Council on Child Internet Safety, 2016).

There is, then, a significant amount of authoritative information, guidance and support available for schools to develop their own approach to internet safety, and to support pupils' own understanding (Stowell, 2016). As noted above, this is important not least because of statutory responsibilities with respect to the Prevent duty, but also because of the pace of change within relevant pedagogic technologies, and the legislation developed to engage with such advances (Ribble, 2015). An example of this is the 2018 GDPR data regulations, to which this essay now turns.

The GDPR regulations address the handling of personal data. Schools process an immense amount of such data in many different ways: enrolment and attendance records, medical information, job applications, software which supports homework completion payments for school meals are just a few examples of the ways in which personal data is collected and processed. The key shift in the new regulations – effective May 2018 – is a move from lawful holding and processing of such data to one where organisations need to be able to evidence compliance with data protection laws (Lock, 2018). Requirements for schools include: mapping computers systems' use of personal data and the ways in which legal compliance is satisfied; the appointment of a Data Protection Officer to oversee compliance; having agreements in place with third parties processing data on behalf of the setting which evidence GDPR compliance; training for all staff so that there is a cultural shift and personal ownership of the issues raised by the new regulations; and effective monitoring and reporting systems in case of a data breach (Lock, 2018). There also needs to be a publication scheme in place so that it is clear what information is made available to the public (such as examination results) as well as guidance on related issues, such as how to approach the use of personal computing devices by staff to process personal data when, for example, marking from home (Information Commissioner's Office, 2018). The post of Data Protection Officer – which might be shared across sites for large academy organisations – is crucial, not least because the impacts of the new legislation are wide-ranging and there is a need for local expertise; however, the responsibilities for safe and compliant handling of personal data impact on all staff working within educational contexts (Information Commissioner's Office, 2018). The GDPR regulations offer a reminder that internet safety relates not only to the more obvious dangers of extreme content, of inappropriate material being accessed, or the potential for radicalisation, but also of informational security (Attai, 2018). The regulations also offer reminders to practitioners of the value of supporting learners to appreciate for themselves the value of their personal data, and to be proactive in their use of online resources in protecting their identity and other data resources accordingly across the curriculum (Lau, 2017).

This short essay has worked to discuss issues connected to internet safety in educational contexts in the UK. As the essay has shown, there is a mix of legal requirements and good practice standards for settings to engage with, and a proactive and setting-wide approach is only appropriate. The centrality of online engagement to contemporary education, and the importance of teaching and learning in ways which recognise both the opportunities and potential issues of online worlds, both mean that a cohesive, detailed and proactive approach which involves all operational and strategic aspects of the setting is appropriate. There is a spectrum of support available through relevant educational, charitable and governmental sources. However, the onus is on the setting to engage with these support mechanisms to not only ensure compliance and safety, but to be proactive so that staff and learners alike are aware of potential dangers, but can still work and learn safely and productively within agreed guidelines.

Source: UKEssays. (2018b, November). *Sample undergraduate 1st education essay*. https://www.ukessays.com/services/samples/1st-education-essay. php. Accessed on 26 November 2020.

Boxes to tick

Introduction

- Is there a discernible hook, in your opinion?
- Is adequate background information provided?
- Is there an essay plan (though this is not an absolute requirement)?
- Is there a clear argument sentence **or** a clear sense of an implied argument?

Body

- Does each body paragraph begin with a topic sentence?
- Does each topic progress in a logical sequence?

- Does each topic relate to the content of the argument sentence/implied argument and by extension to the overall focus of the essay?
- Is there only one topic per body paragraph?
- Is there evidence of 'doing something' with the references used, whether quote, paraphrase or summary (i.e. agree, disagree, illustrate or explain)?
- Are broad words illustrated?

Conclusion

- Does the conclusion arrive at a conclusion – a statement of the overall findings, opinion and/or main point?
- Does the conclusion recap the topics, or certainly some of them?
- Does the conclusion introduce a new topic (which it shouldn't do, of course)?
- Does the conclusion end with a 'closing thought' of some kind?

Finally . . .

- Is there evidence of any kind of justification, if applicable?
- Does the writer hedge where necessary?
- Are phrasal verbs used in excess, in your opinion?
- If figures of speech are used, do you feel they fit the context of the discipline and essay subject?
- Is there an avoidance of empty and/or intuitive expressions and statements?
- In terms of grammar, punctuation and style:
  - Do you find the word choices appropriate for academic writing (e.g. a use of both technical and everyday language, but language overall that is neither too formal nor too casual)?
  - Do you feel that appropriate verb tense is used?

Finally, are there any other boxes that need to be ticked? Is there anything else that you would be on the lookout for, whether positive or negative, if you were marking the essay?

We've covered a lot of ground and a lot of material, and it is my hope that you can now approach your academic assessments with a sense of confidence, strategic planning and, above all, a clear and concrete understanding of just what it means to be 'critical'. Use the book, and any notes you've made, as a permanent guide for all of your future assessments, as well as the tick box exercise above. You may or may not enjoy academic assessments, whatever type of assessment is involved, but you can be better equipped to approach your assessments with the skills needed.

Good luck!

References

Bintliff, A. (2020, September 8). How COVID-19 has influenced teachers' well-being. *Psychology Today*. https://www.psychologytoday.com/intl/blog/multidimensional-aspects-adolescent-well-being/202009/how-covid-19-has-influenced-teachers-well. Accessed on 1 October 2020.

Briz-Redón, A., Belenguer-Sapiña, C., & Serrano-Aroca, A. (2020). Changes in air pollution during COVID-19 lockdown in Spain: A multi-city study. *Journal of Environmental Sciences, 101*, 16–26. https://doi.org/10.1016/j.jes.2020.07.029

Cole, J. (2020). Coronavirus: why changing human behaviour is the best defence in tackling the virus. *The Conversation*. March 26th 2020.

Crawley, M. (2006). Mr. Sorkin goes to Washington: Shaping the President on television's the west wing. Jefferson, NC: McFarland.

Das, E., Medley, G. and Michie, S. (2020). COVID-19: how our behaviour can help stop the coronavirus. https://sciencemediahub.eu/" EUROPEAN SCIENCE-MEDIA HUB. https://sciencemediahub.eu/2020/05/28/covid-19-how-our-behaviour-can-help-stop-the-coronavirus/" COVID-19: how our behaviour can help stop the coronavirus - European Science-Media Hub (sciencemediahub.eu).

Edström, K. (2018). Academic and professional values in engineering education: Engaging with history to explore a persistent tension. *Engineering Studies, 10*(1), 38–65. https://doi.org/10.1080/19378629.2018.1424860

Gentili, C. and Cristea, I. (2020). Challenges and Opportunities for Human Behavior Research in the Coronavirus Disease (COVID-19) Pandemic. Front. Psychol. 11. Frontiers | Challenges and Opportunities for Human Behavior Research in the Coronavirus Disease (COVID-19) Pandemic | Psychology (frontiersin.org). https://www.frontiersin.org/articles/10.3389/fpsyg.2020.01786/full

Harlan, B. (2020). Art critique as social pedagogy. *International Journal of Arts Education, 15*(1), 1–10. https://doi.org/10.18848/2326-9944/CGP/v15i01/1-10

Helmenstine, A. M. (2019, December 9). Scientific hypothesis examples. *ThoughtCo*. https://www.thoughtco.com/scientific-hypothesis-examples-3975979. Accessed on 7 April, 2021.

Khitrov, A. (2020). Hollywood experts: A field analysis of knowledge production in American entertainment television. *British Journal of Sociology, 71*(5), 939–951. https://doi.org/10.1111/1468-4446.12775

Kuo, C. H. (1999). The use of personal pronouns: Role relationships in scientific journal articles. *English for Specific Purposes, 18*(2), 121–138. https://doi.org/10.1111/1468-4446.12775

Matrajt, L., & Leung, T. (2020). Evaluating the Effectiveness of Social Distancing Interventions to Delay or Flatten the Epidemic Curve of Coronavirus Disease. *Emerging Infectious Diseases*, 26(8), 1740–1748.

McCabe, J. (2012). The west wing. Detroit, MI: Wayne State University Press.

Milne, G. and Xie, S. (2020). The Effectiveness of Social Distancing in Mitigating COVID-19 Spread: a modelling analysis. The Effectiveness of Social Distancing in Mitigating COVID-19 Spread: a modelling analysis | medRxiv. https://www.medrxiv.org/content/10.1101/2020.03.20.20040055v1

Paulin, D., & Suneson, K. (2015). Knowledge transfer, knowledge sharing and knowledge barriers-three blurry terms in KM. Leading Issues in Knowledge Management, 73(2).

Petersen, H., Kecklund, G., Nilsson, J., & Åkerstedt, T. (2012). Stress vulnerability and the effects of moderate daily stress on sleep polysomnography and subjective sleepiness. *Journal of Sleep Research*, 22(1), 50–57. https://doi.org/10.1111/j.1365-2869.2012.01034.x

Pignard, O. (2020). Black holes in the theory of the dynamic medium of reference. *Physics Essays*, 33(4), 395–399. https://doi.org/10.4006/0836-1398-33.4.395

Reisch, L., Sunstein, C., Andor, M., Doebbe, F., Meier, J., & Haddaway, N. (2021). Mitigating climate change via food consumption and food waste: A systematic map of behavioral interventions. *Journal of Cleaner Production, 279*. https://doi.org/10.1016/j.jclepro.2020.123717

Robson, D. (2020). The fear of coronavirus is changing our psychology. BBC Future. The fear of coronavirus is changing our psychology - BBC Future. https://www.bbc.com/future/article/20200401-covid-19-how-fear-of-coronavirus-is-changing-our-psychology

Schneider, F. W., Gruman, J. A., & Coutts, L. M. (Eds.). (2012). *Applied Social Psychology: Understanding and Addressing Social and Practical Problems*. Thousand Oaks, CA: SAGE Publications, Inc.

Schwartz, D. G. (2006). Aristotelian view of knowledge management. Encyclopedia of knowledge management, 10–16.

UKEssays. (n.d.-a). *Art essay questions*. https://www.ukessays.com/essay-questions/art/. Accessed on 17 November 2020.

UKEssays. (n.d.-b). *History essay questions*. https://www.ukessays.com/essay-questions/history/. Accessed on 14 November 2020.

UKEssays. (2018a, November). *Sample masters merit nursing dissertation. Findings – effects of acupuncture on hypertension*. https://www.ukessays.com/services/samples/merit-nursing-dissertation.php#_Toc14424824. Accessed on 22 November 2020.

UKEssays. (2018b, November). *Sample undergraduate 1st education essay*. https://www.ukessays.com/services/samples/1st-education-essay.php. Accessed on 26 November 2020.

UKEssays. (2018c, November). *Sample undergraduate 1st education report*. https://www.ukessays.com/services/samples/1st-education-report.php. Accessed on 21 November 2020.

UKEsssays. (2018d, November). *Sample undergraduate 1st health and social care assignment*. https://www.ukessays.com/services/samples/1st-hsc-assignment.php. Accessed on 14 November 2020.

UKEsssays. (2018e, November). *Sample undergraduate 1st health and social care essay*. https://www.ukessays.com/services/samples/1st-hsc-essay.php. Accessed on 14 November 2020.

UKEssays. (2018f, November). *Sample undergraduate 1st HRM essay*. https://www.ukessays.com/services/samples/1st-hrm-essay.php. Accessed on 20 November 2020.

UKEssays. (2018g, November). *Sample undergraduate 1st psychology assignment*. https://www.ukessays.com/services/samples/1st-psychology-assignment.php. Accessed on 21 November 2020.

UKEssays. (2018h, November). *Sample undergraduate 2:1 business dissertation*. https://www.ukessays.com/services/samples/2-1-business-dissertation.php. Accessed on 14 November 2020.

UKEssays. (2018i, November). *Sample undergraduate 2:1 construction dissertation*. https://www.ukessays.com/services/samples/2-1-construction-dissertation.php. Accessed on 22 November 2020.

UKEssays. (2018j, November). *Sample undergraduate 2:1 education dissertation. Summary of further research areas*. https://www.ukessays.com/services/samples/2-1-education-dissertation.php#_Toc526165386. Accessed on 21 November 2020.

UKEssays. (2018k, November). *Sample undergraduate 2:1 environmental sciences dissertation*. https://www.ukessays.com/services/samples/2-1-environmental-science-dissertation.php. Accessed on 28 November 2020.

UKEssays. (2018l, November). *Sample undergraduate 2:1 finance dissertation*. https://www.ukessays.com/services/samples/2-1-finance-dissertation.php. Accessed on 21 November 2020.

UKEssays. (2018m, November). *Sample undergraduate 2:1 marketing dissertation. Chapter III. Methodology*. https://www.ukessays.com/services/samples/2-1-marketing-dissertation.php#_Toc526111372. Accessed on 20 November 2020.

UKEssays. (2018n, November). *Sample undergraduate 2:1 medicine dissertation: Research question*. https://www.ukessays.com/services/samples/2-1-medicine-dissertation.php#_Toc527021272. Accessed on 21 November 2020.

UKEssays. (2018o, November). *Sample undergraduate 2:1 medicine dissertation: Strengths and limitations*. https://www.ukessays.com/services/samples/2-1-medicine-dissertation.php#_Toc527021295. Accessed on 21 November 2020.

UKEssays. (2018p, November). *Sample undergraduate 2:1 nursing essay*. https://www.ukessays.com/services/samples/2-1-nursing-essay.php. Accessed on 12 November 2020.

UKEssays. (2018q, November). *Sample undergraduate 2:1 tourism dissertation on the role of tourism in the economic development of host destinations*. https://www.ukessays.com/services/samples/2-1-tourism-dissertation.php. Accessed on 21 November 2020.

UKEssays. (2020a, February 9). *Impact of linguistic imperialism*. https://www.ukessays.com/essays/linguistics/impact-of-linguistic-imperialism.php. Accessed on 21 November 2020.

UKEssays. (2020b, May 18). *Cultural and societal impacts of the selfie*. https://www.ukessays.com/essays/anthropology/cultural-and-societal-impacts-of-the-selfie.php. Accessed on 12 November 2020.

UKEssays. (2020c, May 18). *Effect of sodium hypochlorite on red food dye reaction rates*. https://www.ukessays.com/essays/chemistry/effect-of-sodium-hypochlorite-on-red-food-dye-reaction-rates.php. Accessed on 21 November 2020.

UKEssays. (2020d, May 18). *Pleasure and pain: Aristotle's theory of moral development*. https://www.ukessays.com/essays/philosophy/pleasure-and-pain-aristotles-theory-of-moral-development.php. Accessed on 20 November 2020.

UKEssays. (2020e, May 18). *To what extent does string theory present a possibility of a unified theory of quantum gravity?* https://www.ukessays.com/essays/physics/to-what-extent-does-string-theory-present-a-possibility-of-a-unified-theory-of-quantum-gravity.php. Accessed on 12 November 2020.

UKEssays. (2020f, June 1). *Case studies on childhood neglect*. https://www.ukessays.com/essays/psychology/childhood-neglect-its-impact-later-in-life.php. Accessed on 21 November 2020.

UKEssays. (2020g, June 1). *Example biology essay – 2:1 level*. https://www.ukessays.com/essays/biology/example-biology-essay.php. Accessed on 12 November 2020.

UKEssays. (2020h, June 1). *Race in the 19th and 20th centuries*. https://www.ukessays.com/essays/sociology/ideas-race-century.php. Accessed on 22 November 2020.

UKEssays. (2020i, June 1). *Structure and functions of microtubules*. https://www.ukessays.com/essays/biology/microtubules-structure-functions.php. Accessed on 20 November 2020.

UKEssays. (2020j, June 1). *Theme of isolation in Jane Eyre*. https://www.ukessays.com/essays/english-literature/isolation-theme-jane-eyre-wide-sargasso-sea.php. Accessed on 22 November 2020.

UKEssays. (2020k, June 1). *True altruism does not exist*. https://www.ukessays.com/essays/psychology/true-altruism-does-not-exist.php. Accessed on 12 November 2020.

Uni Learning. (n.d.). Report writing https://unilearning.uow.edu.au/report/2bii1.html. Accessed on 20 November 2020.

Wagner, S. (2018). *Electoral conflict in Kawe: Perceptions of constituents*. The Pennsylvania State University. https://guides.libraries.psu.edu/c.php?g=882127&p=6338035, under a Creative Commons 4.0 license. Accessed on 1 December 2020.

Wescott, D. (2018). Recent advances in forensic anthropology: Decomposition research. *Forensic Sciences Research*, 3(4), 327–342. https://doi.org/10.1080/20961790.2018.1488571

Index